C000129114

Tucholsky Wagner Zola Scott Sydow Freud Schlegel
Turgenev Wallace Fonatne
Twain Walther von der Vogelweide Fouqué Friedrich II. von Preußen
Weber Freiligrath Frey
Fechner Fichte Weiße Rose von Fallersleben Kant Ernst Frommel
Richthofen
Engels Fielding Hölderlin Tacitus Dumas
Fehrs Faber Flaubert Eichendorff
Feuerbach Maximilian I. von Habsburg Fock Eliasberg Zweig Ebner Eschenbach
Ewald Eliot Vergil
Goethe Elisabeth von Österreich London
Mendelssohn Balzac Shakespeare Dostojewski Ganghofer
Trackl Lichtenberg Rathenau Doyle Gjellerup
Mommsen Stevenson Tolstoi Hambruch
Thoma Lenz Hanrieder Droste-Hülshoff
Dach Verne von Arnim Hägele Hauff Humboldt
Karrillon Reuter Rousseau Hagen Hauptmann Gautier
Garschin
Damaschke Defoe Hebbel Baudelaire
Descartes Hegel Kussmaul Herder
Wolfram von Eschenbach Schopenhauer
Bronner Darwin Dickens Grimm Jerome Rilke George
Melville Bebel Proust
Campe Horváth Aristoteles
Bismarck Vigny Voltaire Federer Herodot
Gengenbach Barlach Heine
Storm Casanova Lessing Tersteegen Gilm Grillparzer Georgy
Chamberlain Langbein Gryphius
Brentano Lafontaine
Strachwitz Claudius Schiller Schilling Kralik Iffland Sokrates
Katharina II. von Rußland Bellamy Gerstäcker Raabe Gibbon Tschechow
Löns Hesse Hoffmann Gogol Wilde Gleim Vulpius
Luther Heym Hofmannsthal Morgenstern
Roth Heyse Klopstock Klee Hölty Kleist Goedicke
Luxemburg Puschkin Homer Mörike
Machiavelli La Roche Horaz Musil
Navarra Aurel Musset Kierkegaard Kraft Kraus
Nestroy Marie de France Lamprecht Kind Kirchhoff Hugo Moltke
Laotse Ipsen Liebknecht
Nietzsche Nansen Ringelnatz
Marx Lassalle Gorki Klett Leibniz
von Ossietzky May vom Stein Lawrence Irving
Petalozzi Platon Knigge
Sachs Poe Pückler Michelangelo Kock Kafka
Liebermann Korolenko
de Sade Praetorius Mistral Zetkin

The Voyages of Captain Scott : Retold from the Voyage of the Discovery and Scott's Last Expedition

Charles Turley

Imprint

This book is part of the TREDITION CLASSICS series.

Author: Charles Turley
Cover design: toepferschumann, Berlin (Germany)

Publisher: tredition GmbH, Hamburg (Germany)
ISBN: 978-3-8495-0075-7

www.tredition.com
www.tredition.de

THE VOYAGES OF CAPTAIN SCOTT

Retold from 'The Voyage of the "Discovery"' and 'Scott's Last Expedition'

BY

CHARLES TURLEY

Author of 'Godfrey Marten, Schoolboy,' 'A Band of Brothers,' etc.

With an introduction by

SIR J. M. BARRIE, BART.

Numerous illustrations in colour and black and white and a map

CONTENTS

THE LAST EXPEDITION

Chapter

ILLUSTRATIONS

INTRODUCTION

BY SIR J. M. BARRIE, BART.

On the night of my original meeting with Scott he was but lately home from his first adventure into the Antarctic and my chief recollection of the occasion is that having found the entrancing man I was unable to leave him. In vain he escorted me through the streets of London to my home, for when he had said good-night I then escorted him to his, and so it went on I know not for how long through the small hours. Our talk was largely a comparison of the life of action (which he pooh-poohed) with the loathsome life of those who sit at home (which I scorned); but I also remember that he assured me he was of Scots extraction. As the subject never seems to have been resumed between us, I afterwards wondered whether I had drawn this from him with a promise that, if his reply was satisfactory, I would let him go to bed. However, the family traditions (they are nothing more) do bring him from across the border. According to them his great-great-grandfather was the Scott of Brownhead whose estates were sequestered after the '45. His dwelling was razed to the ground and he fled with his wife, to whom after some grim privations a son was born in a fisherman's hut on September 14, 1745. This son eventually settled in Devon, where he prospered, Page 2 for it was in the beautiful house of Oatlands that he died. He had four sons, all in the Royal Navy, of whom the eldest had as youngest child John Edward Scott, father of the Captain Scott who was born at Oatlands on June 6, 1868. About the same date, or perhaps a little earlier, it was decided that the boy should go into the Navy like so many of his for-bears.

I have been asked to write a few pages about those early days of Scott at Oatlands, so that the boys who read this book may have some slight acquaintance with the boy who became Captain Scott; and they may be relieved to learn (as it holds out some chance for themselves) that the man who did so many heroic things does not make his first appearance as a hero. He enters history aged six, blue-eyed, long-haired, inexpressibly slight and in velveteen, being held out at arm's length by a servant and dripping horribly, like a half-drowned kitten. This is the earliest recollection of him of a sister, who was too young to join in a children's party on that fatal day. But Con, as he was always called, had intimated to her that from a window she would be able to see him taking a noble lead in the festivities in the garden, and she looked; and that is what she saw. He had been showing his guests how superbly he could jump the leat, and had fallen into it.

Leat is a Devonshire term for a running stream, and a branch of the leat ran through the Oatlands garden while there was another branch, more venturesome, at the bottom of the fields. These were the waters first ploughed by Scott, and he invented many ways of being in them accidentally, it being forbidden Page 3 to enter them of intent. Thus he taught his sisters and brother a new version of the oldest probably of all pastimes, the game of 'Touch.' You had to touch 'across the leat,' and, with a little good fortune, one of you went in. Once you were wet, it did not so much matter though you got wetter.

An easy way of getting to the leat at the foot of the fields was to walk there, but by the time he was eight Scott scorned the easy ways. He invented parents who sternly forbade all approach to this dangerous waterway; he turned them into enemies of his country and of himself (he was now an admiral), and led parties of gallant tars to the stream by ways hitherto unthought of. At foot of the avenue was an oak tree which hung over the road, and thus by dropping from this tree you got into open country. The tree was (at this time) of an enormous size, with sufficient room to conceal a navy, and the navy consisted mainly of the sisters and the young brother. All had to be ready at any moment to leap from the tree and join issue with the enemy on the leat. In the fields there was also a mighty ocean, called by dull grown-ups 'the pond,' and here Scott's battleship lay moored. It seems for some time to have been an English vessel, but by and by he was impelled, as all boys are, to blow something up, and he could think of nothing more splendid for his purpose than the battleship. Thus did it become promptly a ship of the enemy doing serious damage to the trade of those parts, and the valiant Con took to walking about with lips pursed, brows frowning as he cogitated how to remove the Page 4 Terror of Devon. You may picture the sisters and brother trotting by his side and looking anxiously into his set face. At last he decided to blow the accursed thing up with gunpowder. His crew cheered, and then waited to be sent to the local shop for a pennyworth of gunpowder. But Con made his own gunpowder, none of the faithful were ever told how, and on a great day the train was laid. Con applied the match and ordered all to stand back. A deafening explosion was expected, but a mere puff of flame was all that came; the Terror of Devon, which to the unimaginative was only a painted plank, still rode the waters. With many boys this would be the end of the story, but not with Con. He again retired to the making of gunpowder, and did not desist from his endeavors until he had blown that plank sky-high.

His first knife is a great event in the life of a boy: it is probably the first memory of many of them, and they are nearly always given it on condition that they keep it shut. So it was with Con, and a few minutes after he had sworn that he would not open it he was begging for permission to use it on a tempting sapling. 'Very well,' his father said grimly, 'but remember, if you hurt yourself, don't expect any sympathy from me.' The knife was opened, and to cut himself rather badly proved as easy as falling into the leat. The father, however, had not noticed, and the boy put his bleeding hand into his pocket and walked on unconcernedly. He was really considerably damaged; and this is a good story of a child of seven who all his life suffered extreme nausea from Page 5 the sight of blood; even in the *Discovery* days, to get accustomed to 'seeing red,' he had to force himself to watch Dr. Wilson skinning his specimens.

When he was about eight Con passed out of the hands of a governess, and became a school-boy, first at a day school in Stoke Damerel and later at Stubbington House, Fareham. He rode grandly between Oatlands and Stoke Damerel on his pony, Beppo, which bucked in vain when he was on it, but had an ingratiating way of depositing other riders on the road. From what one knows of him later this is a characteristic story. One day he dismounted to look over a gate at a view which impressed him (not very boyish this), and when he recovered from a brown study there was no Beppo to be seen. He walked the seven miles home, but what was characteristic was that he called at police-stations on the way to give practical details of his loss and a description of the pony. Few children would have thought of this, but Scott was naturally a strange mixture of

the dreamy and the practical, and never more practical than immediately after he had been dreamy. He forgot place and time altogether when thus abstracted. I remember the first time he dined
with me, when a number of well-known men had come to meet
him, he arrived some two hours late. He had dressed to come out,
then fallen into one of his reveries, forgotten all about the engage-
ment, dined by himself and gone early to bed. Just as he was falling
asleep he remembered where he should be, arose hastily and joined
us as speedily as possible. It was equally characteristic of him to say
Page 6 of the other guests that it was pleasant to a sailor to meet so
many interesting people. When I said that to them the sailor was by
far the most interesting person in the room he shouted with mirth. It
always amused Scott to find that anyone thought him a person of
importance.

ROBERT F. SCOTT AT THE AGE OF 13 AS A NAVAL CADET.

I suppose everyone takes for granted that in his childhood, as later when he made his great marches, Scott was muscular and strongly built. This was so far from being the case that there were many anxious consultations over him, and the local doctor said he could not become a sailor as he could never hope to obtain the necessary number of inches round the chest. He was delicate and inclined to be pigeon-breasted. Judging from the portrait of him here printed, in his first uniform as a naval cadet, all this had gone by the time he was thirteen, but unfortunately there are no letters of this period extant and thus little can be said of his years on the *Britannia* where 'you never felt hot in your bunk because you could always twist, and sleep with your feet out at port hole.' He became a cadet captain, a post none can reach who is not thought well of by the other boys as well as by their instructors, but none of them foresaw that he was likely to become anybody in particular. He was still 'Old Mooney,' as his father had dubbed him, owing to his dreamy mind; it was an effort to him to work hard, he cast a wistful eye on 'slackers,' he was not a good loser, he was untidy to the point of slovenliness, and he had a fierce temper. All this I think has been proved to me up to the Page 7 hilt, and as I am very sure that the boy of fifteen or so cannot be very different from the man he grows into it leaves me puzzled. The Scott I knew, or thought I knew, was physically as hard as nails and flung himself into work or play with a vehemence I cannot remember ever to have seen equaled. I have fished with him, played cricket and football with him, and other games, those of his own invention being of a particularly arduous kind, for they always had a moment when the other players were privileged to fling a hard ball at your undefended head. 'Slackness,' was the last quality you would think of when you saw him bearing down on you with that ball, and it was the last he asked of you if you were bearing down on him. He was equally strenuous of work; indeed I have no clearer recollection of him than his way of running from play to work or work to play, so that there should be the least possible time between. It is the 'time between' that is the 'slacker's' kingdom, and Scott lived less in it than anyone I can recall. Again, I found him the best of losers, with a shout of delight for every good stroke by an opponent: what is called an ideal sportsman. He was very neat and correct in his dress, quite a model for the youth who come after him, but that we take as a matter of course; it is 'good form' in the Navy. His temper I should have said was bullet-proof. I have never seen him begin to lose it for a second of time, and I have seen him in circumstances where the loss of it would have been excusable.

However, 'the boy makes the man,' and Scott was Page 8 none of those things I saw in him but something better. The faults of his youth must have lived on in him as in all of us, but he got to know they were there and he took an iron grip of them and never let go his hold. It was this self-control more than anything else that made the man of him of whom we have all become so proud. I get many proofs of this in correspondence dealing with his manhood days which are not strictly within the sphere of this introductory note. The horror of slackness was turned into a very passion for keeping himself 'fit.' Thus we find him at one time taking charge of a dog, a 'Big Dane,' so that he could race it all the way between work and home, a distance of three miles. Even when he was getting the *Discovery* ready and doing daily the work of several men, he might have been seen running through the streets of London from Savile Row or the Admiralty to his home, not because there was no time for other method of progression, but because he must be fit, fit, fit. No more 'Old Mooney' for him; he kept an eye for ever on that gentleman, and became doggedly the most practical of men. And practical in the cheeriest of ways. In 1894 a disastrous change came over the fortunes of the family, the father's money being lost and then Scott was practical indeed. A letter he wrote I at this time to his mother, tenderly taking everything and everybody on his shoulders, must be one of the best letters ever written by a son, and I hope it may be some day published. His mother was the great person of his early life, more to him even than his brother Page 9 or his father, whom circumstances had deprived of the glory of following the sailor's profession and whose ambitions were all bound up in this son, determined that Con should do the big things he had not done himself. For the rest of his life Con became the head of the family, devoting his time and his means to them, not in an it-must-be-done manner, but with joy and even gaiety. He never seems to have shown a gayer front than when the troubles fell, and at a farm to which they retired for a time he became famous as a provider of concerts. Not only must there be no 'Old Mooney' in him, but it must be driven out of everyone. His concerts, in which he took a leading part, became celebrated in the district, deputations called to beg for another, and once in these words, 'Wull 'ee gie we a concert over our way when the comic young gentleman be here along?'

Some servants having had to go at this period, Scott conceived the idea that he must even help domestically in the house, and took his own bedroom under his charge with results that were satisfactory to the casual eye, though not to the eyes of his sisters. It was about this time that he slew the demon of untidiness so far as his own dress was concerned and doggedly became a model for still younger officers. Not that his dress was fine. While there were others to help he would not spend his small means on himself, and he would arrive home in frayed garments that he had grown out of and in very tarnished lace. But neat as a pin. In the days when he returned from Page 10 his first voyage in the Antarctic and all England was talking of him, one of his most novel adventures was at last to go to a first-class tailor and be provided with a first-class suit. He was as elated by the possession of this as a child. When going about the country lecturing in those days he traveled third class, though he was sometimes met at the station by mayors and corporations and red carpets.

The hot tempers of his youth must still have lain hidden, but by now the control was complete. Even in the naval cadet days of which unfortunately there is so little to tell, his old friends who remember the tempers remember also the sunny smile that dissipated them. When I knew him the sunny smile was there frequently, and was indeed his greatest personal adornment, but the tempers never reached the surface. He had become master of his fate and captain of his soul.

In 1886 Scott became a middy on the *Boadicea*, and later on various ships, one of them the *Rover*, of which Admiral Fisher was at that time commander. The Admiral has a recollection of a little black pig having been found under his bunk one night. He cannot swear that Scott was the leading culprit, but Scott was certainly one of several who had to finish the night on deck as a punishment. In 1888 Scott passed his examinations for sub-lieutenant, with four first-class honours and one second, and so left his boyhood behind. I cannot refrain however from adding as a conclusion to these notes a letter from Sir Courtauld Page 11 Thomson that gives a very attractive glimpse of him in this same year:

'In the late winter a quarter of a century ago I had to find my way from San Francisco to Alaska. The railway was snowed up and the only transport available at the moment was an ill-found tramp steamer. My fellow passengers were mostly Californians hurrying off to a new mining camp and, with the crew, looked a very unpleasant lot of ruffians. Three singularly unprepossessing Frisco toughs joined me in my cabin, which was none too large for a single person. I was then told that yet another had somehow to be wedged in. While I was wondering if he could be a more ill-favored or dirtier specimen of humanity than the others the last comer suddenly appeared — the jolliest and breeziest English naval Second Lieutenant. It was Con Scott. I had never seen him before, but we at once became friends and remained so till the end. He was going up to join his ship which, I think, was the *Amphion*, at Esquimault, B. C.

'As soon as we got outside the Golden Gates we ran into a full gale which lasted all the way to Victoria, B. C. The ship was so overcrowded that a large number of women and children were allowed to sleep on the floor of the only saloon there was on condition that they got up early, so that the rest of the passengers could come in for breakfast and the other meals.

'I need scarcely say that owing to the heavy weather hardly a woman was able to get up, and the Page 12 saloon was soon in an indescribable condition. Practically no attempt was made to serve meals and the few so-called stewards were themselves mostly out of action from drink or sea-sickness.

'Nearly all the male passengers who were able to be about spent their time drinking and quarrelling. The deck cargo and some of our top hamper were washed away and the cabins got their share of the waves that were washing the deck.

'Then it was I first knew that Con Scott was no ordinary human being. Though at that time still only a boy he practically took command of the passengers and was at once accepted by them as their Boss during the rest of the trip. With a small body of volunteers he led an attack on the saloon — dressed the mothers, washed the children, fed the babies, swabbed down the floors and nursed the sick, and performed every imaginable service for all hands. On deck he settled the quarrels and established order either by his personality, or, if necessary, by his fists. Practically by day and night he worked for the common good, never sparing himself, and with his infectious smile gradually made us all feel the whole thing was jolly good fun.

'I daresay there are still some of the passengers like myself who, after a quarter of a century, have imprinted on their minds the vision of this fair-haired English sailor boy with the laughing blue eyes who at that early age knew how to sacrifice himself for the welfare and happiness of others.'

THE VOYAGE OF THE 'DISCOVERY'

THE 'DISCOVERY'.

Reproduced from a drawing by Dr. E. A. Wilson.

Page 15 CHAPTER I

THE *DISCOVERY*

> Do ye, by star-eyed Science led, explore
> Each lonely ocean, each untrodden shore.

In June, 1899, Robert Falcon Scott was spending his short leave in London, and happened to meet Sir Clements Markham in the Buckingham Palace Road. On that afternoon he heard for the first time of a prospective Antarctic expedition, and on the following day he called upon Sir Clements and volunteered to command it. Of this eventful visit Sir Clements wrote: 'On June 5, 1899, there was a remarkable coincidence. Scott was then torpedo lieutenant of the *Majestic*. I was just sitting down to write to my old friend Captain Egerton[1] about him, when he was announced. He came to volunteer to command the expedition. I believed him to be the best man for so great a trust, either in the navy or out of it. Captain Egerton's reply and Scott's testimonials and certificates most fully confirmed a foregone conclusion.'

[Footnote 1: Now Admiral Sir George Egerton, K.C.B.]

The tale, however, of the friendship between Sir Page 16 Clements and Scott began in 1887, when the former was the guest of his cousin, the Commodore of the Training Squadron, and made the acquaintance of every midshipman in the four ships that comprised it. During the years that followed, it is enough to say that Scott more than justified the hopes of those who had marked him down as a midshipman of exceptional promise. Through those years Sir Clements had been both friendly and observant, until by a happy stroke of fortune the time came when he was as anxious for this Antarctic expedition to be led by Scott as Scott was to lead it. So when, on June 30, 1900, Scott was promoted to the rank of Commander, and shortly afterwards was free to undertake the work that was waiting for him, one great anxiety was removed from the shoulders of the man who had not only proposed the expedition, but had also resolved that nothing should prevent it from going.

Great difficulties and troubles had, however, to be encountered before the *Discovery* could start upon her voyage. First and foremost was the question of money, but owing to indefatigable efforts the financial horizon grew clearer in the early months of 1899. Later on in the same year Mr. Balfour expressed his sympathy with the objects of the undertaking, and it was entirely due to him that the Government eventually agreed to contribute £45,000, provided that a similar sum could be raised by private subscriptions.

In March, 1900, the keel of the new vessel, that the Page 17 special Ship Committee had decided to build for the expedition, was laid in the yard of the Dundee Shipbuilding Company. A definite beginning, at any rate, had been made; but very soon after Scott had taken up his duties he found that unless he could obtain some control over the various committees and subcommittees of the expedition, the only day to fix for the sailing of the ship was Doomsday. A visit to Norway, where he received many practical suggestions from Dr. Nansen, was followed by a journey to Berlin, and there he discovered that the German expedition, which was to sail from Europe at the same time as his own, was already in an advanced state of preparation. Considerably alarmed, he hurried back to England and found, as he had expected, that all the arrangements, which were in full swing in Germany, were almost at a standstill in England. The construction of the ship was the only work that was progressing, and even in this there were many interruptions from the want of some one to give immediate decisions on points of detail.

A remedy for this state of chaos had to be discovered, and on November 4, 1900, the Joint Committee of the Royal Society and the Royal Geographical Society passed a resolution, which left Scott practically with a free hand to push on the work in every department, under a given estimate of expenditure in each. To safeguard the interests of the two Societies the resolution provided that this expenditure should be supervised by a Finance Committee, Page 18 and to this Committee unqualified gratitude was due. Difficulties were still to crop up, and as there were many scientific interests to be served, differences of opinion on points of detail naturally arose, but as far as the Finance Committee was concerned, it is mere justice to record that no sooner was it formed than its members began to work ungrudgingly to promote the success of the undertaking.

In the meantime Scott's first task was to collect, as far as possible, the various members of the expedition. Before he had left the *Majestic* he had written, 'I cannot gather what is the intention as regards the crew; is it hoped to be able to embody them from the R.N.? I sincerely trust so.' In fact he had set his heart on obtaining a naval crew, partly because he thought that their sense of discipline would be invaluable, but also because he doubted his ability to deal with any other class of men.

The Admiralty, however, was reluctant to grant a concession that Scott considered so necessary, and this reluctance arose not from any coldness towards the enterprise, but from questions of principle and precedent. At first the Admiralty assistance in this respect was limited to two officers, Scott himself and Royds, then the limit was extended to include Skelton the engineer, a carpenter and a boatswain, and thus at least a small naval nucleus was obtained. But it was not until the spring of 1901 that the Admiralty, thanks to Sir Anthony Hoskins and Sir Archibald Douglas, gave in altogether, and as the selection of Page 19 the most fitting volunteers had not yet been made, the chosen men did not join until the expedition was almost on the point of sailing.

For many reasons Scott was obliged to make his own headquarters in London, and the room that had been placed at his disposal in Burlington House soon became a museum of curiosities. Sledges, ski, fur clothing and boots were crowded into every corner, while tables and shelves were littered with correspondence and samples of tinned foods. And in the midst of this medley he worked steadily on, sometimes elated by the hope that all was going well, sometimes depressed by the thought that the expedition could not possibly be ready to start at the required date.

During these busy months of preparation he had the satisfaction of knowing that the first lieutenant, the chief engineer and the carpenter were in Dundee, and able to look into the numerous small difficulties that arose in connection with the building of the ship. Other important posts in the expedition had also been filled up, and expeditionary work was being carried on in many places. Some men were working on their especial subjects in the British Museum, others were preparing themselves at the Physical Laboratory at Kew, and others, again, were traveling in various directions both at home and abroad. Of all these affairs the central office was obliged to take notice, and so for its occupants idle moments were few and very far between. Nansen said once that the hardest work Page 20 of a Polar voyage came in its preparation, and during the years 1900-1, Scott found ample cause to agree with him. But in spite of conflicting interests, which at times threatened to wreck the well-being of the expedition, work, having been properly organized, went steadily forward; until on March 21, 1901, the new vessel was launched at Dundee and named the '*Discovery*' by Lady Markham.

In the choice of a name it was generally agreed that the best plan was to revive some time-honoured title, and that few names were more distinguished than 'Discovery.' She was the sixth of that name, and inherited a long record of honourable and fortunate service.

The *Discovery* had been nothing more than a skeleton when it was decided that she should be loaded with her freight in London; consequently, after she had undergone her trials, she was brought round from Dundee, and on June 3, 1901, was berthed in the East India Docks. There, during the following weeks, all the stores were gathered together, and there the vessel, which was destined to be the home of the expedition for more than three years, was laden.

Speaking at the Geographical Congress at Berlin in 1899, Nansen strongly recommended a vessel of the *Fram* type with fuller lines for South Polar work, but the special Ship Committee, appointed to consider the question of a vessel for this expedition, had very sound reasons for not following his advice. Nansen's Page 21 celebrated *Fram* was built for the specific object of remaining safely in the North Polar pack, in spite of the terrible pressures which were to be expected in such a vast extent of ice. This object was achieved in the simplest manner by inclining the sides of the vessel until her shape resembled a saucer, and lateral pressure merely tended to raise her above the surface. Simple as this design was, it fulfilled so well the requirements of the situation that its conception was without doubt a stroke of genius. What, however, has been generally forgotten is that the safety of the *Fram* was secured at the expense of her sea-worthiness and powers of ice-penetration.

Since the *Fram* was built there have been two distinct types of Polar vessels, the one founded on the idea of passive security in the ice, the other the old English whaler type designed to sail the high seas and push her way through the looser ice-packs. And a brief consideration of southern conditions will show which of these types is more serviceable for Antarctic exploration, because it is obvious that the exploring ship must first of all be prepared to navigate the most stormy seas in the world, and then be ready to force her way through the ice-floes to the mysteries beyond.

By the general consent of those who witnessed her performances, the old *Discovery* (the fifth of her name) of 1875 was the best ship that had ever been employed on Arctic service, and the Ship Committee eventually decided that the new vessel should be built on more Page 22 or less the same lines. The new *Discovery* had the honour to be the first vessel ever built for scientific exploration, and the decision to adopt well-tried English lines for her was more than justified by her excellent qualities.

The greatest strength lay in her bows, and when ice-floes had to be rammed the knowledge that the keel at the fore-end of the ship gradually grew thicker, until it rose in the enormous mass of solid wood which constituted the stem, was most comforting. No single tree could provide the wood for such a stem, but the several trees used were cunningly scarfed to provide the equivalent of a solid block. In further preparation for the battle with ice-floes, the stem itself and the bow for three or four feet on either side were protected with numerous steel plates, so that when the ship returned to civilization not a scratch remained to show the hard knocks received by the bow.

The shape of the stem was also a very important consideration. In the outline drawing of the *Discovery* will be seen how largely the stem overhangs, and this was carried to a greater extent than in any former Polar vessel. The object with which this was fitted was often fulfilled during the voyage. Many a time on charging a large ice-floe the stem of the ship glided upwards until the bows were raised two or three feet, then the weight of the ship acting downwards would crack the floe beneath, the bow would drop, and gradually the ship would forge ahead to tussle against the Page 23 next obstruction.

Nothing but a wooden structure has the elasticity and strength to thrust its way without injury through the thick Polar ice.

In Dundee the building of the *Discovery* aroused the keenest interest, and the peculiar shape of her overhanging stern, an entirely new feature in this class of vessel, gave rise to the strongest criticism. All sorts of misfortunes were predicted, but events proved that this overhanging rounded form of stem was infinitely superior for ice-work to the old form of stem, because it gave better protection to the rudder, rudder post and screw, and was more satisfactory in heavy seas.

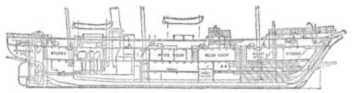

PROFILE DRAWING OF 'DISCOVERY'.

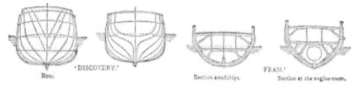

OUTLINE DRAWINGS OF 'DISCOVERY' AND 'FRAM'.

Both in the building and in the subsequent work of the *Discovery* the deck-house, marked on the drawing 'Magnetic Observatory,' was an important place. For the best of reasons it was important that the magnetic observations taken on the expedition should be as accurate as possible, and it will be readily understood that magnetic observations cannot be taken in a place closely surrounded by iron. The ardor of the magnetic experts on the Ship Committee had led them at first to ask that there should be neither iron nor steel in the vessel, but after it had been pointed out that this could scarcely be, a compromise was arrived at and it was agreed that no magnetic materials should be employed within thirty feet of the observatory. This decision caused immense trouble and expense, but in the end it was justified, for the magnetic observations taken on board throughout the voyage Page 25 required very little correction. And if the demands of the magnetic experts were a little exacting, some amusement was also derived from them. At one time those who lived within the circle were threatened with the necessity of shaving with brass razors; and when the ship was on her way home from New Zealand a parrot fell into dire disgrace, not because it was too talkative, but because it had been hanging on the mess-deck during a whole set of observations, and the wires of its cage were made of iron.

The *Discovery* was, in Scott's opinion, the finest vessel ever built for exploring purposes, and he was as enthusiastic about his officers and men as he was about the ship herself.

The senior of the ten officers who messed with Scott in the small wardroom of the *Discovery* was Lieutenant A. B. Armitage, R.N.R. He brought with him not only an excellent practical seamanship training in sailing ships, but also valuable Polar experience; for the P. and O. Company, in which he held a position, had in 1894 granted him leave of absence to join the Jackson-Harmsworth Expedition to Franz-Josef Land.

Reginald Koettlitz, the senior doctor, had also seen Arctic service in the Jackson-Harmsworth Expedition. As his medical duties were expected to be light, he combined them with those of official botanist.

The task of Thomas V. Hodgson, biologist, was to collect by hook or crook all the strange beasts Page 26 that inhabit the Polar seas, and no greater enthusiast for his work could have been chosen.

Charles W. R. Royds was the first lieutenant, and had all to do with the work of the men and the internal economy of the ship in the way that is customary with a first lieutenant of a man-of-war. Throughout the voyage he acted as meteorologist, and in face of great difficulties he secured the most valuable records.

Michael Barne, the second naval lieutenant, had served with Scott in the Majestic. 'I had thought him,' Scott wrote after the expedition had returned, 'as he proved to be, especially fitted for a voyage where there were many elements of dangers and difficulty.'

The original idea in appointing two doctors to the *Discovery* was that one of them should be available for a detached landing-party.

This idea was practically abandoned, but the expedition had reason to be thankful that it ever existed, for the second doctor appointed was Edward A. Wilson. In view of the glorious friendship which arose between them, and which in the end was destined to make history, it is of inestimable value to be able to quote what is believed to be Scott's first written opinion of Wilson. In a letter headed 'At sea, Sept. 27,' he said: 'I now come to the man who will do great things some day—Wilson. He has quite the keenest intellect on board and a marvelous capacity for work. You know his artistic talent, but would be surprised at Page 27 the speed at which he paints, and the indefatigable manner in which he is always at it. He has fallen at once into ship-life, helps with any job that may be in hand... in fact is an excellent fellow all round.

Wilson, in addition to his medical duties, was also vertebrate zoologist and artist to the expedition. In the first capacity he dealt scientifically with the birds and seals, and in the second he produced a very large number of excellent pictures and sketches of the wild scenes among which he was living.

One of Scott's earliest acts on behalf of the expedition was to apply for the services of Reginald W. Skelton as chief engineer. At the time Skelton was senior engineer of the Majestic, and his appointment to the *Discovery* was most fortunate in every way. From first to last there was no serious difficulty with the machinery or with anything connected with it.

The geologist, Hartley T. Ferrar, only joined the expedition a short time before the *Discovery* sailed, and the physicist, Louis Bernacchi, did not join until the ship reached New Zealand.

In addition there were two officers who did not serve throughout the whole term. Owing to ill-health Ernest H. Shackleton was obliged to return from the Antarctic in 1903, and his place was taken by George F. A. Mulock, who was a sub-lieutenant in the Navy when he joined.

Apart from Koettlitz, who was forty, and Hodgson, Page 28 who was thirty-seven, the average age of the remaining members of the wardroom mess was just over twenty-four years, and at that time Scott had little doubt as to the value of youth for Polar service. Very naturally, however, this opinion was less pronounced as the years went by, and on August 6, 1911, he wrote during his last expedition: 'We (Wilson and I) both conclude that it is the younger people who have the worst time... Wilson (39) says he never felt cold less than he does now; I suppose that between 30 and 40 is the best all-round age. Bower is a wonder of course. He is 29. When past the forties it is encouraging to remember that Peary was 52!'

The fact that these officers lived in complete harmony for three years was proof enough that they were well and wisely chosen, and Scott was equally happy in his selection of warrant officers, petty officers and men, who brought with them the sense of naval discipline that is very necessary for such conditions as exist in Polar service. The *Discovery*, it must be remembered, was not in Government employment, and so had no more stringent regulations to enforce discipline than those contained in the Merchant Shipping Act. But everyone on board lived exactly as though the ship was under the Naval Discipline Act; and as the men must have known that this state of affairs was a fiction, they deserved as much credit as the officers, if not more, for continuing rigorously to observe it.

Page 29 Something remains to be said about the *Discovery's* prospective course, and of the instructions given to Captain Scott.

For purposes of reference Sir Clements Markham had suggested that the Antarctic area should be divided into four quadrants, to be named respectively the Victoria, the Ross, the Weddell, and the Enderby, and when he also proposed that the Ross quadrant should be the one chosen for this expedition, his proposal was received with such unanimous approval that long before the *Discovery* was built her prospective course had been finally decided. In fact every branch of science saw a greater chance of success in the Ross quadrant than in any other region. Concerning instructions on such a voyage as the *Discovery's* it may be thought that, when once the direction is settled, the fewer there are the better. Provided, however, that they leave the greatest possible freedom to the commander, they may be very useful in giving him a general view of the situation, and in stating the order in which the various objects are held. If scientific interests clash, it is clearly to the commander's advantage to know in what light these interests are regarded by those responsible for the enterprise. Of such a nature were the instructions Scott received before sailing for the South.

During the time of preparation many busy men gave most valuable assistance to the expedition; but even with all this kindly aid it is doubtful if the *Discovery* would ever have started had it not been Page 30 that among these helpers was one who, from the first, had given his whole and undivided attention to the work in hand. After all is said and done Sir Clements Markham conceived the idea of this Antarctic Expedition, and it was his masterful personality which swept aside all obstacles and obstructions.

Page 31 CHAPTER II

SOUTHWARD HO!

They saw the cables loosened, they saw the gangways cleared,
They heard the women weeping, they heard the men who cheered.
Far off-far off the tumult faded and died away.
And all alone the sea wind came singing up the Bay.
—NEWBOLT.

On July 31, 1901, the *Discovery* left the London Docks, and slowly wended her way down the Thames; and at Cowes, on August 5, she was honoured by a visit from King Edward VII and Queen Alexandra. This visit must be ever memorable for the interest their Majesties showed in the minutest details of equipment; but at the same time it was natural for the members of the expedition to be obsessed by the fear that they might start with a flourish of trumpets and return with failure. The grim possibilities of the voyage were also not to be forgotten—a voyage to the Antarctic, the very map of which had remained practically unaltered from 1843-93.

With no previous Polar experience to help him, Scott was following on the track of great Polar explorers, notably of James Cook and James Ross, of whom it has been well said that the one defined the Antarctic region and the other discovered it. Can it be wondered therefore that his great anxieties were Page 32 to be off and doing, to justify the existence of the expedition at the earliest possible moment, and to obey the instructions which had been given him?

Before the *Discovery* had crossed the Bay of Biscay it was evident that she did not possess a turn of speed under any conditions, and that there must be none but absolutely necessary delays on the voyage, if she was to arrive in the Antarctic in time to take full advantage of the southern summer of 1901-2 for the first exploration in the ice. This proved a serious drawback, as it had been confidently expected that there would be ample time to make trial of various devices for sounding and dredging in the deep sea, while still in a temperate climate. The fact that no trials could be made on the outward voyage was severely felt when the Antarctic was reached.

On October 2 the *Discovery* arrived within 150 miles of the Cape, and on the 5th was moored off the naval station at Simon's Bay. The main object of staying at the Cape was to obtain comparisons with the magnetic instruments, but Scott wrote: 'It is much to be deplored that no permanent Magnetic Station now exists at the Cape. The fact increased the number and difficulty of our own observations, and it was quite impossible to spare the time for such repetitions and verifications as, under the circumstances, could alone have placed them beyond dispute.' Armitage and Barne, however, worked like Trojans in taking observations, and received so much valuable assistance 'that they were able to accomplish a maximum Page 33 amount of work in the limited time at their disposal.' In every way, indeed, the kindliest sympathy was shown at the Cape.

The magnetic work was completed on October 12, and two days later the *Discovery* once more put out to sea; and as time went on those on board became more and more satisfied with her seaworthy qualities. Towards the end of October there was a succession of heavy following gales, but she rose like a cork to the mountainous seas that followed in her wake, and, considering her size, she was wonderfully free of water on the upper deck. With a heavy following sea, however, she was, owing to her buoyancy, extremely lively, and rolls of more than 40° were often recorded. The peculiar shape of the stern, to which reference has been made, was now well tested. It gave additional buoyancy to the after-end, causing the ship to rise more quickly to the seas, but the same lifting effect was also directed to throwing the ship off her course, and consequently she was difficult to steer. The helmsmen gradually became more expert, but on one occasion when Scott and some other officers were on the bridge the ship swerved round, and was immediately swept by a monstrous sea which made a clean breach over her. Instinctively those on the bridge clutched the rails, and for several moments they were completely submerged while the spray dashed as high as the upper topsails.

On November 12 the *Discovery* was in lat. 51 S., long. 131 E., and had arrived in such an extremely Page 34 interesting magnetic area that they steered to the south to explore it. This new course took them far out of the track of ships and towards the regions of ice, and they had scarcely arrived in those lonely waters when Scott was aroused from sleep by a loud knocking and a voice shouting, 'Ship's afire, sir.' Without waiting to give any details of this alarming news the informant fled, and when Scott appeared hastily on the scenes he found that the deck was very dark and obstructed by numerous half-clad people, all of whom were as ignorant as he was. Making his way forward he discovered that the fire had been under the forecastle, and had been easily extinguished when the hose was brought to bear on it. In these days steel ships and electric light tend to lessen the fear of fire, but in a wooden vessel the possible consequences are too serious not to make the danger very real and alarming. Henceforth the risk of fire was constantly in Scott's thoughts, but this was the first and last occasion on which an alarm was raised in the *Discovery*.

On November 15 the 60th parallel was passed, and during the following morning small pieces of sea-ice, worn into fantastic shape by the action of the waves, appeared and were greeted with much excitement and enthusiasm. As the afternoon advanced signs of a heavier pack were seen ahead, and soon the loose floes were all about the ship, and she was pushing her way amongst them and receiving her baptism of ice.

Page 35 This was Scott's first experience of pack-ice, and he has recorded how deeply he was impressed by the novelty of his surroundings. 'The wind had died away; what light remained was reflected in a ghostly glimmer from the white surface of the pack; now and again a white snow petrel flitted through the gloom, the grinding of the floes against the ship's side was mingled with the more subdued hush of their rise and fall on the long swell, and for the first time we felt something of the solemnity of these great Southern solitudes.'

The *Discovery* was now within 200 miles of Adélie Land, and with steam could easily have pushed on towards it. But delays had already been excessive, and they could not be added to if New Zealand was to be reached betimes. Reluctantly the ship's head was again turned towards the North, and soon passed into looser ice.

One great feature of the tempestuous seas of these southern oceans is the quantity and variety of their bird life. Not only are these roaming, tireless birds to be seen in the distance, but in the majority of cases they are attracted by a ship and for hours gather close about her. The greater number are of the petrel tribe, and vary in size from the greater albatrosses, with their huge spread of wing and unwavering flight, to the small Wilson stormy petrel, which flits under the foaming crests of the waves. For centuries these birds have been the friends of sailors, and as Wilson was able to distinguish and Page 36 name the various visitors to the *Discovery*, the interest of the voyage was very greatly increased.

'At 11 A.M. on the 22nd,' Scott wrote in his official report of the Proceedings of the expedition, 'we sighted Macquarie Island, exactly at the time and in the direction expected, a satisfactory fact after so long an absence from land. As the island promised so much of interest to our naturalists I thought a delay of the few hours necessary for landing would be amply justified.... A landing was effected without much difficulty, and two penguin rookeries which had been observed from the ship were explored with much interest. One proved to be inhabited by the beautifully marked King penguin, while the other contained a smaller gold-crested broad-billed species.... At 8 P.M. the party returned to the ship, and shortly after we weighed anchor and proceeded. Including those collected in the ice, we had no fewer than 50 birds of various sorts to be skinned, and during the next few days several officers and men were busily engaged in this work under the superintendence of Dr. Wilson. The opportunity was taken of serving out the flesh of the penguins for food. I had anticipated considerable prejudice on the part of the men to this form of diet which it will so often be essential to enforce, and was agreeably surprised to find that they were by no means averse to it. Many pronounced it excellent, and all seemed to appreciate the necessity of cultivating a taste for it. I found no prejudice more difficult to conquer than my own.'

Page 37 Perhaps the most excited member of the party over this visit to Macquarie Island was Scott's Aberdeen terrier 'Scamp,' who was most comically divided between a desire to run away from the penguins, and a feeling that in such strange company it behooved him to be very courageous. This, however, was Scamp's first and last experience of penguins, for it was felt that he would be unable to live in the Antarctic, and so a comfortable home was found for him in New Zealand.

Late on November 29 the *Discovery* arrived off Lyttelton Heads, and on the following day she was berthed alongside a jetty in the harbor. For both the private and the public kindness which was shown to the expedition in New Zealand, no expressions of gratitude can be too warm. On every possible occasion, and in every possible way, efficient and kindly assistance was given, and this was all the more valuable because a lot of work had to be done before the ship could sail from Lyttelton. The rigging had to be thoroughly overhauled and refitted; the magneticians had to undertake the comparison of their delicate instruments, and as this was the last occasion on which it could be done special attention was necessary; and a large quantity of stores had to be shipped, because some of those in the *Discovery* had been damaged by the leaky state of the ship. This leak had never been dangerous, but all the same it had entailed many weary hours of pumping, and had caused much waste of time and of provisions. Among the many skilled Page 38 workmen, whose united labour had produced the solid structure of the *Discovery*'s hull, had been one who had shirked his task, and although the ship was docked and most determined and persistent efforts were made to find the leak, it succeeded in avoiding detection.

As the month of December advanced the scene on the ship was a very busy one, but at last the day for sailing from Lyttelton arrived, though not for the final departure from civilization, because a short visit was to be paid to Port Chalmers in the south to complete the stock of coal. On Saturday, December 21, the ship lay alongside the wharf ready for sea and very deeply laden. 'One could reflect that it would have been impossible to have got more into her, and that all we had got seemed necessary for the voyage, for the rest we could only trust that Providence would vouch-safe to us fine weather and an easy passage to the south.'

New Zealand, to the last, was bent on showing its enthusiasm for the expedition. Two men-of-war steamed slowly out ahead of the *Discovery*, while no fewer than five steamers, crowded with passengers, and with bands playing and whistles hooting, also accompanied her, until the open sea was reached and the *Discovery* slowly steamed out between the war-ships that seemed to stand as sentinels to the bay. And then, before the cheers of thousands of friends were hardly out of the ears of those on board, a tragedy happened. Among the ship's company who had crowded into the rigging to wave their farewells was one young seaman, named Charles Bonner, who, Page 39 more venturesome than the rest, had climbed above the crow's-nest to the top of the main-mast. There, seated on the truck, he had remained cheering, until in a moment of madness he raised himself into a standing position, and almost directly afterwards he fell and was instantaneously killed. On the Monday the ship arrived at Port Chalmers, and Bonner was buried with naval honours.

By noon on the following day the *Discovery* was clear of the harbor bar, and was soon bowling along under steam and sail towards the south. The last view of civilization, the last sight of fields and flowers had come and gone on Christmas Eve, 1901, and Christmas Day found the ship in the open expanse of the Southern Ocean, though after such a recent parting from so many kind friends no one felt inclined for the customary festivities.

In good sea trim the *Discovery* had little to fear from the worst gales, but at this time she was so heavily laden that had she encountered heavy seas the consequences must have been very unpleasant. Inevitably much of her large deck cargo must have been lost; the masses of wood on the superstructure would have been in great danger, while all the sheep and possibly many of the dogs would have been drowned. Fine weather, however, continued, and on January 3 Scott and his companions crossed the Antarctic Circle, little thinking how long a time would elapse before they would recross it. At length they had entered the Antarctic regions; before them lay Page 40 the scene of their work, and all the trials of preparation, and the anxiety of delays, were forgotten in the fact that they had reached their goal in time to make use of the best part of the short open season in these icebound regions.

Soon the pack was on all sides of them, but as yet so loose that there were many large pools of open water. And then for several days the ship had really to fight her way, and Scott gave high praise to the way she behaved: 'The "Discovery" is a perfect gem in the pack. Her size and weight behind such a stem seem to give quite the best combination possible for such a purpose. We have certainly tried her thoroughly, for the pack which we have come through couldn't have been looked at by Ross even with a gale of wind behind him.'

Necessarily progress became slow, but life abounds in the pack, and the birds that came to visit the ship were a source of perpetual interest. The pleasantest and most constant of these visitors was the small snow petrel, with its dainty snow-white plumage relieved only by black beak and feet, and black, beady eye. These little birds abound in the pack-ice, but the blue-grey southern fulmar and the Antarctic petrel were also to be seen, and that unwholesome scavenger, the giant petrel, frequently lumbered by; while the skua gull, most pugnacious of bullies, occasionally flapped past, on his way to make some less formidable bird disgorge his hard-earned dinner.

The squeak of the penguin was constantly heard, at Page 41 first afar and often long before the birds were seen. Curiosity drew them to the ship, and as she forced her way onward these little visitors would again and again leap into the water, and journey from floe to floe in their eagerness to discover what this strange apparition could be. Some of the sailors became very expert in imitating their calls, and could not only attract them from a long distance, but would visibly add to their astonishment when they approached. These were busy days for the penguins.

In all parts of the pack seals are plentiful and spend long hours asleep on the floes. The commonest kind is the crab-eater or white seal, but the Ross seal is not rare, and there and there is found the sea-leopard, ranging wide and preying on the penguins and even on the young of its less powerful brethren. It is curious to observe that both seals and penguins regard themselves as safe when out of the water. In the sea they are running risks all the time, and in that element Nature has made them swift to prey or to avoid being preyed upon. But once on ice or land they have known no enemy, and cannot therefore conceive one. The seal merely raises its head when anyone approaches, and then with but little fear; whereas it is often difficult to drive the penguin into the water, for he is firmly convinced that the sea is the sole source of danger. Several seals were killed for food, and from the first seal-meat was found palatable, if not altogether the form of diet to recommend to an epicure. The great drawback to the seal is that there is no fat except blubber, Page 42 and blubber has a very strong taste and most penetrating smell. At this time blubber was an abomination to everyone both in taste and smell, and if the smallest scrap happened to have been cooked with the meat, dinner was a wasted meal. Later on, however, this smell lost most of its terrors, while seal-steaks and seal-liver and kidneys were treated almost as luxuries.

On the morning of January 8 a strong water sky could be seen, and soon afterwards the officer of the watch hailed from aloft the glad tidings of an open sea to the south. Presently the ship entered a belt where the ice lay in comparatively small pieces, and after pushing her way through this for over a mile, she reached the hard line where the ice abruptly ended, and to the south nothing but a clear sky could be seen. At 10.30 P.M. on the same evening the joy of being again in the open sea was intensified by a shout of 'Land in sight,' and all who were not on deck quickly gathered there to take their first look at the Antarctic Continent. The sun, near the southern horizon, still shone in a cloudless sky, and far away to the south-west the blue outline of the high mountain peaks of Victoria Land could be seen. The course was now directed for Robertson Bay, and after some difficulty, owing to the reappearance of loose streams of pack-ice, the ship was eventually steered into the open water within the bay.

Robertson Bay is formed by the long peninsula of Cape Adare, within which, standing but slightly above the level of the sea, is a curious triangular Page 43 spit, probably the morainic remains of the vaster ice conditions of former ages. It was on this spit that the expedition sent forth by Sir George Newnes and commanded by Borchgrevink spent their winter in 1896, the first party to winter on the shores of the Antarctic Continent. Here Scott decided to land for a short time, and very soon Armitage, Bernacchi and Barne were at work among the thousands of penguins that abounded, while the naturalists wandered further afield in search of specimens. In the center of Cape Adare beach the hut used by the members of Borchgrevink's party was still found to be standing in very good condition, though at the best of times deserted dwellings are far from cheerful to contemplate. Bernacchi had been a member of this small party of eight, and on the spot he recalled the past, and told of the unhappy death of Hanson — one of his comrades.

Later on Bernacchi and some others landed again to visit Hanson's grave, and to see that all was well with it. They took a tin cylinder containing the latest report of the voyage with them, and were told to place it in some conspicuous part of the hut. In the following year this cylinder was found by the *Morning*,[1] and so the first information was given that the *Discovery* had succeeded in reaching these southern regions.

[Footnote 1: The relief ship.]

On January 10, when the weather was still calm and bright, the ship again stood out to sea, and was steered close around Cape Adare in the hope of finding Page 44 a clear channel near at hand. Very soon, however, the tidal stream began to make from the south, and the whole aspect of the streams of heavy pack-ice rapidly changed. Almost immediately the pack was about the ship, and she was being rapidly borne along with it. Across the entrance to the bay was a chain of grounded icebergs, and it was in this direction that she was being carried. For the first time they faced the dangers of the pack, and realized its mighty powers. Little or nothing could be done, for the floes around them were heavier than anything they had yet encountered. Twist and turn as they would no appreciable advance could be made, and in front of one colossal floe the ship was brought to a standstill for nearly half an hour. But they still battled on; Armitage remained aloft, working the ship with admirable patience; the engine-room, as usual, answered nobly to the call for more steam, and the *Discovery* exerted all her powers in the struggle; but, in spite of these efforts, progress was so slow that it looked almost certain that she would be carried down among the bergs. 'It was one of those hours,' Scott says, 'which impress themselves for ever on the memory. Above us the sun shone in a cloudless sky, its rays were reflected from a myriad points of tire glistening pack; behind us lay the lofty snow-clad mountains, the brown sun-kissed cliffs of the Cape, and the placid glassy waters of the bay; the air about us was almost breathlessly still; crisp, clear and sun-lit, it seemed an atmosphere in which all Nature should rejoice; Page 45 the silence was broken only by the deep panting of our engines and the slow, measured hush of the grinding floes; yet, beneath all, ran this mighty, relentless tide, bearing us on to possible destruction. It seemed desperately unreal that danger could exist in the midst of so fair a scene, and as one paced to and fro on the few feet of throbbing plank that constituted our bridge, it was difficult to persuade oneself that we were so completely impotent.'

With the exception of Scott himself only those who were actually on watch were on deck during this precarious time, for the hour was early, and the majority were asleep in their bunks below, happily oblivious of the possible dangers before them. And the fact that they were not aroused is a proof that a fuss was rarely made in the *Discovery*, if it could by any conceivable means be avoided.

At last, however, release came from this grave danger, and it came so gradually that it was difficult to say when it happened. Little by little the tidal stream slackened, the close-locked floes fell slightly apart, and under her full head of steam the ship began to forge ahead towards the open sea and safety. 'For me,' Scott adds, 'the lesson had been a sharp and, I have no doubt, a salutary one; we were here to fight the elements with their icy weapons, and once and for all this taught me not to undervalue the enemy.' During the forenoon the ship was within seven or eight miles of the high bold coast-line to the south of Cape Adare, but later she had to be turned outwards Page 46 so that the heavy stream of pack-ice drifting along the land could be avoided. By the morning of the 11th she was well clear of the land, but the various peaks and headlands which Sir James Ross had named could be distinctly seen, and gave everyone plenty to talk and think about. Progress, however, was slow, owing to a brisk S. E. wind and the fact that only one boiler was being used.

Of all economies practiced on board the most important was that of coal, but Scott was not at all sure that this decision to use only one boiler was really economical. Certainly coal was saved but time was also wasted, and against an adverse wind the *Discovery* could only make fifty-five miles on the 11th, and on the 12th she scarcely made any headway at all, for the wind had increased and a heavy swell was coming up from the south.

To gain shelter Scott decided to turn in towards the high cliffs of Coulman Island, the land of which looked illusively near as they approached it. So strong was this deception that the engines were eased when the ship was still nearly two miles away from the cliffs. Later on, in their winter quarters and during their sledge journeys, they got to know how easy it was to be deluded as regards distance, and what very false appearances distant objects could assume. This matter is of interest, because it shows that Polar explorers must be exceedingly cautious in believing the evidence of their own eyes, and it also explains the errors which the *Discovery* expedition found to Page 47 have been made by former explorers, and which they knew must have been made in all good faith.

During the night of the 13th the ship lay under the shelter of Coulman Island, but by the morning the wind had increased to such a furious gale, and the squalls swept down over the cliffs with such terrific violence, that in spite of every effort to keep her in her station she began to lose ground. In the afternoon the wind force was ninety miles an hour, and as they continued to lose ground they got into a more choppy sea, which sent the spray over them in showers, to freeze as it fell.

Again the situation was far from pleasant; to avoid one berg they were forced to go about, and in doing so they ran foul of another. As they came down on it the bowsprit just swept clear of its pinnacled sides, and they took the shock broad on their bows. It sent the ship reeling round, but luckily on the right tack to avoid further complications. The following night was dismal enough; again and again small bergs appeared through the blinding spray and drift, and only with great difficulty could the unmanageable ship be brought to clear them. Even gales, however, must have an end, and towards morning the wind moderated, and once more they were able to steam up close to the island. And there, between two tongues of ice off Cape Wadworth, they landed on the steep rocks and erected a staff bearing a tin cylinder with a further record of the voyage. By the time this had been done the wind had fallen completely, and in Page 48 the evening the ship entered a long inlet between Cape Jones and the barrier-ice, and later turned out, of this into a smaller inlet in the barrier-ice itself. She was now in a very well-sheltered spot, and night, as often happened in the Antarctic regions, was turned into day so that several seals could be killed. 'It, seemed a terrible desecration,' Scott says, 'to come to this quiet spot only to murder its innocent inhabitants, and stain the white snow with blood.' But there was the best of all excuses, namely necessity, for this massacre, because there was no guarantee that seals would be found near the spot in which the ship wintered, and undoubtedly the wisest plan was to make sure of necessary food.

While the seal carcasses and some ice for the boilers were being obtained, Scott turned in to get some rest before putting out to sea again, and on returning to the deck at 7.30 he was told that the work was completed, but that some five hours before Wilson, Ferrar, Cross and Weller had got adrift of a floe, and that no one had thought of picking them up. Although the sun had been shining brightly all night, the temperature had been down to 18°, and afar off Scott could see four disconsolate figures tramping about, and trying to keep themselves warm on a detached floe not more than fifteen yards across.

When at length the wanderers scrambled over the side it was very evident that they had a grievance, and not until they had been warmed by hot cocoa could they talk with ease of their experiences. They Page 49 had been obliged to keep constantly on the move, and when they thought of smoking to relieve the monotony they found that they had pipes and tobacco, but no matches. While, however, they were dismally bemoaning this unfortunate state of affairs Wilson, who did not smoke, came to the rescue and succeeded in producing fire with a small pocket magnifying glass—a performance which testified not only to Wilson's resource, but also to the power of the sun in these latitudes.

On the 17th the ship had to stand out farther and farther from the land to clear the pack, and when on the 18th she arrived in the entrance to Wood Bay it was also found to be heavily packed. A way to the N. and N.W. the sharp peaks of Monteagle and Murchison, among bewildering clusters of lesser summits, could be seen; across the bay rose the magnificent bare cliff of Cape Sibbald, while to the S.W. the eye lingered pleasantly upon the uniform outline of Mount Melbourne. This fine mountain rears an almost perfect volcanic cone to a height of 9,000 feet, and with no competing height to take from its grandeur, it constitutes the most magnificent landmark on the coast. Cape Washington, a bold, sharp headland, projects from the foot of the mountain on its eastern side, and finding such heavy pack in Wood Bay, Scott decided to turn to the south to pass around this cape.

From this point the voyage promised to be increasingly interesting, since the coast to the south of Cape Washington was practically unknown. Pack-ice was Page 50 still a formidable obstacle, but on the 20th the *Discovery* pushed her way into an inlet where she met ice which had been formed inside and but recently broken up. The ice was perfectly smooth, and as it showed absolutely no sign of pressure there was no doubting that this inlet would make a secure wintering harbor. Already a latitude had been reached in which it was most desirable to find safe winter quarters for the ship. In England many people had thought that Wood Bay would be the most southerly spot where security was likely to be found, but Scott had seen enough of the coast-line to the south of that place to realize the impossibility of traveling along it in sledges, and to convince him that if any advance to the south was to be made, a harbor in some higher latitude must be found.

This inlet was afterwards named Granite Harbor, and so snug and secure a spot was it to winter in that Scott expressed his thankfulness that he did not yield to its allurements. 'Surrounded as we should have been by steep and lofty hills, we could have obtained only the most local records of climatic conditions, and our meteorological observations would have been comparatively valueless; but the greatest drawback would have been that we should be completely cut off from traveling over the sea-ice beyond the mouth of our harbor.... It is when one remembers how naturally a decision to return to this place might have been made, that one sees how easily the results of the expedition might have been missed.'

Page 51 It was, however, consoling at the time to know that, in default of a better place, a safe spot had been found for wintering, so with Granite Harbor in reserve the ship again took up her battle with the ice; and on the 21st she was in the middle of McMurdo Sound, and creeping very slowly through the pack-ice, which appeared from the crow's-nest to extend indefinitely ahead. They were now within a few miles of the spot where they ultimately took up their winter quarters, but nearly three weeks were to pass before they returned there. 'At 8 P.M. on the 21st,' Scott says, 'we thought we knew as much of this region as our heavy expenditure of coal in the pack-ice would justify us in finding out, and as before us lay the great unsolved problem of the barrier and of what lay beyond it, we turned our course with the cry of Eastward ho!'

Page 52 CHAPTER III

IN SEARCH OF WINTER QUARTERS

> Beholde I see the haven near at hand
> To which I mean my wearie course to bend;
> Vere the main sheet and bear up to the land
> To which afore is fairly to be ken'd.
> —SPENSER, Faerie Queene.

In their journey from Cape Washington to the south something had already been done to justify the dispatch of the expedition. A coast-line which hitherto had been seen only at a great distance, and reported so indefinitely that doubts were left with regard to its continuity, had been resolved into a concrete chain of mountains; and the positions and forms of individual heights, with the curious ice formations and the general line of the coast, had been observed. In short the map of the Antarctic had already received valuable additions, and whatever was to happen in the future that, at any rate, was all to the good.

At 8 P.M. on the 22nd the ship arrived off the bare land to the westward of Cape Crozier, where it was proposed to erect a post and leave a cylinder containing an account of their doings, so that the chain of records might be completed. After a landing had Page 53 been made with some difficulty, a spot was chosen in the center of the penguin rookery on a small cliff overlooking the sea, and here the post was set up and anchored with numerous boulders. In spite of every effort to mark the place, at a few hundred yards it was almost impossible to distinguish it; but although this small post on the side of a vast mountain looked a hopeless clue, it eventually brought the *Morning* into McMurdo Sound.

While Bernacchi and Barne set up their magnetic instruments and began the chilly task of taking observations, the others set off in twos and threes to climb the hillside. Scott, Royds and Wilson scrambled on until at last they reached the summit of the highest of the adjacent volcanic cones, and were rewarded by a first view of the Great Ice Barrier.[1]

[Footnote 1: The immense sheet of ice, over 400 miles wide and of still greater length.]

'Perhaps,' Scott says, 'of all the problems which lay before us in the south we were most keenly interested in solving the mysteries of this great ice-mass.... For sixty years it had been discussed and rediscussed, and many a theory had been built on the slender foundation of fact which alone the meager information concerning it could afford. Now for the first time this extraordinary ice-formation was seen from above.... It was an impressive sight and the very vastness of what lay at our feet seemed to add to our sense of its mystery.'

Early on the 23rd they started to steam along the Page 54 ice-face of the barrier; and in order that nothing should be missed it was arranged that the ship should continue to skirt close to the ice-cliff, that the officers of the watch should repeatedly observe and record its height, and that three times in the twenty-four hours the ship should be stopped and a sounding taken. In this manner a comparatively accurate survey of the northern limit of the barrier was made.

On steaming along the barrier it was found that although they were far more eager to gain new information than to prove that old information was incorrect, a very strong case soon began to arise against the Parry Mountains, which Ross had described as 'probably higher than we have yet seen'; and later on it was known with absolute certainty that these mountains did not exist. This error on the part of such a trustworthy and cautious observer, Scott ascribes to the fact that Ross, having exaggerated the height of the barrier, was led to suppose that anything seen over it at a distance must be of great altitude. 'But,' he adds, 'whatever the cause, the facts show again how deceptive appearances may be and how easily errors may arise. In fact, as I have said before, one cannot always afford to trust the evidence of one's own eyes.' Though the ship was steaming along this ice-wall for several days, the passage was not in the least monotonous, because new variations were continually showing themselves, and all of them had to be carefully observed and recorded. This work continued for several days until, on January 29, they arrived at a particularly interesting place, to Page 55 the southward and eastward of the extreme position reached by Ross in 1842. From that position he had reported a strong appearance of land to the southeast, and consequently all eyes were directed over the icy cliffs in that direction. But although the afternoon was bright and clear, nothing from below or from aloft could be seen, and the only conclusion to be made was that the report was based on yet another optical illusion.

But in spite of the disappointment at being unable to report that Ross's 'appearance of land' rested on solid foundations, there was on the afternoon of the 29th an indescribable sense of impending change. 'We all felt that the plot was thickening, and we could not fail to be inspirited by the fact that we had not so far encountered the heavy pack-ice which Ross reported in this region, and that consequently we were now sailing in an open sea into an unknown world.'

The course lay well to the northward of east, and the change came at 8 P.M. when suddenly the ice-cliff turned to the east, and becoming more and more irregular continued in that direction for about five miles, when again it turned sharply to the north. Into the deep bay thus formed they ran, and as the ice was approached they saw at once that it was unlike anything yet seen. The ice-foot descended to various heights of ten or twenty feet above the water, and behind it the snow surface rose in long undulating slopes to rounded ridges, the heights of which could only be guessed. Whatever doubt remained in their minds that this was snow-covered land, a sounding of 100 fathoms quickly removed it.

Page 56 But what a land! On the swelling mounds of snow above them there was not one break, not a feature to give definition to the hazy outline. No scene could have been more perfectly devised to produce optical illusions. And then, while there was so much to observe, a thick fog descended, and blotted out all hope of seeing what lay beyond the ice-foot. During the afternoon of January 30 the fog was less dense, but still no sign of bare land could be seen, and it was not until the bell had sounded for the evening meal that two or three little black patches, which at first were mistaken for detached cloud, appeared. 'We gazed idly enough at them till someone remarked that he did not believe they were clouds; then all glasses were leveled; assertions and contradictions were numerous, until the small black patches gradually assumed more and more definite shape, and all agreed that at last we were looking at real live rock, the actual substance of our newly discovered land.... It is curious to reflect now on the steps which led us to the discovery of King Edward's Land, and the chain of evidence which came to us before the actual land itself was seen: at first there had been the shallow soundings, and the sight of gently rising snow-slopes, of which, in the nature of things, one is obliged to retain a doubt; then the steeper broken slopes of snow, giving a contrast to convey a surer evidence to the eye; and, finally the indubitable land itself, but even then surrounded with such mystery as to leave us far from complete satisfaction with our discovery.'

Page 57 The temptation to push farther and farther to the east was almost irresistible, but with the young ice forming rapidly around them, Scott, on February 1, decided to return, and on their way back along the barrier they experienced much lower temperatures than on the outward journey. During the return journey they landed on the barrier, and on February 4 preparations for a balloon ascent were made. 'The honour,' Scott says, 'of being the first aeronaut to make an ascent in the Antarctic Regions, perhaps somewhat selfishly, I chose for myself, and I may further confess that in so doing I was contemplating the first ascent I had made in any region, and as I swayed about in what appeared a very inadequate basket and gazed down on the rapidly diminishing figures below, I felt some doubt as to whether I had been wise in my choice.[1]

If, however, this ascent was not altogether enjoyed by the aeronaut, it, at any rate, gave him considerable information about the barrier surface towards the south; and, to his surprise, he discovered that instead of the continuous level plain that he had expected, it continued in a series of long undulations running approximately east and west, or parallel to the barrier surface. Later on, however, when the sledge-party taken out by Armitage returned, they reported that these undulations were not gradual as had been supposed from the balloon, but that the crest of each wave was flattened into a long plateau, from which the descent into the succeeding valley was comparatively sharp. On the evening of the 4th they put out Page 58 to sea again, and on the 8th they were once more in McMurdo Sound, with high hopes that they would soon find a sheltered nook in which the *Discovery* could winter safely, and from which the sledge-parties could set forth upon the task of exploring the vast new world around them.

Without any delay they set out to examine their immediate surroundings, and found a little bay which promised so well for the winter that Scott's determination to remain in this region was at once strengthened. The situation, however, was surrounded with difficulties, for although the ice had broken far afield it refused to move out of the small bay on which they had looked with such eager eyes; consequently they were forced to cling to the outskirts of the bay with their ice-anchors, in depths that were too great to allow the large anchors to be dropped to the bottom. The weather also was troublesome, for after the ship had lain quietly during several hours a sudden squall would fling her back on her securing ropes, and, uprooting the ice-anchors, would ultimately send her adrift.

In spite, however, of the difficulty of keeping the ship in position, steady progress was made with the work on shore, and this consisted mainly in erecting the various huts which had been brought in pieces. The original intention had been that the *Discovery* should not winter in the Antarctic, but should land a small party and turn northward before the season closed, and for this party a large hut had been carried south. But even when it had been decided to keep the Page 59 ship as a home, it was obvious that a shelter on shore must be made before exploring parties could be safely sent away; since until the ship was frozen in a heavy gale might have driven her off her station for several days, if not altogether. In seeking winter quarters so early in February, Scott had been firmly convinced that the season was closing in. 'With no experience to guide us, our opinion could only be based on the very severe and unseasonable conditions which we had met with to the east. But now to our astonishment we could see no sign of a speedy freezing of the bay; the summer seemed to have taken a new lease, and for several weeks the fast sea-ice continued to break silently and to pass quietly away to the north in large floes.'

In addition to the erection of the main hut, two small huts which had been brought for the magnetic instruments had to be put together. The parts of these were, of course, numbered, but the wood was so badly warped that Dailey, the carpenter, had to use a lot of persuasion before the joints would fit.

On February 14 Scott wrote in his diary: 'We have landed all the dogs, and their kennels are ranged over the hillside below the huts.... It is surprising what a number of things have to be done, and what an unconscionable time it takes to do them. The hut-building is slow work, and much of our time has been taken in securing the ship.... Names have been given to the various landmarks in our vicinity. The end of our peninsula is to be called "Cape Armitage," after our excellent navigator. The sharp hill above it Page 60 is to be "Observation Hill."... Next comes the "Gap," through which we can cross the peninsula at a comparatively low level. North of the "Gap" are "Crater Heights," and the higher volcanic peak beyond is to be "Crater Hill"; it is 1,050 feet in height. Our protecting promontory is to be "Hut Point," with "Arrival Bay" on the north and "Winter Quarter Bay" on the south; above "Arrival Bay" are the "Arrival Heights," which continue with breaks for about three miles to a long snow-slope, beyond which rises the most conspicuous landmark on our peninsula, a high, precipitous-sided rock with a flat top, which has been dubbed "Castle Rock"; it is 1,350 feet in height.

'In spite of the persistent wind, away up the bay it is possible to get some shelter, and here we take our ski exercise.... Skelton is by far the best of the officers, though possibly some of the men run him close.'

On the 19th the first small reconnoitering sledge party went out, and on their return three days later they were so excited by their experiences that some time passed before they could answer the questions put to them. Although the temperature had not been severe they had nearly got into serious trouble by continuing their march in a snowstorm, and when they did stop to camp they were so exhausted that frost-bites were innumerable. The tent had been difficult to get up, and all sorts of trouble with the novel cooking apparatus had followed. 'It is strange now,' Scott wrote three years later, 'to look back on Page 61 these first essays at sledding, and to see how terribly hampered we were by want of experience.'

By February 26 the main hut was practically finished, and as a quantity of provisions and oil, with fifteen tons of coal, had been landed, the ship could be left without anxiety, and arrangements for the trip, which Scott hoped to lead himself, were pushed forward. The object of this journey was to try and reach the record at Cape Crozier over the barrier, and to leave a fresh communication there with details of the winter quarters. On the following day, however, Scott damaged his right knee while skiing, and had to give up all idea of going to Cape Crozier. 'I already foresaw how much there was to be learnt if we were to do good sledding work in the spring, and to miss such an opportunity of gaining experience was terribly trying; however, there was nothing to be done but to nurse my wounded limb and to determine that never again would I be so rash as to run hard snow-slopes on ski.'

By March 4 the preparation of the sledge party was completed. The party consisted of four officers, Royds, Koettlitz, Skelton and Barne, and eight men, and was divided into two teams, each pulling a single sledge and each assisted by four dogs. But again the want of experience was badly felt, and in every respect the lack of system was apparent. Though each requirement might have been remembered, all were packed in a confused mass, and, to use a sailor's expression, 'everything was on top and nothing handy.'

Page 62 Once more Scott comments upon this lack of experience: 'On looking back I am only astonished that we bought that experience so cheaply, for clearly there were the elements of catastrophe as well as of discomfort in the disorganized condition in which our first sledge parties left the ship.'

The days following the departure of the sledge party were exceptionally fine, but on Tuesday, March 11, those on board the ship woke to find the wind blowing from the east; and in the afternoon the wind increased, and the air was filled with thick driving snow. This Tuesday was destined to be one of the blackest days spent by the expedition in the Antarctic, but no suspicion that anything untoward had happened to the sledge party arose until, at 8.30 P.M., there was a report that four men were walking towards the ship. Then the sense of trouble was immediate, and the first disjointed sentences of the newcomers were enough to prove that disasters had occurred. The men, as they emerged from their thick clothing, were seen to be Wild, Weller, Heald and Plumley, but until Scott had called Wild, who was the most composed of the party, aside, he could not get any idea of what had actually happened, and even Wild was too exhausted, and excited to give anything but a meager account.

Scott, however, did manage to discover that a party of nine, In charge of Barne, had been sent back, and early in the day had reached the crest of the hills somewhere by Castle Rock. In addition, Wild told him, to the four who had returned, the party had Page 63 consisted of Barne, Quartley, Evans, Hare and Vince. They had thought that they were quite close to the ship, and when the blizzard began they had left their tents and walked towards her supposed position. Then they found themselves on a steep slope and tried to keep close together, but it was impossible to see anything. Suddenly Hare had disappeared, and a few minutes after Evans went. Barne and Quartley had left them to try to find out what had become of Evans, and neither of them had come back, though they waited. Afterwards they had gone on, and had suddenly found themselves at the edge of a precipice with the sea below; Vince had shot past over the edge. Wild feared all the others must be lost; he was sure Vince had gone. Could he guide a search party to the scene of the accident? He thought he could — at any rate he would like to try.

The information was little enough but it was something on which to act, and though the first disastrous news had not been brought until 8.30 P.M. the relieving party had left the ship before 9 P.M. Owing to his knee Scott could not accompany the party, and Armitage took charge of it.

Subsequently the actual story of the original sledge party was known, and the steps that led to the disaster could be traced. On their outward journey they had soon come to very soft snow, and after three days of excessive labour Royds had decided that the only chance of making progress was to use snow-shoes; but unfortunately there were only three pairs of ski Page 64 with the party, and Royds resolved to push on to Cape Crozier with Koettlitz and Skelton, and to send the remainder back in charge of Barne.

The separation took place on the 9th, and on the 11th the returning party, having found an easier route than on their way out, were abreast of Castle Rock. Scarcely, however, had they gained the top of the ridge about half a mile south-west of Castle Rock, when a blizzard came on and the tents were hastily pitched.

'We afterwards weathered many a gale,' Scott says, 'in our staunch little tents, whilst their canvas sides flapped thunderously hour after hour.... But to this party the experience was new; they expected each gust that swept down on them would bear the tents bodily away, and meanwhile the chill air crept through their leather boots and ill-considered clothing, and continually some frost-bitten limb had to be nursed back to life.'

At ordinary times hot tea or cocoa would have revived their spirits, but now the cooking apparatus was out of order, and taking everything into consideration it was small wonder that they resolved to make for the ship, which they believed to be only a mile or so distant.

'Before leaving,' Barne wrote in his report, 'I impressed on the men, as strongly as I could, the importance of keeping together, as it was impossible to distinguish any object at a greater distance than ten yards on account of the drifting snow.' But after they had struggled a very short distance, Hare, who Page 65 had been at the rear of the party, was reported to be missing, and soon afterwards Evans 'stepped back on a patch of bare smooth ice, fell, and shot out of sight immediately.'

Then Barne, having cautioned his men to remain where they were, sat down and deliberately started to slide in Evans's track. In a moment the slope grew steeper, and he was going at such a pace that all power to check himself had gone. In the mad rush he had time to wonder vaguely what would come next, and then his flight was arrested, and he stood up to find Evans within a few feet of him. They had scarcely exchanged greetings when the figure of Quartley came hurtling down upon them from the gloom, for he had started on the same track, and had been swept down in the same breathless and alarming manner. To return by the way they had come down was impossible, and so they decided to descend, but within four paces of the spot at which they had been brought to rest, they found that the slope ended suddenly in a steep precipice, beyond which nothing but clouds of snow could be seen. For some time after this they sat huddled together, forlornly hoping that the blinding drift would cease, but at last they felt that whatever happened they must keep on the move, and groping their way to the right they realized that the sea was at their feet, and that they had been saved from it by a patch of snow almost on the cornice of the cliff. Presently a short break in the storm enabled them to see Castle Rock above their heads, and slowly making their way Page 66 up the incline, they sought the shelter of a huge boulder; and there, crouched together, they remained for several hours.

Meanwhile the party had remained in obedience to orders at the head of the slope, and had shouted again and again in the lulls of the whirling storm. But after waiting for a long time they felt that something was amiss, and that it was hopeless to remain where they were. 'As usual on such occasions,' Scott says, 'the leading spirit came to the fore, and the five who now remained submitted themselves to the guidance of Wild, and followed him in single file as he again struck out in the direction in which they supposed the ship to lie.' In this manner they descended for about 500 yards, until Wild suddenly saw the precipice beneath his feet, and far below, through the wreathing snow, the sea. He sprang back with a cry of warning, but in an instant Vince had flashed past and disappeared.

Then, horror-stricken and dazed, they vaguely realized that at all costs they must ascend the slope down which they had just come. All of them spoke afterwards of that ascent with horror, and wondered how it had ever been made. They could only hold themselves by the soles of their boots, and to slip to their knees meant inevitably to slide backwards towards the certain fate below. Literally their lives depended on each foothold. Wild alone had a few light nails in his boots, and to his great credit he used this advantage to give a helping hand in turn to each Page 67 of his companions. When, after desperate exertions, they did reach the top of the slope their troubles were not finished, for they were still ignorant of the position of the ship. Wild, however, again took the lead, and it was largely due to him that the party eventually saw the ship looming through the whirl of snow. 'It is little wonder that after such an experience they should have been, as I have mentioned, both excited and tired.'

The hours following the departure of Armitage and his search party on this fatal night were unforgettable. Scott, hatefully conscious of his inability to help on account of his injured leg, admits that he could not think of any further means to render assistance, but he says, 'as was always my experience in the *Discovery*, my companions were never wanting in resource.' Soon the shrill screams of the siren were echoing among the hills, and in ten minutes after the suggestion had been made, a whaler was swinging alongside ready to search the cliffs on the chance of finding Vince.

But for Scott and those who had to wait inactively on board there was nothing to do but stand and peer through the driving snow, and fully three hours passed before there was a hail from without, and Ferrar appeared leading three of the lost—Barne, Evans and Quartley. An hour later the main search party returned, having done all that men could do in such weather. A more complete search was impossible, but it had to be admitted that the chance of seeing Page 68 Hare or Vince again was very small. Sadly it had to be realized that two men were almost certainly lost, but there was also no disguising the fact that a far greater tragedy might have happened. Indeed, it seemed miraculous that any of the party were alive to tell the tale, and had not Barne, Evans and Quartley heard the faint shrieks of the siren, and in response to its welcome sound made one more effort to save themselves, the sledge party would in all probability not have found them. All three of them were badly frost-bitten, and one of Barne's hands was in such a serious condition that for many days it was thought that his fingers would have to be amputated.

The end of this story, however, is not yet told, for on March 13 Scott wrote in his diary: 'A very extraordinary thing has happened. At 10 A.M. a figure was seen descending the hillside. At first we thought it must be some one who had been for an early walk; but it was very soon seen that the figure was walking weakly, and, immediately after, the men who were working in the hut were seen streaming out towards it. In a minute or two we recognized the figure as that of young Hare, and in less than five he was on board.... We soon discovered that though exhausted, weak, and hungry, he was in full possession of his faculties and quite free from frost-bites. He went placidly off to sleep whilst objecting to the inadequacy of a milk diet.'

Later on Hare, who like Vince had been wearing fur boots, explained that he had left his companions Page 69 to return to the sledges and get some leather boots, and had imagined that the others understood what he intended to do. Soon after he had started back he was wandering backwards and forwards, and knew that he was walking aimlessly to and fro. The last thing he remembered was making for a patch of rock where he hoped to find shelter, and there he must have lain in the snow for thirty-six hours, though he required a lot of persuasion before he could be convinced of this. When he awoke he found himself covered with snow, but on raising himself he recognized Crater Hill and other landmarks, and realized exactly where the ship lay. Then he started towards her, but until his intense stiffness wore off he was obliged to travel upon his hands and knees.

But though Hare was safe, Vince was undoubtedly gone. 'Finally and sadly we had to resign ourselves to the loss of our shipmate, and the thought was grievous to all.... Life was a bright thing to him, and it is something to think that death must have come quickly in the grip of that icy sea.'

This fatal mishap naturally caused increased anxiety about the three men who had gone on, and anxiety was not diminished when, on the 19th, Skelton was seen coming down, the hill alone. The others, however, were close behind him, and all three of them were soon safely on board.

On the 15th Royds had been compelled to abandon the attempt to reach the record at Cape Crozier, but he did not turn back until it was evident that a better Page 70 equipped party with more favorable weather would easily get to it. On comparing notes with his party, Scott recognized what a difference there might be in the weather conditions of places within easy reach of the ship, and not only in temperature but also in the force and direction of the wind. It had not occurred to anyone that within such a short distance of the ship any large difference of temperature was probable, and as the summer was barely over, Royds, Koettlitz and Skelton had only taken a light wolf-skin fur suit for night-wear. This, however, had proved totally inadequate when the thermometer fell to -42°, and on the night of the 16th uncontrollable paroxysms of shivering had prevented them from getting any sleep. The value of proper clothing and the wisdom of being prepared for the unexpected rigors of such a fickle climate, were two of the lessons learnt from the experiences of the Cape Crozier party.

As the days of March went by Scott began really to wonder whether the sea ever intended to freeze over satisfactorily, and at such an advanced date there were many drawbacks in this unexpected state of affairs. Until the ship was frozen in, the security of their position was very doubtful; economy of coal had long since necessitated the extinction of fires in the boilers, and if a heavy gale drove the ship from her shelter, steam could only be raised with difficulty and after the lapse of many hours. There was, too, the possibility that the ship, if once driven off, would not be able to return, and so it was obviously unsafe Page 71 to send a large party away from her, because if she went adrift most of them would be needed.

Another annoying circumstance was that until they had a solid sheet of ice around them they could neither set up the meteorological screen, nor, in short, carry out any of the routine scientific work which was such an important object of the expedition.

At this time Scott was eager to make one more sledding effort before the winter set in. The ostensible reason was to layout a depôt of provisions to the south in preparation for the spring, but 'a more serious purpose was to give himself and those who had not been away already a practical insight into the difficulties of sledge traveling. But as this party would have to include the majority of those on board, he was forced to wait until the ship was firmly fixed, and it may be said that the *Discovery* was as reluctant to freeze-in as she was difficult to get out when once the process had been completed.

On March 28, however, Scott was able to write in his diary: 'The sea is at last frozen over, and if this weather lasts the ice should become firm enough to withstand future gales. We have completed the packing of our sledges, though I cannot say I am pleased with their appearance; the packing is not neat enough, and we haven't got anything like a system.'

Three days later a party of twelve, divided into two teams, each with a string of sledges and nine dogs, made a start. Their loads were arranged on the theory Page 72 of 200 lbs. to each man, and 100 lbs. to each dog, but they very quickly discovered that the dogs were not going to have anything to do with such a theory as this. The best of them would only pull about 50 lbs., and some of the others had practically to be pulled.

Later on Scott learned that it was a bad plan to combine men and dogs on a sledge, because the dogs have their own pace and manner of pulling, and neither of these is adapted to the unequal movement caused by the swing of marching men. And on this occasion another reason for the inefficiency of the dogs was that they were losing their coats, and had but little protection against the bitterly cold wind. 'As a matter of fact, our poor dogs suffered a great deal from their poorly clothed condition during the next week or two, and we could do little to help them; but Nature seemed to realize the mistake, and came quickly to the rescue: the new coats grew surprisingly fast, and before the winter had really settled down on us all the animals were again enveloped in their normally thick woolly covering.

The refusal of the dogs to work on this trip meant that the men had to do far more than their share, and from the first they had no chance of carrying out their intentions. Each hour, however, was an invaluable experience, and when a return was made to the ship Scott was left with much food for thought. 'In one way or another each journey had been a failure; we had little or nothing to show for our labours. The errors were patent; food, clothing, everything was Page 73 wrong, the whole system was bad. It was clear that there would have to be a thorough reorganization before the spring, and it was well to think that before us lay a long winter in which this might be effected.'

But in a sense even these failures were successful, for everyone resolved to profit by the mistakes that had been made and the experience that had been gained, and the successful sledge journeys subsequently made in the spring were largely due to the failures of the autumn.

Page 74 CHAPTER IV

THE POLAR WINTER

> The cold ice slept below,
> Above the cold sky shone,
> And all around
> With a chilling sound
> From caves of ice and fields of snow
> The breath of night like death did flow
> Beneath the sinking moon. —SHELLEY.

The sun was due to depart before the end of April, and so no time could be wasted if the outside work, which had been delayed by the tardy formation of the ice-sheet, was to be completed before the daylight vanished.

One of the most urgent operations was to get up the meteorological screen, which had been made under the superintendence of Royds. The whole of this rather elaborate erection was, placed about 100 yards astern of the ship, and consequently in a direction which, with the prevalent south-easterly winds, would be to windward of her. To obtain a complete record of meteorological observations was one of the most important scientific objects of the expedition, and it was decided that the instruments should be read and recorded every two hours. Consequently in calm or storm Page 75 some member of the community had to be on the alert, and every other hour to make the rounds of the various instruments. On a fine night this was no great hardship, but in stormy weather the task was not coveted by anyone. On such occasions it was necessary to be prepared to resist the wind and snowdrift, and the round itself was often full of exasperating annoyances. In fact the trials and tribulations of the meteorological observers were numerous, and it was arranged that throughout the winter each officer should take it in turn to make the night observations from 10 P.M. to 6 A.M. Wilson nobly offered always to take the 8 A.M. observation, but the lion's share of the work fell on Royds himself, since besides taking his share of the night work he also, throughout the first winter and a great part of the second, took all the observations between 10 A.M. and 10 P.M.

The magnetic huts and all that appertained to them were Bernacchi's special business, and many times daily he was to be seen journeying to and fro in attendance upon his precious charge. The general reader may well ask why so much trouble should be taken to ascertain small differences in the earth's magnetism, and he can scarcely be answered in a few words. Broadly speaking, however, the earth is a magnet, and its magnetism is constantly changing. But why it is a magnet, or indeed what magnetism may be, is unknown, and obviously the most hopeful way of finding an explanation of a phenomenon is to study it. For many reasons the *Discovery*'s winter station in the Page 76 Antarctic was an especially suitable place in which to record the phenomenon of magnetism.

Besides establishing the routine of scientific work many preparations had to be made for the comfort and well-being of the ship during the winter, and long before the sun had disappeared the little company had settled down to a regular round of daily life.

Later in the year Scott wrote in his diary: 'The day's routine for the officers gives four clear hours before tea and three after; during these hours all without exception are busily employed except for the hour or more devoted to exercise.... It would be difficult to say who is the most diligent, but perhaps the palm would be given to Wilson, who is always at work; every rough sketch made since we started is reproduced in an enlarged and detailed form, until we now possess a splendid pictorial representation of the whole coastline of Victoria Land.... At home many no doubt will remember the horrible depression of spirit that has sometimes been pictured as a pendant to the long polar night. We cannot even claim to be martyrs in this respect; with plenty of work the days pass placidly and cheerfully.'

Nearly seven months before Scott wrote in this cheerful spirit of the winter, he had expressed himself warmly about those who were to spend it with him. 'I have,' he said in a letter dispatched from Port Chalmers on the voyage out, 'the greatest admiration for the officers and men, and feel that their allegiance to me is a thing assured. Our little society in the wardroom is governed by a spirit of good fellowship and patience which is all that the heart of man could desire; I am everlastingly glad to be one of the company and not forced to mess apart.... The absence of friction and the fine comradeship displayed throughout is beyond even my best expectation.'

This spirit of good-fellowship and give-and-take was a remarkable feature of life during the time spent in the *Discovery*, and the only man Scott had a word to say against was the cook. 'We shipped him at the last moment in New Zealand, when our trained cook became too big for his boots, and the exchange was greatly for the worse; I am afraid he is a thorough knave, but what is even worse, he is dirty — an unforgivable crime in a cook.'

Under such circumstances it is obvious that tempers might have been overstrained, and apart from the sins of the cook the weather was unexpectedly troublesome. Almost without exception the North Polar winter has been recorded as a period of quiescence, but in the Antarctic the wind blew with monotonous persistency, and calm days were very few and far between. Nevertheless Scott had little reason to change his original opinion about his companions, all of whom were prepared to put up with some unavoidable discomforts, and to make the best of a long job.

During the winter a very regular weekly routine was kept up, each day having its special food and its special tasks. The week's work ended on Friday, and Saturday was devoted to 'clean ship,' the officers doing Page 78 their share of the scrubbing. In the forenoon the living-spaces were thoroughly cleaned, holes and corners were searched, and while the tub and scrubber held sway the deck became a 'snipe marsh.' At this time the holds also were cleared up, the bilges pumped out, the upper deck was 'squared up,' and a fresh layer of clean snow was sprinkled over that which had been soiled by the traffic of the week. Then a free afternoon for all hands followed, and after dinner in the wardroom the toast was the time-honoured one of 'Sweethearts and Wives.'

On Sunday a different garment was put on, not necessarily a newer or a cleaner one, the essential point being that it should be different from that which had been worn during the week. By 9.30 the decks had been cleared up, the tables and shelves tidied, and the first lieutenant reported 'All ready for rounds.' A humble imitation of the usual man-of-war walk-round Sunday inspection followed, and Scott had the greatest faith in this system of routine, not only because it had a most excellent effect on the general discipline and cleanliness of the ship, but also because it gave an opportunity to raise and discuss each new arrangement that was made to increase the comfort of all on board.

After this inspection of both ship and men, the mess-deck was prepared for church; harmonium, reading-desk and chairs were all placed according to routine, and the bell was tolled. Scott read the service, Koettlitz the lessons, and Royds played the harmonium.

Page 79 Service over, all stood off for the day and looked forward to the feast of mutton which was limited to Sunday. 'By using it thus sparingly the handsome gift of the New Zealand farmers should last us till the early spring. But it is little use to think of the sad day when it will fail; for the present I must confess that we always take an extra walk to make quite sure of our appetites on Sunday.'

On June 23 the festival of mid-winter was celebrated, and the mess-deck was decorated with designs in coloured papers and festooned with chains and ropes of the same materials. Among the messes there was a great contest to have the best decorations, and some astonishing results were achieved with little more than brightly coloured papers, a pair of scissors and a pot of paste. On each table stood a grotesque figure or fanciful erection of ice, which was cunningly lighted up by candles from within and sent out shafts of sparkling light. 'If,' Scott wrote in his diary, 'the light-hearted scenes of to-day can end the first period of our captivity, what room for doubt is there that we shall triumphantly weather the whole term with the same general happiness and contentment?'

During the winter months the *South Polar Times*, edited by Shackleton, appeared regularly, and was read with interest and amusement by everyone. At first it had been decided that each number should contain, besides the editorial, a summary of the events and meteorological conditions of the past month, some scientifically instructive articles dealing with the work Page 80 and surroundings, and others written in a lighter vein; but, as the scheme developed, it was found that such features as caricatures and acrostics could be added. One of the pleasantest points in connection with the *Times* was that the men contributed as well as the officers; in fact some of the best, and quite the most amusing, articles were written by the occupants of the mess-deck. But beyond all else the journal owed its excellence to Wilson, who produced drawings that deserved — and ultimately obtained — a far wider appreciation than could be given to them in the Antarctic. So great was the desire to contribute to the first number of the *S. P. T.* that the editor's box was crammed with manuscripts by the time the date for sending in contributions had arrived. From these there was no difficulty in making a selection, but as there was also some danger of hurting the feelings of those whose contributions had been rejected, a supplementary journal named *The Blizzard* was produced. This publication, however, had but a brief career, for in spite of some good caricatures and a very humorous frontispiece by Barne, it was so inferior to the *S. P. T.* that even its contributors realized that their mission in life did not lie in the paths of literary composition. *The Blizzard*, in short, served its purpose, and then ceased to exist.

In considering the arrangements to make the ship comfortable during the dark months, the question of artificial light was as difficult as it was important. Paraffin had from the first been suggested as the most Page 81 suitable illuminant, its main disadvantage being that it is not a desirable oil to carry in quantities in a ship. 'Our luckiest find,' Scott says, 'was perhaps the right sort of lamp in which to burn this oil. Fortunately an old Arctic explorer, Captain Egerton, presented me with a patent lamp in which the draught is produced by a fan worked by clockwork mechanism, and no chimney is needed. One can imagine the great mortality there would be in chimneys if we were obliged to employ them, so that when, on trial, this lamp was found to give an excellent light, others of the same sort were purchased, and we now use them exclusively in all parts of the ship with extremely satisfactory results.'

There was, however, a still brighter illuminant within their reach in the shape of acetylene, but not until it became certain that they would have to spend a second winter in the Antarctic, did their thoughts fly to the calcium carbide which had been provided for the hut, and which they had not previously thought of using. 'In this manner the darkness of our second winter was relieved by a light of such brilliancy that all could pursue their occupations by the single burner placed in each compartment. I lay great stress on this, because I am confident that this is in every way the best illuminant that can be taken for a Polar winter, and no future expedition should fail to supply themselves with it.'

As has already been said, the meteorological observations had to be read and recorded every two hours, and on July 21 Scott gave in his diary a full and Page 82 graphic account of the way he occupied himself during his 'night on.' 'Each of us has his own way of passing the long, silent hours. My own custom is to devote some of it to laundry-work, and I must confess I make a very poor fist of it. However, with a bath full of hot water, I commence pretty regularly after the ten o'clock observation, and labour away until my back aches. There is little difficulty with the handkerchiefs, socks and such-like articles, but when it comes to thick woolen vests and pajamas, I feel ready to own my incapacity; one always seems to be soaping and rubbing at the same place, and one is forced to wonder at the area of stuff which it takes to cover a comparatively small body. My work is never finished by midnight, but I generally pretend that it is, and after taking the observations for that hour, return to wring everything out. I am astonished to find that even this is no light task; as one wrings out one end the water seems to fly to the other; then I hang some heavy garment on a hook and wring until I can wring no more; but even so, after it has been hung for a few minutes on the wardroom clothes-line, it will begin to drip merrily on the floor, and I have to tackle it afresh. I shall always have a high respect for laundry-work in future, but I do not think it can often have to cope with such thick garments as we wear.

'Washing over, one can devote oneself to pleasanter occupations. The night-watchman is always allowed a box of sardines, which are scarce enough to be a great luxury, and is provided with tea or cocoa and a spirit-lamp.

Page 83 Everyone has his own ideas as to how sardines should be prepared... and I scarcely like to record that there is a small company of *gourmets*, who actually wake one another up in order that the night-watchman may present his fellow epicures with a small finger of buttered toast, on which are poised two sardines "done to a turn." The awakened sleeper devours the dainty morsel, grunts his satisfaction, and goes placidly off into dreamland again.

'I find that after my labours at the wash-tub and the pleasing supper that follows, I can safely stretch myself out in a chair without fear of being overcome by sleep, and so, with the ever-soothing pipe and one's latest demand on the library book-shelves, one settles down in great peace and contentment whilst keeping an eye on the flying hours, ready to sally forth into the outer darkness at the appointed time.

'The pleasure or pain of that periodic journey is of course entirely dependent on the weather. On a fine night it may be quite a pleasure, but when, as is more common, the wind is sweeping past the ship, the observer is often subjected to exasperating difficulties, and to conditions when his conscience must be at variance with his inclination.

'Sometimes the lantern will go out at the screen, and he is forced to return on board to light it; sometimes it will refuse to shine on the thin threads of mercury of the thermometer until it is obvious that his proximity has affected the reading, and he is forced to stand off until it has again fallen to the air temperature.... Page 84 These and many other difficulties in taking observations which may be in themselves valueless are met in the right spirit. I think we all appreciate that they are part of a greater whole whose value must stand or fall by attention to detail.'

At the end of July a most unpleasant fact had to be faced in a mishap to the boats. Early in the winter they had been hoisted out to give more room for the awning, and had been placed in a line about a hundred yards from the ice-foot on the sea-ice. The earliest gale drifted them up nearly gunwale high, and thus for the next two months they remained in sight. But then another gale brought more snow, and was so especially generous with it in the neighborhood of the boats, that they were afterwards found to be buried three or four feet beneath the surface. With no feelings of anxiety, but rather to provide occupation, Scott ordered the snow on the top of them to be removed, and not until the first boat had been reached was the true state of affairs revealed. She was found lying in a mass of slushy ice with which she was nearly filled, and though for a moment there was a wild hope that she could be pulled up, this soon vanished; for the air temperature promptly converted the slush into hardened ice, and so she was stuck fast.

Nothing more could be done at that time to recover the boats, because as fast as the sodden ice could be dug out, more sea-water would have come in and frozen. But to try and prevent bad going to worse before the summer brought hope with it, parties were Page 85 engaged day after day in digging away at the snow covering, and in the course of months many tons must have been removed. The danger was that fresh gales bringing more snow might have sunk the boats so far below the surface that they could never be recovered, and after each gale the diggers were naturally despondent, as to all appearances they had to begin all over again. The prospect, however, of having to leave the Antarctic without a single boat in the ship, and also the feeling that so much labour must tell in the end, spurred on the diggers to renewed vigour, but it was not until December that the boats were finally liberated.

Early in August another gale with blinding drift was responsible for an experience to Bernacchi and Skelton that once again emphasized the bewildering effect of a blizzard. They were in the smaller compartment of the main hut completing a set of pendulum observations, while Royds was in the larger compartment—the hut was used for many and various purposes — rehearsing his nigger minstrel troupe. Either because nigger minstrelsy and scientific work did not go hand in hand, or because their work was finished, Bernacchi and Skelton, soon after the rehearsal began, left the hut to return to the ship. Fully an hour and a half afterwards Royds and his troupe, numbering more than a dozen, started back, and found that the gale had increased and that the whirling snow prevented them from seeing anything. Being, however, in such numbers, they were able to join hands and sweep along until they caught the guide-rope leading to the gangway; Page 86 and then as they traveled along it they heard feeble shouts, and again extending their line suddenly fell upon Bernacchi and Skelton, who, having entirely lost their bearings, had been reduced to shouting on the chance of being heard and rescued.

The hut was scarcely 200 yards from the ship, and the latter was not only a comparatively big object but was surrounded by guide-ropes and other means of direction, which if encountered would have informed the wanderers of their position. Additionally Bernacchi and Skelton could be trusted to take the most practical course in any difficulty, and so it seems the more incredible that they could actually have been lost for two hours. Both of them were severely frostbitten about the face and legs, but bitter as their experience was it served as yet another warning to those who were to go sledding in the spring that no risks could be taken in such a capricious climate. Had not Royds been rehearsing his troupe on this occasion the results to Bernacchi and Skelton must have been more disastrous than they were; consequently the idea of using the large hut as a place of entertainment was fortunate in more ways than one.

During the first week of May a concert had been given in the hut, but this was more or less in the nature of an experiment; for Royds, who took infinite pains over these entertainments, had arranged a long program with the object of bringing to light any possible talent. The result of this was that even the uncritical had to confess that most of the performers would have Page 87 been less out of place among the audience. So much dramatic ability, however, was shown that Barne was entrusted with the work of producing a play, which, after many rehearsals conducted with due secrecy, was produced on June 25.

This play was entitled 'The Ticket of Leave,' 'a screaming comedy in one act,' and was produced with unqualified success. 'I for one,' Scott says, 'have to acknowledge that I have rarely been so gorgeously entertained.'

Later on Royds began to organize his nigger minstrel troupe, and when the doors of the Royal Terror Theatre opened at 7.30 on August 6, the temperature outside them was -40°, while inside it was well below zero. Under these conditions it is small wonder that the audience was glad when the curtain went up.

'There is no doubt,' Scott says in reference to this performance, 'that sailors dearly love to make up; on this occasion they had taken an infinity of trouble to prepare themselves.... "Bones" and "Skins" had even gone so far as to provide themselves with movable top-knots which could be worked at effective moments by pulling a string below.... To-night the choruses and plantation-songs led by Royds were really well sung, and they repay him for the very great pains he has taken in the rehearsals.'

So with entertainments to beguile the time, and with blizzards to endure, and with preparations to make for sledding, the days passed by until on August 21 the sun was once more due to return. But on that Page 88 day a few hours of calm in the morning were succeeded by whirling snow-squalls from the south, and each lull was followed by a wild burst of wind. Scott was glad enough to have everyone on board in such weather, and at noon when he had hoped to be far over the hills only vast sheets of gleaming snow could be seen. The following day, however, was an ideal one for the first view of the long-absent sun, and Scott went to the top of Crater Hill to watch and welcome. 'Over all the magnificent view the sunlight spreads with gorgeous effect after its long absence; a soft pink envelops the western ranges, a brilliant red gold covers the northern sky; to the north also each crystal of snow sparkles with reflected light. The sky shows every gradation of light and shade; little flakes of golden sunlit cloud float against the pale blue heaven, and seem to hover in the middle heights, whilst far above them a feathery white cirrus shades to grey on its unlit sides.'

But when the men were told that the sun could be seen from Hut Point, to Scott's astonishment they displayed little or no enthusiasm. Everyone seemed glad to think that it had been punctual in keeping its appointment, but after all they had seen the sun a good many times before, and in the next few months they would in all probability see it a good many times again, and there was no sense in getting excited about it. Some of them did set off at a run for the point, while others, since it seemed the right thing to do, followed at a walk, but a good Page 89 number remained on board and had their dinner. On August 25 the Feast of the Sun was duly celebrated, and the days that followed were fuller than ever with preparations for the spring journeys. The only sewing-machine clattered away all day long, and the whole company plied their needles as if they were being sweated by iron-handed taskmasters. The long winter was at an end, and everyone, in the best of spirits, was looking forward eagerly to the spring sledge journeys, and making garments in which to bid defiance to the wind and the weather. As regards the actual sledge equipment which was taken to the south, Scott had depended on the experience of others, and especially on that of Armitage, but owing to a variety of reasons the difficulty of providing an efficient sledding outfit had been immense.

In England twenty-five years had passed since any important sledding expedition had been accomplished, and during that time not a single sledge, and very few portions of a sledge equipment, had been made in the country. The popular accounts of former expeditions were not written to supply the minute details required, and no memory could be expected to retain these details after such a lapse of time. In fact the art of sledge-making was lost in England, but fortunately the genius of Nansen had transferred it to Norway. In the autumn of 1900 Scott had visited Christiania, and there received much advice and assistance from Nansen himself. It was not, however, until Armitage agreed to serve as second in Page 90 command of the expedition that Scott had anyone on whom he could rely to provide the sledding outfit.

In making these preparations for long journeys in the south, there was no previous experience to go upon except that which had been gained in the north; indeed it was necessary to assume that southern conditions would be more or less similar to those of the north,

73

and in so far as they proved different the sledding outfit ran the risk of failure. Experience taught Scott that in many respects the sledding conditions of the south were different from those of the north, and so it is only fair to consider the sledge journeys taken by the *Discovery* expedition as pioneer efforts. These differences are both climatic and geographical. For instance, the conditions in the south are more severe than those in the north, both in the lowness of the temperatures and in the distressing frequency of blizzards and strong winds. And the geographical difference between the work of the northern and the southern sledge-traveler is as great as the climatic, if not greater, for the main part of northern traveling has been and will be done on sea-ice, while the larger part of southern traveling has been and will be done over land surfaces, or what in this respect are their equivalents.

LOOKING UP THE GATEWAY FROM PONY DEPÔT.
Photo by Capt. R. F. Scott.

So impressed was Scott by the impossibility of dragging a sledge over the surfaces of the Great Barrier to the South at the rate maintained by the old English travelers on the northern sea-ice, that he began seriously to think that the British race of explorers Page 91 must have deteriorated rapidly and completely in stamina. But later on, in carrying out exploration to the west, he had to travel over the sea-ice of the strait, and then he discovered that—given the surface there was nothing wrong with the pace at which his sledge parties could travel. Probably, however, the distances recorded by the northern travelers will never be exceeded in the south, for the Antarctic explorer has to meet severer climatic conditions, and while pulling his sledge over heavier surfaces he is not likely to meet with fewer obstacles in his path. To make marching records is not, of course, the main purpose of sledge-travelers, but all the same, where conditions are equal, speed and the distance traveled are a direct test of the efficiency of sledding preparations, and of the spirit of those who undertake this arduous service.

The main differences between the sledges used by the *Discovery* expedition and those used by other explorers were a decrease in breadth and an increase in runner surface. Measured across from the center of one runner to the center of the other Scott's sledges were all, with one exception, 1 foot 5 inches. The runners themselves were 3-3/4 inches across, so that the sledge track from side to side measured about 1 foot 8-3/4 inches. The lengths varied from 12 feet to 7 feet, but the 11-foot sledges proved to be by far the most convenient—a length of 12 feet seeming to pass just beyond the limit of handiness.

Taking then 11 feet as about the best length for this type of sledge, it will be seen that it differed Page 92 considerably from the old Arctic type, which was 10 feet long and 3 feet broad. The weight of such all 11-foot sledge was anything between 40 and 47 lbs., and this was none too light when the full strength of the structure was required. Generally speaking, the full load that could be put upon them was about 600 lbs. The most important part of the sledge is the runner, in which the grain must be perfectly straight and even, or it will splinter very easily; but it surprised Scott to find what a lot of wear a good wood runner would stand, provided that it was only taken over snow. 'Some of our 9-foot sledges must,' he says, 'have traveled 1,000 miles, and there was still plenty of wear left in the runners.'

In point of numbers the *Discovery*'s crew was far behind the old Northern expeditions; and it was this fact that made Scott decide, in arranging a sledge equipment where men and not dogs would do most of the haulage, to divide his parties into the smallest workable units. The old Northern plan had allowed for parties of at least eight, who, having a common tent and cooking arrangements, could not be subdivided. Scott's plan was not necessarily to limit the number of men in his parties, but to divide them into units of three, which should be self-contained, so that whenever it was advisable a unit could be detached from the main party. Under such a system it is obvious that each unit must have its own tent, sleeping-bag, cooker, and so on; and therein lay a disadvantage, as economy of material and weight can Page 93 be better carried out with a large unit than with a small one.

The weights of a party naturally divide themselves under two headings: the permanent, which will not diminish throughout the trip, and the consumable, including food, oil, &c. The following is a list of the permanent weights carried on Scott's journey to the west, and it will give some idea of the variety of articles, exclusive of provisions. The party numbered six.

		lbs.
2	Sledges with fittings complete	130
	Trace	5
2	Cookers, pannikins and spoons	30
2	Primus lamps, filled	10
2	Tents complete	60
2	Spades	9
2	Sleeping-bags with night-gear	100
	Sleeping jackets, crampons, spare finnesko[1]	50
	Medical bag	6
3	Ice-axes	8
	Bamboos and marks	11.5
	Instruments and camera	50
	Alpine rope	9
	Repair and tool bags, sounding-line, tape, sledge brakes	15
	Ski boots for party	15
	Ski for party	60

Total	568.5

[Footnote 1: Reindeer-fur boots.]

Page 94 Roughly speaking, a man can drag from 200 to 240 lbs., but his load was rarely above 200 lbs. This for six men gave a total carrying capacity of 1,200 lbs. and hence about 630 lbs. could be devoted to provisions.

Again, speaking very roughly, this amount is about six weeks' food for a party of six, but as such a short period is often not long enough to satisfy sledge-travelers, they are compelled to organize means by which their journey can be prolonged. This can be done in two ways; they may either go out earlier in the season and lay a depôt at a considerable distance towards their goal, or they may arrange to receive assistance from a supporting party, which accompanies them for a certain distance on the road and helps their advance party to drag a heavier load than they can accomplish alone.

Both of these plans were adopted by Scott on the more important journeys, and his parties were able to be absent from the ship for long periods and to travel long distances.

Page 95 CHAPTER V

THE START OF THE SOUTHERN JOURNEY

> Hold hard the breath and bend up every spirit
> To its full height...

...Shew us here
That you are worth your breeding, which I doubt not.
For there is none so mean or base
That have not noble lustre in your eyes.
I see you stand like greyhounds in the slips,
Straining upon the start.
 —SHAKESPEARE.

During the later months of the dark season all thoughts had been turned to the prospects of the spring journeys, and many times the advantages and disadvantages of dogs for sledding were discussed. This question of the sacrifice of animal life was one on which Scott felt strongly from the time he became an explorer to the end of his life. Argue with himself as he might, the idea was always repugnant to his nature.

'To say,' he wrote after his first expedition, that dogs do not greatly increase the radius of action is absurd; to pretend that they can be worked to this end without pain, suffering, and death, is equally futile. The question is whether the latter can be justified by the gain, and I think that logically it may be; Page 96 but the introduction of such sordid necessity must and does rob sledge-traveling of much of its glory. In my mind no journey ever made with dogs can approach the height of that fine conception which is realized when a party of men go forth to face hardships, dangers, and difficulties with their own unaided efforts, and by days and weeks of hard physical labour succeed in solving some problem of the great unknown. Surely in this case the conquest is more nobly and splendidly won.'

When the spring campaign opened in 1902 the original team of dogs had been sadly diminished. Of the nineteen that remained for the southern journey, all but one—and he was killed at an earlier period—left their bones on the great southern plains. This briefly is the history of the dogs, but the circumstances under which they met their deaths will be mentioned later on.

SLEDDING.

Before Scott started on the southern journey he decided to make a short trip to the north with the dogs and a party of six officers and men, his main purposes being to test the various forms of harness, and to find out whether the dogs pulled best in large or small teams. During part of this journey, which only lasted from September 2 to 5, the four sledges were taken independently with four dogs harnessed to each, and it was discovered that if the first team got away all right, the others were often keen to play the game of 'follow my leader.' Sometimes, indeed, there was a positive spirit of rivalry, and on one occasion two Page 97 competing teams got closer and closer to each other, with the natural result that when they were near enough to see what was happening, they decided that the easiest way to settle the matter was by a free fight. So they turned inwards with one accord and met with a mighty shock. In a moment there was a writhing mass of fur and teeth, and an almost hopeless confusion of dog traces. But even in this short trip some experience had been gained; for results showed how unwise it was to divide the dogs into small parties, and also there was no mistaking which were the strong and which the weak dogs, and, what was of more importance, which the willing and which the lazy ones.

On September 10, Royds and Koettlitz started off to the southwest with Evans, Quartley, Lashly and Wild. And of this party Scott wrote: 'They looked very workmanlike, and one could see at a glance the vast improvement that has been made since last year. The sledges were uniformly packed.... One shudders now to think of the slovenly manner in which we conducted things last autumn; at any rate here is a first result of the care and attention of the winter.'

Armitage and Ferrar with four men left for the west on the following day, but owing to the necessity of making fresh harness for the dogs and to an exasperating blizzard, Scott was not able to start on his southern reconnaissance journey until September 17.

On the morning of that day he and his two companions, Page 98 Barne and Shackleton, with thirteen dogs divided into two teams, left the ship in bright sunshine; but by 1.15 P.M., when they camped for lunch, the wind was blowing from the east and the thermometer was down to -43°.

The sledges carried a fortnight's food for all concerned, together with a quantity of stores to form a depôt, the whole giving a load of about 90 lbs. per dog; but this journey was destined to be only a short and bitter experience.

The reason was that on the night of the 17th the travelers were so exhausted that they did not heap enough snow on the skirting of the tent, and when Scott woke up on the following morning he found himself in the open. 'At first, as I lifted the flap of my sleeping-bag, I could not think what had happened. I gazed forth on a white sheet of drifting snow, with no sign of the tent or my companions. For a moment I wondered what in the world it could mean, but the lashing of the snow in my face very quickly awoke me to full consciousness, and I sat up to find that in some extraordinary way I had rolled out of the tent.'

At the time a violent gale was raging, and through the blinding snow Scott could only just see the tent, though it was flapping across the foot of his bag; but when he had wriggled back to the tent the snow was whirling as freely inside as without, and the tent itself was straining so madly at what remained of its securing, that something had to be done at once to prevent it from blowing away altogether.

Page 99 So with freezing fingers they gripped the skirting and gradually pulled it inwards, and half sitting upon it, half grasping it, they tried to hold it against the wild blasts of the storm, while they discussed the situation. Discussion, however, was useless. An attempt to secure the tent properly in such weather was impossible, while they felt that if once they loosed their grip, the tent would hasten to leave them at once and for ever. Every now and then they were forced to get a fresh hold, and lever themselves once more over the skirt. And as they remained hour after hour grimly hanging on and warning each other of frostbitten features, their sleeping-bags became fuller and fuller of snow, until they were lying in masses of chilly slush. Not until 6 P.M. had they by ceaseless exertions so far become masters of the situation, that there was no further need for the tent to be held with anything except the weight of their sleeping-bags. Then an inspection of hands showed a number of frostbites, but Barne, whose fingers had not recovered from the previous year, had suffered the most. 'To have hung on to the tent through all those hours must have been positive agony to him, yet he never uttered a word of complaint.'

By 10 P.M. the worst of the storm had passed, and after a few hours' sleep and a hot meal, they soon decided that to push on after this most miserable experience was very unwise, since by returning to the ship they would only lose one day's march and everything could be dried for a fresh start.

Page 100 Apart from 'Brownie,' who spent his time inside the tent, the rest of the dogs never uttered a sound during the storm, and were found quite happily sleeping in their nests of snow. On the journey back the thermometer recorded -53°, and the effect of such a temperature upon wet clothing may be imagined. 'I shall remember the condition of my trousers for a long while; they might have been cut out of sheet iron. It was some time before I could walk with any sort of ease, and even when we reached the ship I was conscious of carrying an armor plate behind me.... It will certainly be a very long time before I go to sleep again in a tent which is not properly secured.'

On September 24 Scott was ready to start again, but Barne's fingers had suffered so severely that his place was taken by the boatswain, Feather, who had taken a keen interest in every detail of sledding. Owing to the dogs refusing to do what was expected of them, and to gales, slow progress was made, but the wind had dropped by the morning of September 29, and Scott was so anxious to push on that he took no notice of a fresh bank of cloud coming up from the south, with more wind and drift. Taking the lead himself, he gave orders to the two teams to follow rigidly in his wake, whatever turns and twists he might make. Notwithstanding the bad light he could see the bridged crevasses, where they ran across the bare ice surface, by slight differences in shade, and though he could not see them where they dived into the valleys, he found that the bridges were strong enough to bear. In Page 101 his desire to use the snowy patches as far as possible, the course he took was very irregular, and the dogs invariably tried to cut corners. In this manner they proceeded for some time, until Scott suddenly heard a shout, and looking back saw to his horror that Feather had vanished. The dog team and sledges were there all right, but their leader was lost to sight. Hurrying back he found that the trace had disappeared down a formidable crevasse, but to his great relief Feather was at the end of the trace, and was soon hauled up. One strand of Feather's harness was cut clean through where it fell across the ice-edge, and although, being a man of few words, he was more inclined to swear at 'Nigger' for trying to cut a corner than to marvel at his own escape, there is no doubt that he had a very close call.

After this accident the dog teams were joined, and reluctant to give up they advanced again; but very soon the last of the four sledges disappeared, and was found hanging vertically up and down in an ugly-looking chasm. To the credit of the packing not a single thing had come off, in spite of the jerk with which it had fallen. It was, however, too heavy to haul up as it was, but, after some consultation, the indefatigable Feather proposed that he should be let down and undertake the very cold job of unpacking it. So he was slung with one end of the Alpine rope, while the other was used for hauling up the various packages; and at last the load was got up, and the lightened sledge soon followed.

After this incident they thought it prudent to treat these numerous crevasses with more respect, and on Page 102 proceeding they roped themselves together; but although no more mishaps occurred, Scott afterwards was more inclined to attribute this to good luck than to good judgment. 'Looking back on this day, I cannot but think our procedure was extremely rash. I have not the least doubt now that this region was a very dangerous one, and the fact that we essayed to cross it in this light-hearted fashion can only be ascribed to our ignorance. With us, I am afraid, there were not a few occasions when one might have applied the proverb that "Fools rush in where angels fear to tread."'

The depôt, leaving six weeks' provision for three men and 150 lbs. of dog-food, was made on the morning of October 1, and besides marking it with a large black flag, Scott was also careful to take angles with a prismatic compass to all the points he could see. Then they started home, and the dogs knowing at once what was meant no longer required any driving. On the homeward march the travelers went for all they were worth, and in spite of perpetual fog covered eighty-five statute miles in less than three days.

On returning to the ship Scott admits that he found it a most delightful place. The sense of having done what he wanted to do had something to do with this feeling of satisfaction, but it was the actual physical comfort after days of privation that chiefly affected him. The joy of possessing the sledding appetite was sheer delight, and for many days after the travelers returned from their sledding-trips, they retained a hunger which it seemed impossible to satisfy.

Page 103 In short Scott, on the night of his return, was very pleased with himself and the world in general, but before he went to bed all his sense of comfort and peace had gone. For he had discovered what Armitage, wishing to give him some hours of unmixed enjoyment, had not meant to mention until the following morning, and this was that there had been an outbreak of scurvy — the disease that has played a particularly important, and often a tragic, part in the adventures of Polar travelers, and the seriousness of which everyone who has read the history of Polar explorations cannot fail to realize.

This outbreak had occurred during Armitage's journey, and when he, after much anxiety, had got his men back to the ship, Wilson's medical examination proved that Ferrar, Heald and Cross were all attacked, while the remainder of the party were not above suspicion.

Very soon, however, symptoms of the disease began to abate, but the danger lurking around them was continually in Scott's thoughts, and he was determined not to give the dreaded enemy another chance to break out.

Everything possible was done to make the ship and everything in her sweet and clean, and after a large seal-killing party, sent out at Wilson's suggestion, had returned, the order was given that no tinned meat of any description should be issued. By October 20 this grave disease had to all intents and purposes passed away, but although evidence showed that it was Page 104 caused by tinned meats which were to all appearances of the best quality, and by apparently fresh mutton taken in small quantities, there was no positive proof that these were the causes of the trouble.

This attack of scurvy came as a great surprise to everyone, for when the long winter was over and all of them were in good health and high spirits, they had naturally congratulated themselves on the effectiveness of their precautions. The awakening from this pleasant frame of mind was rude, and though the disease vanished with astonishing rapidity, it was—quite apart from the benefit lost to medical science—very annoying not to be able to say definitely from what the evil had sprung.

But although the seriousness of this outbreak was not underrated, and every precaution was taken to prevent its recurrence, preparations for the various journeys were pushed on with no less vigour and enthusiasm. The game to play was that there was nothing really to be alarmed about, and everyone played it with the greatest success.

Scott's journey to the south had indicated that the main party would have to travel directly over the snow-plain at a long distance from, and perhaps out of sight of, land; and as in all probability no further depôts could be established, it was desirable that this party should be supported as far as possible on their route. To meet these requirements it was decided that Barne, with a party of twelve men, should accompany the dog-team, until the weights were reduced to an amount Page 105 which the dogs could drag without assistance.

Then Barne was to return to the ship, and after a short rest start again with six men, to follow the coast-line west of the Bluff. As soon as this was in train, Armitage was to have at his disposal all the men and material left in the ship for his attack on the western region.

On Friday, October 24, Royds, who had left the ship three weeks before with Skelton, Lashly, Evans, Quartley and Wild, returned with the good news that he had been able to communicate with the 'Record' post at Cape Crozier. If a relief ship was going to be sent out, Scott now had the satisfaction of knowing that she had a good prospect of being guided to the winter quarters of the expedition. It was also a great source of satisfaction to find that although Royds and his party had left almost immediately after the outbreak of scurvy, they had all returned safe and with no symptom of the disease.

From the 13th to the 18th this party had been kept in their tents by a most persistent blizzard, and before the blizzard ceased they were practically buried in the heart of a snowdrift; in fact one tent had literally to be dug out before its occupants could be got into the open, while the sledges and everything left outside were completely buried. As the snow gradually accumulated round the tents it became heavier and heavier on every fold of canvas, and reduced the interior space to such an extent that those inside were obliged to lie with their knees bent double. Royds, whose reports were invariably very brief and to Page 106 the point, dismissed the tale of these five days in half a page, but no great effort of imagination is needed to grasp the horrible discomforts everyone must have endured. And yet when this party recounted their adventures on board the ship, the hardships were scarcely mentioned, and all that the men seemed to remember were the amusing incidents that had happened.

On this journey a colony of Emperor penguins was discovered, and among them were several which were nursing chicks. 'I will only testify,' Scott says, 'to the joy which greeted this discovery on board the ship. We had felt that this penguin was the truest type of our region. All other birds fled north when the severity of winter descended upon us: the Emperor alone was prepared to face the extremest rigors of our climate; and we gathered no small satisfaction from being the first to throw light on the habits of a creature, which so far surpasses in hardihood all others of the feathered tribe.'

Before the end of October everything was prepared for the southern journey; every eventuality seemed to be provided for, and as it was expected that the dogs would travel faster than the men Barne and his party started off on October 30, while the dog team left a few days later. 'The supporting party started this morning, amidst a scene of much enthusiasm; all hands had a day off, and employed it in helping to drag the sledges for several miles... Barne's banner floated on the first, the next bore a Union Jack, and Page 107 another carried a flag with a large device stating "*No dogs needs apply*"; the reference was obvious. It was an inspiriting sight to see nearly the whole of our small company step out on the march with ringing cheers, and to think that all work of this kind promised to be done as heartily.'

And then the day that Scott had been so eagerly looking forward to arrived, and at ten o'clock on the morning of November 2, he, Shackleton and Wilson, amidst the wild cheers of their comrades, started on the southern journey. 'Every soul was gathered on the floe to bid us farewell, and many were prepared to accompany us for the first few miles.' The dogs, as if knowing that a great effort was expected of them, had never been in such form, and in spite of the heavy load and the fact that at first two men had to sit on the sledges to check them, it was as much as the rest of the party could do to keep up. By noon the volunteers had all tailed off, and the three travelers were alone with the dogs, and still breathlessly trying to keep pace with them. Soon afterwards they caught sight of a dark spot ahead and later on made this out to be the supporting party, who, when they were overtaken on the same evening, reported that they had been kept in their tents by bad weather. Having relieved them of some of their loads, Scott camped, while they pushed on to get the advantage of a night march.

During the next few days the two parties constantly passed and re-passed each other, since it was Page 108 impossible for Scott to push on ahead of Barne's party, and the latter's progress was very slow, as they could get no hold with their fur boots, and they found their ski leather boots dreadfully cold for their feet. To add to the slowness of the journey the weather was very unfavorable, and the greater parts of the 8th and 9th were entirely wasted by a blizzard. On the 10th Depôt A, that had previously been laid, was reached and Scott wrote: 'Already it seems to me that the dogs feel the monotony of a long march over the snow more than we do; they seem easily to get dispirited, and that it is not due to fatigue is shown when they catch a glimpse of anything novel.... To-day, for instance, they required some driving until they caught sight of the depôt flag, when they gave tongue loudly and dashed off as though they barely felt the load behind them.'

The names of the dogs were:

Nigger	Birdie	Wolf
Jim	Nell	Vic
Spud	Blanco	Bismarck
Snatcher	Grannie	Kid
Fitzclarence	Lewis	Boss
Stripes	Gus	Brownie
	Joe	

Each of them had his peculiar characteristics, and what the Southern party did not already know concerning their individualities, they had ample opportunities of finding out in the course of the next few weeks.

Page 109 Nigger was the leader of the team; a place he chose naturally for himself, and if he was put into any other position he behaved so unpleasantly to his neighbors, and so generally upset things, that he was quickly shifted. A more perfect sledge-dog could scarcely be imagined. He seemed to know the meaning of every move, and in camp would be still as a graven image until he saw the snow being shoveled from the skirting of the tent, when he would spring up and pace to and fro at his picket, and give a low throaty bark of welcome if anyone approached him. A few minutes later, when the leading man came to uproot his picket, he would watch every movement, and a slow wagging of the tail quite obviously showed his approval: then, as the word came to start, he would push affectionately against the leader, as much as to say, 'Now come along!' and brace his powerful chest to the harness. At the evening halt after a long day he would drop straight in his tracks and remain perfectly still, with his magnificent black head resting on his paws. Other dogs might clamor for food, but Nigger knew perfectly well that the tent had first to be put up. Afterwards, however, when the dog-food was approached his deep bell-like note could always be distinguished amid the howling chorus, and if disturbance was to be avoided it was well to attend to him first of all.

Of the other dogs Lewis was noisily affectionate and hopelessly clumsy; Jim could pull splendidly when he chose, but he was up to all the tricks of the trade and was extraordinarily cunning at pretending to pull; Page 110 Spud was generally considered to be daft; Birdie evidently had been treated badly in his youth and remained distrustful and suspicious to the end; Kid was the most indefatigable worker in the team; Wolf's character possessed no redeeming point of any kind, while Brownie though a little too genteel for very hard work was charming as a pet, and it may also be said of him that he never lost an opportunity of using his pleasant appearance and delightful ways to lighten his afflictions. The load for this dog team after Depôt A had been passed was 1,850 lbs., which, considering that some of the dogs were of little use, was heavy. But it must not be forgotten that the men also expected to pull, and that each night the weight would be reduced by thirty or forty pounds. By the 13th the travelers were nearly up to the 79th parallel, and therefore farther south than anyone had yet been. 'The announcement of the fact caused great jubilation, and I am extremely glad that there are no fewer than fifteen of us to enjoy this privilege of having broken the record.' A photograph of the record-breakers was taken, and then half of the supporting party started to return, and the other half stepped out once more on a due south line, with the dogs following.

By the 15th, however, when the rest of the supporting party turned back, Scott had begun to be anxious about the dogs. 'The day's work has cast a shadow on our high aspirations, and already it is evident that if we are to achieve much it will be only by extreme toil, for the dogs have not pulled well to-day....

Page 111 We have decided that if things have not improved in the morning we will take on half a load at a time; after a few days of this sort of thing the loads will be sufficiently lightened for us to continue in the old way again.'

On the following day an attempt to start with the heavy loads promptly and completely failed, and the only thing to do was to divide the load into two portions and take half on at a time. This meant, of course, that each mile had to be traveled three times, but there was no alternative to this tedious form of advance. Even, however, with the half-loads the dogs seemed to have lost all their spirit, and at the end of the march on the 18th they were practically 'done.' Only five geographical miles[1] were gained on that day, but to do it they had to cover fifteen.

[Footnote 1: 7 geographical miles = a little more than 8 statute miles.]

On the night of the 19th matters had gone from bad to worse, and it had to be acknowledged that the fish diet the dogs were eating permanently disagreed with them. Originally Scott had intended to take ordinary dog-biscuits for the animals, but in an unlucky moment he was persuaded by an expert in dog-driving to take fish. The fish taken was the Norwegian stock-fish, such as is split, dried and exported from that country in great quantities for human food. But one important point was overlooked, namely the probability of the fish being affected on passing through the tropics. The lesson, Scott said, was obvious, that in future travelers in the south should safeguard their Page 112 dogs as carefully as they do their men, for in this case it was the dogs that called the halts; and so the party had to spend hours in their tent which might have been devoted to marching.

Day after day relay work continued, the only relief from the monotony of their toil being that land was sighted on the 21st, and as the prospects of reaching a high latitude were steadily disappearing, it was decided to alter their course to S. S. W. and edge towards it. Then the surface over which they were traveling showed signs of improvement, but the travelers themselves were beginning to suffer from blistered noses and cracked lips, and their eyes were also troubling them. Appetites, however, were increasing by leaps and bounds. 'The only thing to be looked to on our long marches is the prospect of the next meal.'

On November 24 a new routine was started which made a little variation in the dull toil of relay work. After pushing on the first half-load one of the three stopped with it, and got up the tent and prepared the meal while the other two brought up the second half-load. And then on the following day came one of those rewards which was all the sweeter because it had been gained by ceaseless and very monotonous toil.

'Before starting to-day I took a meridian altitude,' Scott wrote, 'and to my delight found the latitude to be 80° 1'. All our charts of the Antarctic region show a plain white circle beyond the eightieth parallel... It has always been our ambition to get inside that white Page 113 space, and now we are there the space can no longer be a blank; this compensates for a lot of trouble.'

A blizzard followed upon this success, but the dogs were so exhausted that a day's rest had been thought of even if the weather had not compelled it. Wilson, to his great discomfort, was always able to foretell these storms, for when they were coming on he invariably suffered from rheumatism; so, however reluctant, he could not help being a very effective barometer.

After the storm had passed an attempt was made on the morning of the 27th to start with the full load, but it took next to no time to discover that the dogs had not benefited by their rest, and there was nothing to do except to go on with the old routine of relay work. As the days passed with no signs of improvement in the dogs, it became more and more necessary to reach the land in hopes of making a depôt; so the course was laid to the westward of S. W., which brought the high black headland, for which they were making, on their port bow. 'I imagine it to be about fifty miles off, but hope it is not so much; nine hours' work to-day has only given us a bare four miles.'

Then for some days the only change in the toil of relay work and the sickening task of driving tired dogs on and on was that they marched by night, and rested by day. The breakfast hour was between 4 and 5 P.M., the start at 6 P.M., and they came to camp somewhere between three and four in the morning. Thus they rested while the sun was at its greatest Page 114 height; but although there were certainly advantages in this, Scott could not get rid of a curious feeling that something was amiss with such a topsy-turvy method of procedure.

By December 3 they were close enough to the land to make out some of its details. On their right was a magnificent range of mountains, which by rough calculations Scott made out to be at least fifty miles away. By far the nearest point of land was an isolated snow-cape, an immense, and almost dome-shaped, snow-covered mass. At first no rock at all could be seen on it, but as they got nearer a few patches began to appear. For one of these patches they decided to make so that they might establish a depôt, but at the rate at which they were traveling there was little hope of reaching it for several days.

By this time the appetites of the party were so ravenous that when the pemmican bag was slung alongside a tin of paraffin, and both smelt and tasted of oil, they did not really mind. But what saddened them more than this taste of paraffin was the discovery, on December 5, that their oil was going too fast. A gallon was to have lasted twelve days, but on investigation it was found on an average to have lasted only ten, which meant that in the future each gallon would have to last a fortnight. 'This is a distinct blow, as we shall have to sacrifice our hot luncheon meal and to economize greatly at both the others. We started the new routine to-night, and for lunch ate some frozen seal-meat and our allowance of sugar and biscuit.'

Page 115 It was perhaps fortunate that their discovery about the oil was not delayed any longer, but nevertheless it came at a time when the outlook was dreary and dispiriting enough without additional discomforts. On the 6th Spud gnawed through his trace, and when Scott went outside before breakfast, one glance at the dog's balloon-like appearance was enough to show how he had spent his hours of freedom. He had, in fact, eaten quite a week's allowance of the precious seal-meat, and though rather somnolent after his gorge, he did not seem to be suffering any particular discomfort from the enormous increase of his waist. On the next day there was a blizzard, duly predicted by Wilson's twinges of rheumatism, and on the

8th Scott reluctantly records that the dogs were steadily going downhill. 'The lightening of the load is more than counter-balanced by the weakening of the animals, and I can see no time in which we can hope to get the sledges along without pulling ourselves.'

By the 10th they were within ten or twelve miles of the coast, but so exhausted that they felt no certainty of reaching it; and even supposing they did get there and make a depôt, they doubted very much if they would be in any condition to go on. One dog, Snatcher, was already dead, and some of the others had only been got to move with the second load by the ignominious device of carrying food in front of them. To see the dogs suffering was agony to those who had to drive and coax them on, and though Scott refers often in these days to the hunger that was nipping him, Page 116 no one can read his diary without seeing how infinitely more he was concerned over the suffering of the dogs than about his own troubles. 'It is terrible,' he says, 'to see them.'

At last, on December 14, they arrived, when they were almost spent, at a place where dog-food could be left. In their march they had only managed to do two miles after the most strenuous exertions, for the snow became softer as they approached the land, and the sledge-runners sank from three to four inches. On any particularly soft patch they could do little more than mark time, and even to advance a yard was an achievement.

No wonder that Scott, after they had left three weeks' provisions and a quantity of dog-food in Depôt B and had resumed their march, sounded a note of thankfulness: 'As I write I scarcely know how to describe the blessed relief it is to be free from our relay work. For one-and-thirty awful days we have been at it, and whilst I doubt if our human endurance could have stood it much more, I am quite sure the dogs could not. It seems now like a nightmare, which grew more terrible towards its end.' The sense of relief was, however, not destined to last, for on December 21 the dogs were in such a hopeless condition that they might at any moment have completely collapsed. This was a fact that had to be faced, and the question whether under such circumstances it was wise to push on had to be asked and answered. The unanimous answer was that the risk Page 117 of going on should be taken, but on that same night Wilson, in view of future plans, reported to Scott that his medical examinations revealed that Shackleton had decidedly angry-looking gums, and that for some time they had been slowly but surely getting worse. It was decided not to tell Shackleton of these symptoms of scurvy, and as the bacon they were using seemed likely to be the cause of them, it was discarded and an increased allowance of seal given in its place. This was a loss in weight which was serious, for already they were reduced almost to starvation rations of about a pound and a half a day.

Supper was the best meal, for then they had a *hoosh* which ran from between three-quarters to a whole pannikin apiece, but even this they could not afford to make thick. While it was being heated in the central cooker, cocoa was made in the outer, but the lamp was turned out directly the *hoosh* boiled, and by that time the chill was barely off the contents of the outer cooker. Of course the cocoa was not properly dissolved, but they were long past criticizing the quality of their food. All they wanted was something to 'fill up,' but needless to say they never got it. Half an hour after supper was over they were as hungry as ever.

When they had started from the ship, there had been a vague idea that they could go as they pleased with the food, but experience showed that this would not do, and that there must be a rigid system of shares. Consequently they used to take it in turn to divide Page 118 things into three equal portions, and as the man who made the division felt called upon to take the smallest share, the game of 'shut-eye' was invented to stop all arguments and remonstrances. The shares were divided as equally as possible by someone, then one of the other two turned his head away and the divider pointed to a portion and said, 'Whose is this?' He of the averted head named the owner, and thus this simple but useful game was played.

Wilson's examination of Shackleton on December 24 was not encouraging, but they had reached a much harder surface and under those conditions Scott and Wilson agreed that it was not yet time to say 'Turn.' Besides, Christmas Day was in front of them, and for a week they had all agreed that it would be a crime to go to bed hungry on that night. In fact they meant it to be a wonderful day, and everything conspired to make it so.

The sun shone gloriously from a clear sky, and not a breath of wind disturbed the calmness of the morning, but entrancing as the scene was they did not stay to contemplate it, because for once they were going to have a really substantial breakfast, and this was an irresistible counter-attraction.

And afterwards, when they felt more internally comfortable than they had for weeks, the surface continued to be so much better that the sledges could be pulled without any help from the dogs. On that day they had the satisfaction of covering nearly eleven miles, the longest march they had made for a long Page 119 time. So when camp was pitched they were thoroughly pleased with the day, and ready to finish it off with a supper to be remembered. A double 'whack' of everything was poured into the cooking-pot, and in the *hoosh* that followed a spoon would stand without any support, and the cocoa was also brought to boiling-point.

'I am writing,' Scott says, 'over my second pipe. The sun is still circling our small tent in a cloudless sky, the air is warm and quiet. All is pleasant without, and within we have a sense of comfort we have not known for many a day; we shall sleep well tonight—no dreams, no tightening of the belt.

'We have been chattering away gaily, and not once has the conversation turned to food. We have been wondering what Christmas is like in England... and how our friends picture us. They will guess that we are away on our sledge journey, and will perhaps think of us on plains of snow; but few, I think, will imagine the truth, that for us this has been the reddest of all red-letter days.'

Page 120 CHAPTER VI

THE RETURN

How many weary steps
Of many weary miles you have o'ergone,
Are numbered to the travel of one mile.
SHAKESPEARE. i

Some days passed before the pleasing effects of Christmas Day wore off, for it had been a delightful break in an otherwise uninterrupted spell of semi-starvation, and the memories lingered long after hunger had again gripped the three travelers. By this time they knew that they had cut themselves too short in the matter of food, but the only possible alteration that could now be made in their arrangements was to curtail their journey, and rather than do that they were ready cheerfully to face the distress of having an enormous appetite, and very little with which to appease it.

Thinking over the homeward marches after he had returned to the ship, Scott expresses his emphatic opinion that the increasing weariness showed that they were expending their energies at a greater rate than they could renew them, and that the additional Page 121 weight, caused by carrying a proper allowance of food, would have been amply repaid by the preservation of their full strength and vigour.

Apart, however, from the actual pangs of hunger, there was another disadvantage from this lack of food, for try as they would it was impossible not to think and talk incessantly of eating. Before they went to sleep it was almost certain that one of them would give a detailed description of what he considered an ideal feast, while on the march they found themselves counting how many footsteps went to the minute, and how many, therefore, had to be paced before another meal.

But if, during these days of hunger, thoughts of what they could eat if only the chance was given to them kept constantly cropping up, there were also very real compensations for both their mental and physical weariness. Day by day, as they journeyed on, they knew that they were penetrating farther and farther into the unknown. Each footstep was a gain, and made the result of their labours more assured. And as they studied the slowly revolving sledge-meter or looked for the calculated results of their observations, it is not surprising that above all the desires for food was an irresistible eagerness to go on and on, and to extend the line which they were now drawing on the white space of the Antarctic chart.

Day by day, too, the magnificent panorama of the Western land was passing before their eyes. 'Rarely a march passed without the disclosure of some new Page 122 feature, something on which the eye of man had never rested; we should have been poor souls indeed had we not been elated at the privilege of being the first to gaze on these splendid scenes.'

From the point of view of further exploration their position on December 26 was not very hopeful. On their right lay a high undulating snow-cap and the steep irregular coast-line, to the south lay a cape beyond which they could not hope to pass, and to all appearances these conditions were likely to remain to the end of their journey. But on that night they had christened a distant and lofty peak 'Mount Longstaff,' in honour of the man whose generosity had alone made the expedition possible, and although they thought that this was the most southerly land to which they would be able to give a name, they were in no mood to turn back because the outlook was unpromising. Arguing on the principle that it was impossible to tell what may turn up, they all decided to push on; and their decision was wise, for had they returned at that point one of the most important features of the whole coast-line would have been missed.

On the 26th and 27th Wilson had a very bad attack of snow-blindness, which caused him the most intense agony. Some days before Scott had remarked in his diary upon Wilson's extraordinary industry: 'When it is fine and clear, at the end of our fatiguing days he will spend two or three hours seated in the door of the tent sketching each detail of the splendid mountainous coast-scene to the west. His sketches Page 123 are most astonishingly accurate; I have tested his proportions by actual angular measurements and found them correct.... But these long hours in the glare are very bad for the eyes; we have all suffered a good deal from snow-blindness of late, though we generally march with goggles, but Wilson gets the worst bouts, and I fear it is mainly due to his sketching.'

The attack, however, after Christmas was very much worse than anything that had gone before, and all day long during the 27th Wilson was pulling alongside the sledges with his eyes completely covered. To march blindfold with an empty stomach must touch the bottom of miserable monotony, but Wilson had not the smallest intention of giving in. With Scott walking opposite to him and telling him of the changes that were happening around them he plodded steadily on, and during the afternoon of the 27th it happened that a most glorious mountainous scene gradually revealed itself. With some excitement Scott noticed that new mountain ridges were appearing as high as anything they had seen to the north, and his excitement increased when these ridges grew higher and higher. Then, instead of a downward turn in the distant outline came a steep upward line, and as they pressed on apace to see what would happen next, Scott did his best to keep Wilson posted up in the latest details. The end came in a gloriously sharp double peak crowned with a few flecks of cirrus cloud, and all they could think of in camp that night was this splendid twin-peaked mountain, which even in such Page 124 a lofty country looked like a giant among pigmies. 'At last we have found something which is fitting to bear the name of him whom we must always the most delight to honour, and "Mount Markham" it shall be called in memory of the father of the expedition.'

Wilson, in spite of his recent experiences, did not mean to miss this, and however much his eyes had to suffer the scene had to be sketched. Fortunately a glorious evening provided a perfect view of their surroundings, for very soon they knew that the limit of their journey would be reached, and that they would have but few more opportunities to increase their stock of information.

After a day that had brought with it both fine weather and most interesting discoveries, they settled down in their sleeping-bags, full of hope that the morrow would be equally kind. But instead of the proposed advance the whole day had to be spent in the tent while a strong southerly blizzard raged without, and when they got up on the following morning they found themselves enveloped in a thick fog.

Reluctantly the decision was made that this camp must be their last, and consequently their southerly limit had been reached. Observations gave it as between 82.16 S. and 82.17 S., and though this record may have compared poorly with what Scott had hoped for when leaving the ship, it was far more favorable than he anticipated when the dogs had begun to fail. 'Whilst,' he says, 'one cannot help a deep sense of disappointment in reflecting on the "might have been" Page 125 had our team remained in good health, one cannot but remember that even as it is we have made a greater advance towards a pole of the earth than has ever yet been achieved by a sledge party.'

With less than a fortnight's provision to take them back to Depôt B, they turned their faces homewards on the last day of the year, and it was significant of the terrible condition of the surviving dogs that the turn did not cause the smallest excitement. Many of them were already dead, killed to keep the others alive, but those which remained seemed to guess how poor a chance they had of getting back to the ship. Again and again Scott refers to the suffering of the dogs on the homeward march, and how intensely he felt for them is proved beyond all manner of doubt. 'January 3. This afternoon, shortly after starting, "Gus" fell, quite played out, and just before our halt, to our greater grief, "Kid" caved in. One could almost weep over this last case; he has pulled like a Trojan throughout, and his stout little heart bore him up till his legs failed beneath him.' Only seven of the team now remained, and of them Jim seemed to be the strongest, but Nigger, though weak, was still capable of surprising efforts. But at the end of a week on the return journey, all of the remaining dogs were asked to do nothing except walk by the sledges.

For several hours on January 7 the men pulled steadily and covered ten good miles. But the distance they succeeded in traveling was as nothing compared with the relief they felt at no longer having to Page 126 drive a worn-out team. In the future no more cheering and dragging in front would be needed, no more tangled traces would have to be put straight, and above all there would be no more whip. So far steady though rather slow progress had been made, but January 8 brought an unpleasant surprise. Try as they would the sledge could scarcely be made to move, and after three hours of the hardest work only a mile and a quarter had been gained. Sadly they were compelled to admit that the surface had so completely changed that the only thing to do was to remain in camp until it improved. But whether it would improve was an anxious matter, for they had less than a week's provisions and were at least fifty miles from Depôt B.

The next day, however, saw an improvement in the surface, and a fairly good march was done. By this time only four dogs were left,

Nigger, Jim, Birdie and Lewis, and poor Nigger was so lost out of harness that he sometimes got close to the traces and marched along as if he was still doing his share of the pulling. But this more or less ordinary day was followed on the 10th by a march in a blizzard that exhausted Scott and Wilson, and had even a more serious effect upon Shackleton. With the wind behind them they had gained many miles, but the march had tired them out, because instead of the steady pulling to which they were accustomed they had been compelled sometimes to run, and sometimes to pull forwards, backwards, sideways, and always with their senses keenly alert and their muscles strung up for instant action.

Page 127 On that night Scott in no very cheerful frame of mind wrote: 'We cannot now be far from our depôt, but then we do not exactly know where we are; there is not many days' food left, and if this thick weather continues we shall probably not be able to find it.' And after two more days of bad surface and thick weather he wrote again: 'There is no doubt we are approaching a very critical time. The depôt is a very small spot on a very big ocean of snow; with luck one might see it at a mile and a half or two miles, and fortune may direct our course within this radius of it; but, on the other hand, it is impossible not to contemplate the ease with which such a small spot can be missed.... The annoying thing is that one good clear sight of the land would solve all our difficulties.'

At noon on January 13 the outlook was more hopeless than ever. Three hours' incessant labour had gained only three-quarters of a mile, and consequently they had to halt though their food-bag was a mere trifle to lift, and they could have finished all that remained in it at one sitting and still have been hungry. But later on Scott caught a glimpse of the sun in the tent, and tumbled hastily out of his sleeping-bag in the hope of obtaining a meridional altitude; and after getting the very best result he could under the very difficult conditions prevailing, he casually lowered the telescope and swept it round the horizon. Suddenly a speck seemed to flash by, and a vehement hope as suddenly arose. Then he brought the telescope slowly back, and there it was again, and accompanied this Page 128 time by two smaller specks on either side of it. Without a shadow of doubt it was the depôt which meant the means of life to them. 'I sprang up and shouted, "Boys, there's the depôt." We are not a demonstrative party, but I think we excused ourselves for the wild cheer that greeted this announcement.'

In five minutes everything was packed on the sledges, but though the work was as heavy as before the workers were in a very different mood to tackle it. To reach those distant specks as quickly as possible was their one desire and all minor troubles were forgotten as they marched, for before them was the knowledge that they were going to have the fat *hoosh* which would once more give them an internal sense of comfort. In two hours they were at the depôt, and there they found everything as they had left it.

On that same morning they had stripped off the German silver from the runners of one of their sledges, and now fortified by the fat *hoosh* of their dreams they completed the comparison between the two sledges, which respectively had metal and wood runners. Having equalized the weights as much as possible they towed the sledges round singly, and found that two of them could scarcely move the metalled sledge as fast as one could drag the other.

Of course they decided to strip the second sledge, and with only about 130 miles to cover to their next depôt, a full three weeks' provisions, and the prospect of better traveling on wood runners, they went to bed Page 129 feeling that a heavy load of anxiety had been lifted. The chief cause of worry left was the question of health, and the result of a thorough medical examination on the morning of the 14th did nothing to remove this. Shackleton was found to be very far indeed from well, but although Scott and Wilson both showed symptoms of scurvy they still felt that, as far as they were concerned, there was no danger of a breakdown.

On that day they made a fairly good march, but at the end of it Wilson had to warn Scott that Shackleton's condition was really alarming. Commenting on this Scott wrote: 'It's a bad case, but we must make the best of it and trust to its not getting worse; now that human life is at stake, all other objects must be sacrificed.... It went to my heart to give the order, but it had to be done, and the dogs are to be killed in the morning.

'One of the difficulties we foresee with Shackleton, with his restless, energetic spirit, is to keep him idle in camp, so to-night I have talked seriously to him. He is not to do any camping work, but to allow everything to be done for him.... Every effort must be devoted to keeping him on his legs, and we must trust to luck to bring him through.'

With the morning of the 15th came the last scene in the tragic story of the dogs, and poor Nigger and Jim, the only survivors of that team of nineteen, were taken a short distance from the camp and killed. 'I think we could all have wept.... Through our most troublous time we always looked forward to getting Page 130 some of our animals home. At first it was to have been nine, then seven, then five, and at the last we thought that surely we should be able to bring back these two.'

During the part of the return journey which was now beginning, they had promised themselves an easier time, but instead of that it resolved itself into days of grim struggle to save a sick companion. The weather also added to their troubles, because it was so overcast that steering was extremely difficult. For nearly ten consecutive days this gloomy weather continued to harass them, but on the 20th it cleared as they were on their march, and on the following day with a brisk southerly breeze and their sail set they traveled along at a fine rate. The state of Shackleton's health was still a source of acutest anxiety, but each march brought safety nearer and nearer, and on the 23rd Scott was able to write in a much more hopeful spirit. Next day a glimpse of the Bluff to the north was seen, but this encouraging sight was accompanied by a new form of surface which made the pulling very wearisome. An inch or so beneath the soft snow surface was a thin crust, almost, but not quite, sufficient to bear their weight. The work of breaking such a surface as this would, Scott says, have finished Shackleton in no time, but luckily he was able to go on ski and avoid the jars. 'In spite of our present disbelief in ski, one is bound to confess that if we get back safely Shackleton will owe much to the pair he is now using.'

MOUNT EREBUS.

Page 131 But in spite of bad surfaces and increasingly heavy work, Scott and Wilson were determined to leave as little as possible to chance, and to get their invalid along as quickly as his condition would allow. Directly breakfast was over Shackleton started off and got well ahead, while Scott and Wilson packed up camp; and after lunch the same procedure was adopted. By this means he was able to take things easily, and though eager to do his share of the work he was wise enough to see that every precaution taken was absolutely necessary.

Encouragements in this stern struggle were few and far between, but when the smoke of Erebus was seen on the 25th, it cheered them to think that they had seen something that was actually beyond the ship. Probably it was more than a hundred miles away, but they had become so accustomed to seeing things at a distance that they were not in the least astonished by this.

January 26, too, had its consolations, for while plodding on as usual the travelers suddenly saw a white line ahead, and soon afterwards discovered that it was a sledge track. There was no doubt that the track was Barne's on his way back from his survey work to the west, but it was wonderful what that track told them. They could see that there had been six men with two sledges, and that all of the former had been going strong and well on ski. From the state of the track this party had evidently passed about four days before on the homeward route, and from Page 132 the zig-zagging of the course it was agreed that the weather must have been thick at the time. Every imprint in the soft snow added some small fact, and the whole made an excellent detective study. But the main point was that they knew for certain that Barne and his party were safe, and this after their own experiences was a great relief.

Another day and a half of labour brought them to the depôt, and the land of plenty. 'Directly,' Scott wrote on the 28th, 'our tent was up we started our search among the snow-heaps with childish glee. One after another our treasures were brought forth: oil enough for the most lavish expenditure, biscuit that might have lasted us for a month, and, finally, a large brown provision-bag which we knew would contain more than food alone. We have just opened this pro-vision-bag and feasted our eyes on the contents. There are two tins of sardines, a large tin of marmalade, soup squares, pea soup, and many other delights that already make our mouths water. For each one of us there is some special trifle which the forethought of our kind people has provided, mine being an extra packet of tobacco; and last, but not least, there are a whole heap of folded letters and notes — *billets-doux* indeed. I wonder if a mail was ever more ac-ceptable.'

The news, too, was good; Royds, after desperate labour, had suc-ceeded in rescuing the boats; Blissett had discovered an Emperor penguin's egg, and his messmates expected him to be knighted. But the meal itself, though 'pure joy' at first, was not an Page 133 un-qualified success, for after being accustomed to starvation or semi-starvation rations, they were in no condition either to resist or to digest any unstinted meal, and both Scott and Wilson suffered acutely.

On the next morning they awoke to find a heavy blizzard, and the first thought of pushing on at all hazards was abandoned when Shackleton was found to be extremely ill. Everything now depend-ed upon the weather, for should the blizzard continue Scott doubt-ed if Shackleton would even be well enough to be carried on the sledge. 'It is a great disappointment; last night we thought ourselves out of the wood with all our troubles behind us, and to-night matters seem worse than ever. Luckily Wilson and I are pretty fit, and we have lots of food.' By great luck the weather cleared on the morning of the 30th, and as Shackleton after a very bad night revived a little it was felt that the only chance was to go on. 'At last he was got away, and we watched him almost tottering along with frequent painful halts. Re-sorting our provisions, in half an hour we had packed our camp, set our sail, and started with the sledges. It was not long before we caught our invalid, who was so exhausted that we thought it wiser he should sit on the sledges, where for the remainder of the forenoon, with the help of our sail, we carried him.'

In Wilson's opinion Shackleton's relapse was mainly due to the blizzard, but fortune favored them during the last stages of the struggle homewards, and the glorious weather had a wonderful effect upon the Page 134 sick man. By the night of February 2 they were within ten or twelve miles of their goal, and saw a prospect of a successful end to their troubles. During the afternoon they had passed round the corner of White Island, and as they did so the old familiar outline of the friendly peninsula suddenly opened up before them. On every side were suggestions of home, and their joy at seeing the well-known landmarks was increased by the fact that they were as nearly 'spent as three persons can well be.'

Shackleton, it is true, had lately shown an improvement, but his companions placed but little confidence in that, for they knew how near he had been, and still was, to a total collapse. And both Scott and Wilson knew also that their scurvy had again been advancing rapidly, but they scarcely dared to admit either to themselves or each other how 'done' they were. For many a day Wilson had suffered from lameness, and each morning had vainly tried to disguise his limp, but from his set face Scott knew well enough how much he suffered before the first stiffness wore off. 'As for myself, for some time I have hurried through the task of changing my foot-gear in an attempt to forget that my ankles are considerably swollen. One and all we want rest and peace, and, all being well, tomorrow, thank Heaven, we shall get them.'

These are the final words written in Scott's sledge-diary during this remarkable journey, for on the next morning they packed up their camp for the last time and set their faces towards Observation Hill. Brilliant Page 135 weather still continued, and after plodding on for some hours two specks appeared, which at first were thought to be penguins, but presently were seen to be men hurrying towards them. Early in the morning they had been reported by watchers on the hills, and Skelton and Bernacchi had hastened out to meet them.

Then the tent was put up, and while cocoa was made they listened to a ceaseless stream of news, for not only had all the other travelers returned safe and sound with many a tale to tell, but the relief ship, the *Morning*, had also arrived and brought a whole year's news.

So during their last lunch and during the easy march that followed, they, gradually heard of the events in the civilized world from December, 1901, to December, 1902, and these kept their thoughts busy until they rounded the cape and once more saw their beloved ship.

Though still held fast in her icy prison the *Discovery* looked trim and neat, and to mark the especial nature of the occasion a brave display of bunting floated gently in the breeze, while as they approached, the side and the rigging were thronged with their cheering comrades.

With every want forestalled, and every trouble lifted from their shoulders by companions vying with one another to attend to them, no welcome could have been more delightful, and yet at the time it appeared unreal to their dull senses. 'It seemed too good to be true that all our anxieties had so completely ended, Page 136 and that rest for brain and limb was ours at last.' For ninety-three days they had plodded over a vast snow-field and slept beneath the fluttering canvas of a tent; during that time they had covered 960 statute miles; and if the great results hoped for in the beginning had not been completely achieved, they knew at any rate that they had striven and endured to the limit of their powers.

A SECOND WINTER

As cold waters to a thirsty soul,
So is good news from a far country.
PROVERBS.

In a very short time Scott discovered that the sledding resources of the ship had been used to their fullest extent during his absence, and that parties had been going and coming and ever adding to the collection of knowledge.

On November 2 Royds had gone again to Cape Crozier to see how the Emperor penguins were faring, and in the meantime such rapid progress had been made in the preparations for the western party that November 9, being King Edward's birthday, was proclaimed a general holiday and given up to the eagerly anticipated athletic sports.

Of all the events perhaps the keenest interest was shown in the toboggan race, for which the men entered in pairs. Each couple had to provide their own toboggan, subject to the rule that no sledge, or part of a sledge, and no ski should be used. The start was high up the hillside, and as the time for it approached the Page 138 queerest lot of toboggans gradually collected. The greater number were roughly made from old boxes and cask staves, but something of a sensation was caused when the canny Scottish carpenter's mate arrived with a far more pretentious article, though built from the same material. In secret he had devoted himself to making what was really a very passable sledge, and when he and his companion secured themselves to this dark horse, the result of the race was considered a foregone conclusion. But soon after the start it was seen that this couple had laboured in vain; for although they shot ahead at first, their speed was so great that they could not control their machine. In a moment they were rolling head-over-heels in clouds of snow, and while the hare was thus amusing itself a tortoise slid past and won the race.

By the end of November everything was ready for the western journey, and a formidable party set out on the 29th to cross

McMurdo Sound and attack the mainland. In Armitage's own party were Skelton and ten men, while the supports consisted of Koettlitz, Ferrar, Dellbridge and six men. Excellent pioneer work was done by Armitage and his party during their seven weeks' journey. Without a doubt a practicable road to the interior was discovered and traversed, and the barrier of mountains that had seemed so formidable an obstruction from the ship was conquered. It was equally certain that the party could claim to be the first to set foot on the interior of Victoria Land but they had been forced to turn back at an extremely Page 139 interesting point, and in consequence were unable to supply very definite information with regard to the ice-cap. They had, however, fulfilled their main object, and in doing so had disclosed problems that caused the deepest interest to be focussed upon the direction in which they had traveled.

Perhaps the most promising circumstance of all was that among the rock specimens brought back were fragments of quartz-grits. These, with other observations, showed the strong probability of the existence of sedimentary deposits which might be reached and examined, and which alone could serve to reveal the geological history of this great southern continent. At all hazards Scott determined that the geologist of the expedition must be given a chance to explore this most interesting region.

The extensive preparations for the western journey had practically stripped the ship of sledge equipment, and those who went out on shorter journeys were obliged to make the best of the little that remained. This did not, however, balk their energies, and by resorting to all kinds of shifts and devices they made many useful expeditions.

While these efforts at exploration were being carried out the ship was left in the charge of Royds, who employed everyone on board in the most important task of freeing the boats. Drastic measures had to be taken before they could be released from their beds of ice, and with sawing and blasting going on in the unseen depths, it was not possible Page 140 that the task could be accomplished without doing considerable damage. When at length all of them had been brought to the surface their condition was exceedingly dilapidated; indeed only two of them were in a condition to float; but although it was evident that the carpenter would be busy for many weeks before they would be seaworthy, their reappearance was a tremendous relief.

Long before his departure to the south, Scott had given instructions that the *Discovery* should be prepared for sea by the end of January. Consequently, after the boats had been freed, there was still plenty of employment for everybody, since 'preparations for sea' under such circumstances meant a most prodigious amount of labour. Tons and tons of snow had to be dug out from the deck with pick-axes and shoveled over the side; aloft, sails and ropes had to be looked to, the running-gear to be re-rove, and everything got ready for handling the ship under sail; many things that had been displaced or landed near the shore-station had to be brought on board and secured in position; thirty tons of ice had to be fetched, melted, and run into the boilers; below, steam-pipes had to be rejointed, glands re-packed, engines turned by hand, and steam raised to see that all was in working order.

Not doubting that the ice would soon break up and release the ship, this work was carried on so vigorously that when the southern travelers returned all was ready for them to put to sea again.

Page 141 But eleven days before Scott and his companions struggled back to safety the great event of the season had happened in the arrival of the *Morning*. How the funds were raised by means of which this ship was sent is a tale in itself; briefly, however, it was due to the untiring zeal and singleness of purpose shown by Sir Clements Markham that the *Morning*, commanded by Lieutenant William Colbeck, R.N.R., was able to leave the London Docks on July 9, 1902.

Long before the *Discovery* had left New Zealand the idea of a relief ship had been discussed, and although Scott saw great difficulties in the way, he also felt quite confident that if the thing was to be done Sir Clements was the man to do it. Obviously then it was desirable to leave as much information as possible on the track, and the relief ship was to try and pick up clues at the places where Scott had said that he would attempt to leave them. These places were Cape Adare, Possession Islands, Coulman Island, Wood Bay, Franklin Island and Cape Crozier.

On January 8 a landing was effected at Cape Adare, and there Colbeck heard of the *Discovery's* safe arrival in the south. The Possession Islands were drawn blank, because Scott had not been able to land there, and south of this the whole coast was so thickly packed that the *Morning* could not approach either Coulman Island or Wood Bay.

Franklin Island was visited on January 14, but Page 142 without result; and owing to the quantities of pack ice it was not until four days later that a landing was made at Cape Crozier. Colbeck himself joined the landing party, and after spending several hours in fruitless search, he was just giving up the hunt and beginning despondently to wonder what he had better do next, when suddenly a small post was seen on the horizon. A rush was made for it, and in a few minutes Colbeck knew that he had only to steer into the mysterious depths of McMurdo Sound to find the *Discovery*, and practically to accomplish the work he had set out to do.

On board the *Discovery* the idea had steadily grown that a relief ship would come. For no very clear reason the men had begun to look upon it as a certainty, and during the latter part of January it was not uncommon for wild rumors to be spread that smoke had been seen to the north. Such reports, therefore, were generally received without much excitement, but when a messenger ran down the hill on the night of the 23rd to say that there was actually a ship in sight the enthusiasm was intense. Only the most imperturbable of those on board could sleep much during that night, and early on the 24th a large party set out over the floe. The *Morning* was lying some ten miles north of the *Discovery*, but it was far easier to see her than to reach her. At last, however, the party, after various little adventures, stood safely on deck and received the warmest of welcomes.

During the last week of January the weather was Page 143 in its most glorious mood, and with some of the treacherous thin ice breaking away the *Morning* was able to get a mile nearer. Parties constantly passed to and fro between the two ships, and everyone — with unshaken confidence that the *Discovery* would soon be free — gave themselves up to the delight of fresh companionship, and the joy of good news from the home country. To this scene of festivity and cheeriness Scott, Wilson and Shackleton returned on February

3, and though the last to open their letters they had the satisfaction of knowing that the *Morning* had brought nothing but good news.

By a curious coincidence Colbeck chose the night of the Southern party's return to make his first visit to the *Discovery*, and soon after Scott had come out of his delicious bath and was reveling in the delight of clean clothes, he had the pleasure of welcoming him on board. 'In those last weary marches over the barrier,' Scott says, 'I had little expected that the first feast in our home quarters would be taken with strange faces gathered round our festive table, but so it was, and I can well remember the look of astonishment that dawned on those faces when we gradually displayed our power of absorbing food.'

But however difficult the appetites of the party were to appease, for a fortnight after they had reached the ship their condition was very wretched. Shackleton at once went to bed, and although he soon tried to be out and about again, the least exertion caused a return of his breathlessness, and he still suffered from Page 144 the violent fits of coughing that had troubled him so much on the journey. With Wilson, who at one time had shown the least signs of scurvy, the disease had increased so rapidly at the end that on his return he wisely decided to go to bed, where he remained quietly for ten days. 'Wilson,' Scott wrote on February 16, 'is a very fine fellow, his pluck and go were everything on our southern journey; one felt he wouldn't give in till he dropped.' And this collapse when he got back to the ship was in itself a proof of the determination which must have upheld him during the last marches.

Scott, though the least affected of the three, was also by no means fit and well. Both his legs were swollen and his gums were very uncomfortable, but in addition to these troubles he was attacked by an overwhelming feeling of both physical and mental weariness. 'Many days passed,' he says, 'before I could rouse myself from this slothful humour, and it was many weeks before I had returned to a normally vigorous condition. It was probably this exceptionally relaxed state of health that made me so slow to realize that the ice conditions were very different from what they had been in the previous season.... The prospect of the ice about us remaining fast throughout the season never once entered my head.' His diary, however, for the month shows how he gradually awakened to the true state of affairs, and on February 13 he decided to begin the transport of stores from the *Morning* to the *Discovery*, so that the former ship 'should run no risk of being detained.' And on the 18th when Page 145 he paid his first visit to the *Morning* and found the journey 'an awful grind,' he had begun to wonder whether the floe was ever going to break up.

LUNAR CORONA.

A week later he was clearly alive to the situation. 'The *Morning* must go in less than a week, and it seems now impossible that we shall be free by that time, though I still hope the break-up may come after she has departed.' Some time previously he had decided that if they had to remain the ship's company should be reduced, and on the 24th he had a talk with the men and told them that he wished nobody to stop on board who was not willing. On the following day a list was sent round for the names of those who wanted to go, and the result was curiously satisfactory — for Scott had determined that eight men should go, and not only were there eight names on the list, but they were also precisely those which Scott would have put there had he made the selection. Shackleton also had to be told that he must go, as in his state of health Scott did not think that any further hardships ought to be risked; but in his place Scott requisitioned Mulock who by an extraordinary chance is just the very man we wanted. We have now an immense amount of details for charts... and Mulock is excellent at this work and as keen as possible. It is rather amusing, as he is the only person who is obviously longing for the ice to stop in, though of course he doesn't say so. The other sporting characters are still giving ten to one that it will go out, but I am bound to confess that I am not sanguine.'

Page 146 The letter from which the last extract is taken was begun on February 16, and before the end of the month all hope of the *Discovery* being able to leave with the *Morning* had been abandoned. On March 2 nearly the whole of the *Discovery's* company were entertained on board the *Morning,* and on the following day the relief ship slowly backed away from the ice-edge, and in a few minutes she was turning to the north, with every rope and spar outlined against the black northern sky. Cheer after cheer was raised as she gathered way, and long after she had passed out of earshot the little band stood gazing at her receding hull, and wondering when they too would be able to take the northern track.

In the *Morning* went a letter from Scott which shows that although in a sense disappointed by the prospect of having to remain for another winter, both he and his companions were not by any means dismayed. 'It is poor luck,' he wrote, 'as I was dead keen on getting a look round C. North before making for home. However we all take it philosophically, and are perfectly happy and contented on board, and shall have lots to do in winter, spring and summer. We will have a jolly good try to free the ship next year, though I fear manual labour doesn't go far with such terribly heavy ice as we have here; but this year we were of course unprepared, and when we realized the situation it was too late to begin anything like extensive operations. I can rely on every single man that remains in the ship and I gave them all the option of leaving... Page 147 the ship's company is now practically naval-officers and men—it is rather queer when one looks back to the original gift of two officers.'

Referring to the Southern journey he says, 'We cut our food and fuel too fine.... I never knew before what it was to be hungry; at times we were famished and had to tighten our belts nightly before going to sleep. The others dreamt of food snatched away at the last moment, but this didn't bother me so much.'

But characteristically the greater part of this long letter refers not to his own doings, but to the admirable qualities of those who were with him. Wilson, Royds, Skelton, Hodgson, Barne and Bernacchi are all referred to in terms of the warmest praise, and for the manner in which Colbeck managed the relief expedition the greatest admiration is expressed. But in some way or other Scott discovered good points in all the officers he mentioned, and if they were not satisfactory in every way his object seemed to be rather to excuse than to blame them. He was, however, unaffectedly glad to see the last of the cook, for the latter had shown himself far more capable at talking than at cooking, and had related so many of his wonderful adventures that one of the sailors reckoned that the sum total of these thrilling experiences must have extended over a period of five hundred and ninety years—which, as the sailor said, was a fair age even for a cook.

By March 14 even the most optimistic of the company were compelled to admit the certainty of a second winter, and orders were given to prepare the Page 148 ship for it. Compared with the previous year the weather had been a great deal worse, for there had been more wind and much lower temperatures, and under such conditions it was hopeless to go on expecting the ice to break up. But it was not to be wondered at that they found themselves wondering what their imprisonment meant. Was it the present summer or the last that was the exception? For them this was the gravest question, since on the answer to it their chance of getting away next year, or at all, depended.

While, however, the situation as regards the future was not altogether without anxiety, they sturdily determined to make the best of the present. To ward off any chance of scurvy, it was determined to keep rigidly to a fresh-meat routine throughout the winter, and consequently a great number of seals and skuas had to be killed. At first the skua had been regarded as unfit for human food, but Skelton on a sledding trip had caught one in a noose and promptly put it into the pot. And the result was so satisfactory that the skua at once began to figure prominently on the menu. They had, however, to deplore the absence of penguins from their winter diet, because none had been seen near the ship for a long time.

On Wednesday, April 24, the sun departed, but Scott remarks upon this rather dismal fact with the greatest cheerfulness: 'It would be agreeable to know what is going to happen next year, but otherwise we have no wants. Our routine goes like clock-work; Page 149 we eat, sleep, work and play at regular hours, and are never in lack of employment. Hockey, I fear, must soon cease for lack of light, but it has been a great diversion, although not unattended with risks, for yesterday I captured a black eye from a ball furiously driven by Royds.'

Of the months that followed little need be said, except that Scott's anticipations were fully realized. In fact the winter passed by without a hitch, and their second mid-winter day found them even more cheerful than their first. Hodgson continued to work away with his fish-traps, tow-nets and dredging; Mulock, who had been trained as a surveyor and had great natural abilities for the work, was most useful, first in collecting and re-marking all the observations, and later on in constructing temporary charts; while Barne generally vanished after breakfast and spent many a day at his distant sounding holes.

Throughout the season the routine of scientific observations was carried out in the same manner as in the previous year, while many new details were added; and so engaged was everyone in serviceable work that when the second long Polar night ended, Scott was able to write: 'I do not think there is a soul on board the *Discovery* who would say that it has been a hardship.... All thoughts are turned towards the work that lies before us, and it would be difficult to be blind to the possible extent of its usefulness. Each day has brought it more home to us how little we know and how much there is to be learned, and we Page 150 realize fully that this second year's work may more than double the value of our observations. Life in these regions has lost any terror it ever possessed for us, for we know that, come what may, we can live, and live well, for any reasonable number of years to come.'

Page 151 CHAPTER VIII

THE WESTERN JOURNEY

> Path of advance! but it leads
> A long steep journey through sunk
> Gorges, o'er mountains in snow. — M. ARNOLD.

During the second winter much time and attention had to be given to the sledge equipment, for there was scarcely an article in it that did not need to be thoroughly overhauled and refitted. But in spite of all their efforts, the outfit for the coming season was bound to be a tattered and makeshift affair. Skins of an inferior quality had to be used for sleeping-bags; the tents were blackened with use, threadbare in texture, and patched in many places; the cooking apparatus was considerably the worse for wear; the wind clothes were almost worn out, while for all the small bags, which were required for provisions, they were obliged to fall back on any sheets and tablecloths that could be found. This state of things, however, was very far from daunting their spirits, and long before the winter was over the plan of campaign for the next season had been drawn up.

In making the program Scott knew that extended Page 152 journeys could only be made by properly supported parties, and it was easy to see that his small company would not be able to make more than two supported journeys, though it might be just possible to make a third more or less lengthy journey without support. The next thing to decide was in what direction these parties should go, and in this connection the greatest interest undoubtedly lay in the west. To explore the Ferrar Glacier from a geological point of view and find out the nature of the interior ice-cap must, Scott determined, be attempted at all costs, and this journey to the west he decided to lead himself.

In the south it was evident that without dogs no party could hope to get beyond the point already reached. But Scott's journey had been made a long way from land, and consequently had left many problems unsolved, chief among which were the extraordinary straits that had appeared to run through the mountain ranges without rising in level. It was therefore with the main object of exploring one of them that the second supported party, under the leadership of Barne and Mulock, was to set out.

The credit in arranging the direction in which the unsupported party should go belongs to Bernacchi, who was the first to ask Scott what proof they had that the barrier surface continued on a level to the eastward; and when Scott began to consider this question, he discovered that there was no definite proof, and decided that the only way to get it was to go and see.

PINNACLED ICE AT MOUTH OF FERRAR GLACIER.
Photo by F. Debenham.

PRESSURE RIDGES NORTH SIDE OF DISCOVERY BLUFF.
Photo by F. Debenham.

Page 153 Besides the longer journeys, the program included a number of shorter ones for specific purposes, and the most important of these were the periodic visits to the Emperor penguin rookery, as it was hoped that Wilson would be able to observe these birds from the beginning of their breeding season.

Finally, one important factor was to dominate all the sledding arrangements, for although the *Discovery* was mainly at the mercy of natural causes, Scott made up his mind that everything man could do to free her from the ice should be done. As soon as they could hope to make any impression upon the great ice-sheet around them, the whole force of the company was to set to work at the task of extrication, and so all sledding journeys were to start in time to assure their return to the ship by the middle of December.

On September 9 Scott got away with his own party of Skelton, Dailey, Evans, Lashly and Handsley, their object being to find a new road to the Ferrar Glacier, and on it to place a depôt ready for a greater effort over the ice-cap. The Ferrar Glacier descends gradually to the inlet, which had been named New Harbor, but Armitage had reported most adversely on this inlet as a route for sledges, and in conducting his own party had led it across the high foot-hills. As yet Scott had not been to this region, but in the nature of things he could not help thinking that some practical route must exist up the New Harbour inlet, and that if it could be found the journey to the west would be much easier. And the result of this little journey Page 154 was really important, for whereas Armitage, at the foot of the Ferrar Glacier, had seen the disturbance on the south side, and had concluded that it must extend right across, Scott's party fortunately pushed over this disturbance and found much easier conditions beyond it.

The fact thus discovered, and which was amply supported by further observations, was that invariably in the Antarctic regions where glaciers run more or less east and west, the south side will be found to be much broken up and decayed, while the north side will be comparatively smooth and even. The reason of this, of course, is simple enough, for the sun achieves its highest altitude in the north, and consequently its warmest and most direct rays fall on the south side of a valley. Here, therefore, the greater part of the summer melting takes place, and a wild chaos of ice disturbance is caused.

Scott's party, by taking a different route, laid a depôt at a spot which Armitage had taken three weeks to reach, and was back again at the ship in less than a fortnight.

'We were,' Scott says, 'inclined to be exceedingly self-satisfied; we had accomplished our object with unexpected ease, we had done a record march, and we had endured record temperatures—at least, we thought so, and thought also how pleasant it would be to tell these things in front of a nice bright fire. As we approached the ship, however, Hodgson came out to greet us, and his first question was, "What temperatures Page 155 have you had?" We replied by complacently quoting our array of *minus* fifties, but he quickly cut us short by remarking that we were not in it.'

In fact during those few days there had been a very cold snap throughout the region. Barne's party on the barrier, where they had been laying a depôt, had the coldest time, and after their thermometer had fallen lower and lower its spirit-column broke at -67.7°.

Royds and his party also had to endure -62°, but in other respects they were in luck. For on arriving at Cape Crozier they found that the Emperor penguins had already hatched out their young, and Wilson was delighted to get the opportunity of studying the chicks at such a tender age. Commenting upon this and another journey to Cape Crozier, Wilson wrote: 'The Emperor penguin stands nearly four feet high, and weighs upward of eighty to ninety pounds.... I think the chickens hate their parents, and when one watches the proceedings in a rookery it strikes one as not surprising. In the first place there is about one chick to ten or twelve adults, and each adult has an overpowering desire to "sit" on something. Both males and females want to nurse, and the result is that when a chicken finds himself alone there is a rush on the part of a dozen unemployed to seize him. Naturally he runs away, and dodges here and there till a six-stone Emperor falls on him, and then begins a regular football scrimmage, in which each tries to hustle the other off, and the end is too often disastrous to the chick.... I think it is not Page 156 an exaggeration to say that of the 77 per cent. that die no less than half are killed by kindness.'

From Cape Crozier Cross resolved to try to bring two chickens back to the ship, and by giving up his sleeping jacket to keep them warm and tending them with the utmost care, he succeeded in his attempt. But eventually they died from unnatural feeding, and Wilson says: 'Had we even succeeded in bringing them to the age when they put on their feathers, I fear that the journey home through the tropics would have proved too much for them, as we had no means of making a cool place for them on the ship.'

September 21 brought with it a grievous disappointment, as on that day the nautical almanac announced that nine-tenths of the sun would be obscured. For this event Bernacchi had made the most careful preparations, and everyone was placed under his orders during the day. Telescopes and the spectroscopic camera were trained in the right direction, magnetic instruments were set to run at quick speed, and observers were told off to watch everything on which the absence of sun could possibly have the smallest effect. Everything, in short, was ready except the sun itself which obstinately refused to come out. 'There may,' Scott says, 'have been an eclipse of the sun on September 21, 1903, as the almanac said, but we should none of us have liked to swear to the fact.'

The next three weeks or so were spent in preparations for the long journeys, and on October 12 Scott Page 157 left the ship with a party of twelve, and four 11-foot sledges. First came his own party, which included Skelton, Feather, Evans, Lashly and Handsley; secondly there was a small party for the geologist, Ferrar, who was accompanied by Kennar and Weller; and thirdly there were the supports, consisting of Dailey, Williamson and Plumley.

Scott guessed rightly that in many respects this was going to be the hardest task he had yet undertaken, but he knew also that experience would be a thing to be reckoned upon, and that it would take a good deal to stop the determined men whom he had chosen. At the start their loads were a little over 200 lbs. per man, but most of the party were by this time in thoroughly good condition, and by hard marching they covered the forty-five miles to New Harbour and reached the snow-cape early on the 14th.

This snow-cape in future was to be known as Butter Point, for here on their return journey they could hope to obtain fresh seal-meat, and in preparation for this great event a tin of butter was carried and left at the point for each party.

At first all went well with the travelers, and it was not until the evening of the 17th, when they were camped amid indescribably beautiful scenery, that the first cloud of trouble arose. Then Dailey the carpenter reported that the German silver had split under the runners of two sledges, and this was a most serious blow; for although the wood runners were capable of running on snow without protection, on Page 158 hard, sharp ice, especially if the sledge was heavily laden, they would be knocked to pieces in a very short time. It was, therefore, absolutely necessary to protect the runners on this journey, but unfortunately the German silver protection had already stood a season's work, and had worn thin without giving any outward sign.

From start to finish of the Ferrar Glacier about ninety miles of hard ice were to be expected, and the problem that immediately arose was how to get the sledges over this without damage.

By lunch-time on the 18th they had achieved a height of over 6,000 feet, and by that time the sledges were in such a parlous state that Scott had all of them unpacked and the runners turned up for inspection. Horrid revelations followed; one sledge remained sound, and Scott promptly decided that there was one course and only one to take, and that was to return to the ship as fast as they could. Had two sledges been available the advance party might have struggled on, but with one they could do nothing; so they left the sound sledge with everything else except the half-week's provisions necessary to take them back, and on the following days they 'came as near flying as is possible with a sledge party.' On the morning of the 19th they had eighty-seven miles to cover, and by 8.30 P.M. on the 21st they had reached the ship.

During this march Scott had determined to test his own party to the utmost, but seeing no necessity Page 159 for the supports to be dragged into this effort he told them to take their own time. The supporting party, however, did not mean to be left behind if they could help it, and later on the night of the 21st they also reached the ship. In the hard struggle of the last hours some of the members of the supporting party, though determined not to give in, had been comically astounded by the pace which was set, and Kennar, presumably referring to Scott, kept on repeating, 'If he can do it, I don't see why I can't: my legs are as long as his.

Five days after their flying return they were off again, and although the material for repairing sledges was very scanty, one sound 11-foot sledge had been made and also a 7-foot one for Ferrar's glacier work. Trouble, however, almost at once began with the runners, and on the 29th Ferrar's sledge gave out and caused a long delay. But in spite of being held up by wind for two days, they reached their depôt on November 1, and thought at first that everything was safe. On examination, however, they discovered that a violent gale had forced open the lid of the instrument box, and that several things were missing, among which Scott found to his dismay was the 'Hints to Travelers.'

'The gravity of this blow,' he wrote in his diary on November 1, 'can scarcely be exaggerated; but whilst I realized the blow I felt that nothing would induce me to return to the ship a second time; I thought it fair, however, to put the case to the others, Page 160 and I am, as I expected, fortified by their willing consent to take the risks of pushing on.'

In traveling to the west, Scott expected to be — as indeed he was — out of sight of landmarks for some weeks. In such a case as this the sledge-traveler is in precisely the same position as a ship or a boat at sea: he can only obtain a knowledge of his whereabouts by observation of the sun or stars, and with the help of these observations he finds his latitude and longitude, but to do this a certain amount of data is required. 'Hints to Travelers' supplies these necessary data, and it was on this book that Scott had been relying to help him to work out his sights and fix accurately the position of his party. Unless he went back to the ship to make good his loss, he was obliged to take the risk of marching into the unknown without knowing exactly where he was or how he was to get back. 'If,' he says, 'the loss of our "Hints to Travelers" did not lead us into serious trouble it caused me many a bad half-hour.'

Having, however, decided to push on, they wasted no time about it, and although the sledge-runners continued to need constant attention they arrived at the base of the upper glacier reach on the 2nd, and on the following day gained a height of 7,000 feet.

So far nothing exceptionally eventful had occurred, but November 4 was destined to begin a time that Scott described afterwards as 'the most miserable week I have ever spent.' In the morning of the 4th there was bright sunshine with a cold, increasing wind, Page 161 but later on the sun disappeared and the weather became very threatening. Still, however, they battled on and were half-way up the bare, icy slope they were climbing, when the air became thick with driving snow and the full force of the gale burst upon them. Pushing on at almost a run they succeeded in reaching the top, and hurriedly started to search for a patch of snow on which to camp, but nothing could be found except bare, blue ice. By this time the position was becoming serious, all of them were frost-bitten in the face, and although the runners of the sledges were split again so badly that they could barely pull them over the surface, they did not dare to leave the sledges in the thick drift.

At last a white patch was seen and a rush was made for it, but the snow discovered was so ancient and wind-swept that it was almost as hard as the ice itself. Nevertheless they knew it was this or nothing, and Scott seized a shovel for his own tent-party, and dug for all he was worth without making the least impression. At this moment Feather, the boatswain, luckily came to help him, and being more expert with the shovel managed to chip out a few small blocks. Then they tried to get up a tent, but again and again it and the poles were blown flat, and at least an hour passed before the tents were erected. 'Nothing,' Scott wrote, 'but experience saved us from disaster to-day, for I feel pretty confident that we could not have stood another hour in the open.'

Little, however, did they expect when shelter Page 162 was gained that a week would pass before they could resume their march. From November 4-11 the gale raged unceasingly, and meanwhile not a vision of the outer world came to them, for they were enveloped continuously in a thick fog of driving snow.

In Scott's tent there was one book, Darwin's 'Cruise of the *Beagle*,' and first one and then another would read this aloud, until frozen fingers prevented the pages from being turned over. Only one piece of work were they able to perform, and this on the first day when, thinking the storm would soon blow over, they hauled the sledges beneath one of the tents and stripped the German silver ready for the onward march.

By the fifth day of their imprisonment sleep began to desert them, and Scott, realizing that the long inactivity was telling on the health of the party, determined that whatever the conditions might be he would try to start on the following morning.

This attempt, however, resulted in complete failure. In ten minutes both of Scott's hands were 'gone,' Skelton had three toes and the heel of one foot badly frost-bitten, and Feather lost all feeling in both feet. 'Things are looking serious,' Scott wrote after this unsuccessful effort to be up and doing, 'I fear the long spell of bad weather is telling on us. The cheerfulness of the party is slowly waning; I heard the usual song from Lashly this morning, but it was very short-lived and dolorous.... Something must be done to-morrow, but what it will be, to-morrow only can show.'

Fortunately the next morning brought a lull in the Page 163 storm, and though the air was still as thick as a hedge it was possible at last to break away from 'Desolation Camp.' Then Scott's party separated from Ferrar's, the former making for the ice-fall and eventually and miraculously reaching the top without accident. On starting they could not see half-a-dozen yards ahead, and at once went as nearly as possible into an enormous chasm; and when they began to ascend they crossed numerous crevasses without waiting to see if the bridges would bear. 'I really believe that we were in a state when we none of us really cared much what happened; our sole thought was to get away from that miserable spot.'

But during the succeeding days fortune was with them, and by the night of the 13th the fight was won and the summit reached. With five weeks' provisions in hand, and the prospect of covering many miles before a return to the glacier would be necessary, they were, as they camped at the elevation of 8,900 feet, a very different party from the one which had struggled out of 'Desolation Camp' on the morning of the 11th.

But they had scarcely gained the summit of the icecap and started the journey to the west before troubles again began to gather round them. The long stay in 'Desolation Camp' had covered their sleeping-bags and night-jackets with ice, and with falling temperatures this ice had so little chance to evaporate that camping arrangements were acutely uncomfortable; and as each night the thermometer fell a little lower, Page 164 the chance of relief from this state of things could scarcely be said to exist. The wind, too, was a constant worry, for though it was not very strong, when combined with the low temperature and rarefied air its effect was blighting.

'I do not think,' Scott wrote, 'that it would be possible to conceive a more cheerless prospect than that which faced us at this time, when on this lofty, desolate plateau we turned our backs upon the last mountain peak that could remind us of habitable lands. Yet before us lay the unknown. What fascination lies in that word! Could anyone wonder that we determined to push on, be the outlook ever so comfortless?'

So they plodded forward with all their strength, but in spite of every effort their progress gradually became slower. By the 17th the sledges had been divided, Scott, Feather, and Evans leading with one, while Skelton, Handsley, and Lashly followed with the other. But Scott found very soon that the second sledge had great difficulty in keeping up, and that although he himself felt thoroughly strong and well, some of his companions were beginning to fail. As was natural with such men not one of them would own that he was exhausted, and in consequence it was only by paying the keenest attention that he could detect those who from sheer incapacity were relaxing their strain on the traces. And his position was not pleasant even when he knew, for to tell any of these brave people that they must turn back was a most unenviable Page 165 task. Thus it came about that all six of them marched on, though Scott was sure that better progress would have been made had the party been divided.

Something like a climax was reached on the 20th, when Handsley more or less broke down. Not for a moment, however, did he mean to give up, and when he was relieved of some part of his work he begged Scott not again to make an example of him. In Handsley's opinion his breakdown was a disgrace, and no arguments would make him change it. Small wonder then that Scott wrote in his diary: 'What children these men are, and yet what splendid children! The boatswain has been suffering agonies from his back; he has been pulling just behind me, and in some sympathy that comes through the traces I have got to know all about him, yet he has never uttered a word of complaint, and when he knows my eye is on him he straightens up and pretends he is just as fit as ever. What is one to do with such people?'

What Scott did was to try for another day to go on as before, but on November 22 he had to tell Skelton, Feather, and Handsley that they must turn back, and though 'they could not disguise their disappointment, they all seemed to understand that it had to be.'

From the date on which Scott reluctantly came to this decision, three weeks of the hardest physical toil followed for him and his companions, Evans and Lashly. Nevertheless Scott looked back upon this strenuous time with unmixed satisfaction, and paid a Page 166 high tribute of praise to his companions for their part in the successful work that was done.

'With these two men behind me,' he says, 'our sledge seemed to be a living thing, and the days of slow progress were numbered.... Troubles and discomforts were many, and we could only guess at the progress we made, but we knew that by sticking to our task we should have our reward when our observations came to be worked out on board the ship.'

Regularly each night the temperature fell to -40° or below, while during the marching hours it rarely rose much above -25°, and with this low temperature there was a constant wind. In fact the wind was the plague of their lives and cut them to pieces. So cracked were their faces that laughing hurt horribly, and the first half-hour of the morning march, before they were warmed up to the work, was dreadful, as then all their sore places got frost-bitten. In short the last week of their outward march was a searching test of endurance, but they had resolved to march on until November 30, and in spite of the miserable conditions there was no turning back before the month had ended.

Scott, however, was most undisguisedly glad when November 30 had come and gone. 'We have finished our last outward march, thank heaven! Nothing has kept us going during the past week but the determination to carry out our original intention of going on to the end of the month, and so here we have pitched our last camp.'

Page 167 CHAPTER IX

THE RETURN FROM THE WEST

> Ceaseless frost round the vast solitude
> Bound its broad zone of stillness. — SHELLEY.

'We are all,' Scott wrote in his diary, 'very proud of our march out. I don't know where we are, but I know we must be a long way to the west from my rough noon observation of the compass variation.' But not for anything in the world did he want again to see the interior of Victoria Land. Writing two years after this great march he says: 'For me the long month which we spent on the Victoria Land summit remains as some vivid but evil dream. I have a memory of continuous strain on mind and body, lightened only by the unfailing courage and cheerfulness of my companions.'

From first to last the month of November had been a struggle to penetrate into this barren, deserted, wind-swept, piercingly cold, and fearfully monotonous region, and although on turning homewards the travelers were relieved by having the wind at their backs, the time of trial was by no means over. Only by utilizing all their powers of marching could they hope Page 168 to retreat in safety from their position, and December opened with such overcast weather that valuable time had to be spent in the tent. During the next few days, however, good marches were made, until on December 9 everything changed abruptly for the worse.

On the afternoon of the 9th the surface became so abominably bad, that by pulling desperately they could not get the sledge along at more than a mile an hour. Oil was growing short, and in view of the future Scott had to propose that marching hours should be increased by one hour, that they should use half allowance of oil, and that if they did not sight landmarks within a couple of days their rations should be reduced. 'When I came to the cold lunch and fried breakfast poor Evans' face fell; he evidently doesn't much believe in the virtue of food, unless it is in the form of a *hoosh* and has some chance of sticking to one's ribs.'

Land was sighted on the 10th, 11th, and 12th, but the weather was as overcast as ever, and Scott was still in dreadful uncertainty of their whereabouts, because he was unable to recognize a single point. Ten hours' pulling per day was beginning to tell upon them, and although apart from the increasing pangs of hunger there was no sign of sickness, Scott remarks, on the 12th, that they were becoming 'gaunt shadows.'

During the morning of the 13th Evans' nose, which had been more or less frost-bitten for some weeks, had an especially bad attack. His attitude Page 169 to this unruly member was one of comic forbearance, as though, while it scarcely belonged to him, he was more or less responsible for it and so had to make excuses. On this occasion when told that it had 'gone,' he remarked in a resigned tone, 'My poor old nose again; well, there, it's chronic!' By the time it had been brought round a storm was blowing, and though they continued to march, the drift was so thick that at any moment they might have walked over the edge of a precipice — a fitting prelude to what, by general consent, was admitted to be the most adventurous day in their lives.

Prospects, when they started to march on the next morning, were at first a little brighter, but soon a bitterly cold wind was blowing and high ice hummocks began to appear ahead of them. In this predicament Scott realized that it was both rash to go forward, as the air was becoming thick with snow-drift, and equally rash to stop, for if they had to spend another long spell in a blizzard camp, starvation would soon be staring them in the face. So he asked Evans and Lashly if they were ready to take the risk of going on, and promptly discovered that they were. Then they marched straight for the ice disturbance, and as the surface became smoother and the slope steeper their sledge began to overrun them. At this point Scott put Evans and Lashly behind to hold the sledge back, while he continued in front to guide its course, and what happened afterwards is described most graphically in the diary of the 15th.

Page 170 'Suddenly Lashly slipped, and in an instant he was sliding downward on his back; directly the strain came on Evans, he too was thrown off his feet. It all happened in a moment, and before I had time to look the sledge and the two men hurtled past me; I braced myself to stop them, but might as well have attempted to hold an express train. With the first jerk I was whipped off my legs, and we all three lay sprawling on our backs and flying downward with an ever-increasing velocity. For some reason the first thought that flashed into my mind was that someone would break a limb if he attempted to stop our mad career, and I shouted something to this effect, but might as well have saved my breath. Then there came a sort of vague wonder as to what would happen next, and in the midst of that I was conscious that we had ceased to slide smoothly and were now bounding over a rougher incline, sometimes leaving it for several yards at a time; my thought flew to broken limbs again, for I felt we could not stand much of such bumping.

'At length we gave a huge leap into the air, and yet we traveled with such velocity that I had not time to think before we came down with tremendous force on a gradual incline of rough, hard, windswept snow. Its irregularities brought us to rest in a moment or two, and I staggered to my feet in a dazed fashion, wondering what had happened.

'Then to my joy I saw the others also struggling to their legs, and in another moment I could thank heaven that no limbs were broken. But we had by Page 171 no means escaped scathless; our legs now show one black bruise from knee to thigh, and Lashly was unfortunate enough to land once on his back, which is bruised and very painful.... I, as the lightest, escaped the easiest, yet before the two men crawled painfully to their feet their first question was to ask if I had been hurt.

'As soon as I could pull myself together I looked round, and now to my astonishment I saw that we were well on towards the entrance of our own glacier; ahead and on either side of us appeared well-remembered landmarks, whilst behind, in the rough broken ice-wall over which we had fallen, I now recognized at once the most elevated ice cascade of our valley....

'I cannot but think that this sudden revelation of our position was very wonderful. Half an hour before we had been lost; I could not have told whether we were making for our own glacier or any other, or whether we were ten or fifty miles from our depôt; it was more than a month since we had seen any known landmark. Now in this extraordinary manner the curtain had been raised... and down the valley we could see the high cliffs of the Depôt Nunatak where peace and plenty awaited us.'

The sledge had not capsized until they all rolled over at the end, but the jolting had scattered their belongings and broken open the biscuit box, with the result that they had no provisions left, except the few scraps they could pick up and the meager contents of their food bag. As quickly as stiffening limbs would Page 172 allow they collected their scattered articles, repacked the sledge and marched on towards the depôt. Before them lay a long plateau, at the edge of which Scott knew that they would find a second cascade, and beneath it the region of Desolation Camp and a more gradual icy surface down to the depôt.

Fortune favored them in descending the second cascade, and quite unsuspicious of any further danger they joined up their harness to their usual positions in front of the sledge. This brought

Scott in the middle and a little in advance, with Lashly on his right and Evans on his left. Presently the sledge began to skid, and Scott told Lashly to pull wide to steady it. Scarcely had this order been obeyed when Scott and Evans stepped on nothing and disappeared, while Lashly miraculously saved himself from following and sprang back with his whole weight on the trace. The sledge flashed by him and jumped the crevasse down which Scott and Evans had gone, one side of the sledge being cracked by the jerk but the other side mercifully holding. 'Personally,' Scott says, 'I remember absolutely nothing until I found myself dangling at the end of my trace with blue walls on either side and a very horrid looking gulf below; large ice-crystals dislodged by our movements continued to shower down on our heads. As a first step I took off my goggles; I then discovered that Evans was hanging just above me. I asked him if he was all right, and received a reassuring reply in his calm, matter-of-fact tones.'

Page 173 Then Scott began to grope about on every side with his cramponed feet, but not until his struggles set him swinging did his leg suddenly strike a projection. At a glance he saw that by raising himself he could get a foothold on this, and after a short struggle he stood upon a thin shaft of ice, which was wedged providentially between the walls of the chasm, and could look about him. To the right or left, above or below, there was not the vestige of another such support, nothing, in fact, but the smooth walls of ice. The projection seemed to have got there by a miracle, but miracle or not the thing to do was to help Evans, and when the latter had slipped his harness well up beneath his arms Scott found that he could pilot his feet to the bridge.

'All this had occupied some time, and it was only now that I realized what had happened above us, for there, some twelve feet over our heads, was the outline of the broken sledge. I saw at once what a frail support remained, and shouted to Lashly to ask what he could do, and then I knew the value of such a level-headed companion; for whilst he held on grimly to the sledge and us with one hand, his other was busily employed in withdrawing our ski. At length he succeeded in sliding two of these beneath the broken sledge, and so making our support more secure.'

But clever as this device was it still left them without Lashly's active assistance, because directly he relaxed his hold the sledge began to slip. The only Page 174 possible course, therefore, was for Scott and Evans to climb out unaided, and, after a word with Evans Scott decided to try first; though he confessed afterwards that he never expected to reach the top. Not for a longtime had he swarmed a rope, and to do so in thick clothing, heavy crampons, and with frost-bitten fingers seemed to him impossible. Of the struggle that followed he remembered little except that he got a rest when he could plant his foot in the belt of his own harness, and again when his feet held on the rings of the belt. 'Then came a mighty effort, till I reached the stirrup formed by the rope span of the sledge, and then, mustering all the strength that remained, I reached the sledge itself and flung myself on to the snow beyond. Lashly said, "Thank God!" and it was perhaps then that I realized that his position had been the worst of all.'

But having arrived at the top he was completely out of action for several minutes, for his hands were white to the wrists, and not until their circulation came back could he get to work. With two on top and only one below the position, however, was very different, and presently Evans, badly frost-bitten, was landed on the surface. For a minute or two they could only stand and look at one another. Then Evans said, 'Well, I'm blowed,' which was the first sign of surprise he had shown.

By six o'clock on that same evening they reached their depôt, and passed from abject discomfort to rest and peace. Bruised, sore and tired as they were, Page 175 Lashly sang merrily as he stirred the pot, while Scott and Evans sat on the sledge, shifted their foot-gear, spread out their clothes to dry, and talked cheerily about the happenings of the day.

From this time onward their camp-life was wholly, pleasant, except to Lashly who had an attack of snow-blindness. Apart from that they were in the best of condition for the hard marching in front of them, and when on the night of the 20th they reached their second depôt and could look out towards the sea, they did not care how far round they might have to walk if only that stubborn sheet of ice had broken away. But it was too evident that their homeward track might be as straight as they chose, as only in the far distance was open water to be seen, and with sorrow they realized that there must still be many miles of ice between it and the *Discovery*.

Late on Christmas Eve they were once more on board the ship after an absence of fifty-nine days, during which they had traveled 725 miles. Taking the eighty-one days of absence which had constituted the whole sledding season, Scott, Evans and Lashly had covered 1,098 miles, and, not including minor undulations, had climbed heights which totaled to 19,000 feet. On getting back to the *Discovery* Scott found only Koettlitz, Handsley and Quartley on board, because all the rest of the company had gone to the north to saw through the ice; and during the few days of rest that he allowed himself before going to the sawing-camp, he was able to read the reports of the Page 176 officers who had led the other journeys, and to see what excellent work had been done during his absence.

Ferrar's survey and Skelton's photographic work had added materially to the value of the western journey; the party led by Barne and Mulock to the south had met with ill-fortune from the start, but throughout the journey Mulock used the theodolite indefatigably, with the results that this stretch of coast-line was more accurately plotted than any other part of Victoria Land, and that the positions and height of over two hundred mountain peaks were fixed. Barne also obtained a very good indication of the movement of the Great Barrier ice-sheet. During Royds' journey, on which the party went on very short food allowance, Bernacchi took a most interesting series of magnetic observations. And although to Bernacchi himself belongs the greatest credit, some reflected glory, at any rate, fell upon his companions, because they had to stay shivering outside the tent while he was at work inside it.

Wilson had not only been busy with the penguins at Cape Crozier, but had also made a complete examination of the enormous and interesting pressure ridges which form the junction of the Great Barrier ice-mass with the land, and subsequently had spent much time in studying the windless area to the south of Ross Island. Also, with Armitage and Heald, he had made an excellent little journey, on which Armitage obtained some very good photographs, Page

177 sufficient in themselves to prove the receding glacial conditions of the whole continent.

In short during Scott's absence his companions had been working strenuously to increase the supply of information; so when the second sledding-season ended, they could with reason congratulate themselves that the main part of their work was done.

Page 178 CHAPTER X

RELEASE

> And Thor
> Set his shoulder hard against the stern
> To push the ship through...
> ...and the water gurgled in
> And the ship floated on the waves and rock'd.
> M. ARNOLD.

After a few days on board Scott became restless to see what was going on in the sawing-camp, and on the morning of the 31st he started off with Evans, Lashly and Handsley to march the ten and a half miles to the north. When the instructions for this attempt to free the *Discovery* were drawn up, there had been, of course, no telling how broad the ice-sheet would be when operations began, and Scott had been obliged to assume that it would be nearly the same as in the previous year, when the open water had extended to the Dellbridge Islets about eleven miles from the ship. There he directed that the camp should be made, and Armitage, on whom in Scott's absence the command had devolved, made all preparations in accordance with the instructions he had received.

At the outset, however, a difficulty awaited him, Page 179 as in the middle of December the open water, instead of being up to the islets, ended at least ten miles farther to the north. Under the circumstances he considered it dangerous to take the camp out to the ice-edge, and so the sawing work had been begun in the middle of the ice-sheet instead of at its edge.

Thirty people were in the camp when Scott arrived, and though at first the work had been painful both to arms and backs they were all in splendid condition and spirits. Fortunately this was a land of plenty, penguins and seals abounded, and everyone agreed that, apart from the labour, they were having a most enjoyable time, though no one imagined that the work would be useful.

In two days Scott was as convinced as anyone that the work must be in vain, and ordered the sawing to stop. 'I have been much struck,' he wrote, 'by the way in which everyone has cheerfully carried on this hopeless work until the order came to halt. There could have been no officer or man among them who did not see from the first how utterly useless it was, and yet there has been no faltering or complaint, simply because all have felt that, as the sailor expresses it, "Them's the orders."'

With twenty miles of ice between the *Discovery* and freedom, the possibility of yet another winter had to be considered, so although most of the company returned to the ship, Lashly, Evans, Handsley and Clarke were left behind to make sure of an adequate stock of penguins. And then Scott being unable Page 180 to do any good by remaining in the ship started off to the north with Wilson, the former being anxious to watch the ice-edge and see what chance there was of a break-up, while Wilson wanted to study the life of that region. This journey was to be 'a real picnic,' with no hard marching and plenty to eat; and, pursuing their leisurely way, on January 4 they were within half a mile of the open water when Wilson suddenly said, 'There they are.' Then Scott looked round, and on the rocks of Cape Royds saw a red smudge dotted with thousands of little black and white figures. Without doubt they had stumbled upon a penguin rookery, but interesting as it was to have made the discovery, it was at the same time exasperating to think of the feast of eggs they had missed in the last two years. During the rest of the day they watched the penguins and the skua gulls which were nesting around them; and before supper they took soap and towels down to a rill of thaw-water that ran within a few yards of their tent, and washed in the warm sunlight. 'Then,' Scott says, 'we had a dish of fried penguin's liver with seal kidneys; eaten straight out of the frying-pan, this was simply delicious. I have come to the conclusion that life in the Antarctic Regions can be very pleasant.'

Still in the proper picnic spirit they dawdled over their breakfast on the following day, and were lazily discussing plans when Scott, looking through the open door of the tent to the clear sea beyond, suddenly caught sight of a ship. In a moment haste and bustle reigned supreme, and while they were searching for Page 181 boots and other things necessary for the march, Wilson said, 'Why, there's another,' and without any doubt two vessels were framed in the doorway. It had at once been taken for granted that the first ship was the *Morning*, but what in the name of fortune was the meaning of the other neither Scott nor Wilson could imagine. The easiest and quickest way to find out was to go straight on board, for the ships were making for the ice-edge some five miles to the westward, but if they had followed this simple plan their companions on the *Discovery* would have known nothing about it, and would have been compelled to wait for their mails. So they started southward to find the penguin hunters, and then to send them to establish communications with the ship. For a long time no sight of the men could be seen, but after traveling about six miles Scott and Wilson saw the tent, though without any signs of life about it; indeed they were within a hundred yards before in answer to their shouts four very satisfied figures emerged, still munching the remains of a meal. 'Of course,' Scott says, 'I thought they had not seen the ships, but they had, only, as they explained, they didn't see there was any cause for them to do anything in the matter. I said, "But, good heavens, you want your mails, don't you?" "Oh, yes, sir," they replied, "but we thought that would be all right." In other words, they as good as said that life was so extremely easy and pleasant that there was no possible object in worrying over such a trifle as the arrival of a relief expedition.' When, however, they Page 182 had got their orders they were off at once, and Scott and Wilson went back to the ships and soon found out from Colbeck why the *Terra Nova* had accompanied the *Morning*, and how strangely the aspect of affairs had altered. Writing in his diary on that night Scott says, 'I can only record that in spite of the good home news, and in spite of the pleasure of seeing old friends again, I was happier last night than I am to-night.'

Briefly the reasons for the sending of the two ships instead of one were these. Scott's report taken by the *Morning* had left the strong impression that the relief ship must again be sent to the south in 1903. The 'Morning' fund, however, was inadequate to meet the requirements of another year, and there was not time enough to appeal to the public and to explain the full necessities of the case. In these circumstances there was nothing for the Societies to do but to appeal to the Government, and eventually the latter agreed to undertake the whole conduct of the relief expedition, provided that the *Morning*, as she stood, was delivered over to them. The Government naturally placed the management of affairs in the hands of the Admiralty, and once having taken the responsibility it was felt that two ships must be sent, in order that there should be no risk of the pledge being unfulfilled.

The *Terra Nova*, one of the finest of the whaling ships, was bought, and a whaling crew, under the command of Captain Harry MacKay, was engaged to navigate her. Towards the end of November 1903 she layoff Hobart Town in Tasmania, and in Page 183 December she was joined by the *Morning*, Captain Colbeck being directed to take charge of this joint venture until both ships could come under Scott's command.

Thus it happened that, much to every one's surprise, two ships arrived off the edge of the fast ice on January 4, 1904. It was not, however, the arrival of the *Terra Nova*, whose captain from the first was anxious to help in every way, but quite another matter that made Scott so sad — and naturally sad — at this time.

In England the majority of those competent to judge the situation had formed the opinion that the *Discovery* was stuck fast in the ice for all time. Whether the Admiralty held this opinion or not is of no consequence, because in any case it was their duty to see that the expense of another relief expedition should be avoided. Consequently there was no other course open to them except to tell Scott to abandon the *Discovery*, if she could not be freed in time to accompany the relief ships to the north. But necessary as this order was, it placed Scott and his companions in a very cruel position. Under the most ordinary conditions a sailor would go through much rather than abandon his ship, but the ties which bound Scott and his company to the *Discovery* were very far beyond the ordinary; indeed they involved a depth of sentiment not in the least surprising when their associations with her are remembered.

In spite of their long detention in the ice, the thought of leaving her had never entered their heads. Page 184 Some time she would be free again, and even if they had to spend a third winter in her they had determined to go through with it, and make themselves as comfortable as possible.

It was from this passably contented frame of mind that they were rudely awakened. Now they were obliged to face the fact that unless a twenty-mile plain of ice broke up within six weeks, they must bid a long farewell to their beloved ship and return to their homes as castaways. So with the arrival of the relief ships there fell the first and last cloud of gloom which was ever allowed on board the *Discovery*. And as day followed day with no improvement in the ice conditions, the gloom deepened until anyone might easily have imagined that an Antarctic expedition was a most dismal affair.

On January 10 Scott wrote: 'Reached the ship this morning, and this afternoon assembled all hands on the mess-deck, where I told them exactly how matters stood. There was a stony silence. I have not heard a laugh in the ship since I returned.'

For some time a flagstaff had been erected on Tent Islet, ten miles to the north, and a system of signals had been arranged to notify any changes in the ice, but day after day the only signal was 'No change in the ice conditions.'

On the 15th to relieve the weariness of waiting for something that did not happen, Scott arranged that their collections and instruments should be transported to the relief ships. Whatever the future held in Page 185 store he saw no reason why this should not be done, and to have anything at all to do during this trying time was a blessing; though he had by no means given up hope that the Discovery would be freed.

After a long spell at Cape Royds camp, Wilson returned to the ship on the night of the 21st with news that was all the more welcome at such an anxious time. Strolling over the beach one day to inspect what he thought was a prodigiously large seal he saw that it was quite different from any of the ordinary seals, and went back to the camp for his gun. Two of the *Morning* officers were in camp with him, and all three of them proceeded to stalk this strange new beast. Their great fear was that they might only succeed in wounding it and that it might escape into the sea; so in spite of the temperature of the water they waded round it before they attacked. These tactics were successful, but their quarry when dispatched was far too heavy for them to move, or for Wilson to examine where it lay. On the following day, however, Colbeck came over in the *Morning*, and with the aid of boats and ropes the carcass was landed on his decks. Then Wilson came to the conclusion that the animal was a sea-elephant commonly found at Macquarie Island, but never before seen within the Antarctic circle.

No change in the ice occurred until the 18th when some large pieces broke away, and by the 23rd Scott reckoned that the relief ships were four or five miles nearer than they had been a fortnight before. But, Page 186 if the conditions were to be as they had been two years before, thirteen or fourteen miles of ice must go out in fifteen days, a far more rapid rate than it had been going during the previous fortnight. On the 28th, however, the first sign of real promise occurred, for the whole ice-sheet began to sway very slightly under the action of a long swell, its edge against the land rising and falling as much as 18 inches. 'We are all very restless, constantly dashing up the hill to the lookout station or wandering from place to place to observe the effects of the swell. But it is long since we enjoyed such a cheerful experience as we get on watching the loose pieces of ice jostling one another at Hut Point.'

Days of hope and anxiety followed, until the 14th of February arrived and brought the best of news with it. During the day nothing unusual happened, and it was not until Scott was at dinner that the excitement began. Then he heard a shout on deck, and a voice sang out down the hatchway, 'The ships are coming, sir!'

'There was no more dinner, and in a moment we were racing for Hut Point, where a glorious sight met our view. The ice was breaking up right across the strait, and with a rapidity which we had not thought possible. No sooner was one great floe borne away. Than a dark streak cut its way into the solid sheet that remained and carved out another, to feed the broad stream of pack which was hurrying away to the north-west.

'I have never witnessed a more impressive sight; Page 187 the sun was low behind us, the surface of the ice-sheet in front was intensely white, and in contrast the distant sea and its forking leads looked almost black. The wind had fallen to a calm, and not a sound disturbed the stillness about us. Yet, in the midst of this peaceful silence, was an awful unseen agency rending that great ice-sheet as though it had been none but the thinnest paper.'

But fast as the ice was breaking, it was not fast enough for the relief ships. Evidently there was a race between them to be the first to pass beyond the flagstaff round which the small company of spectators had clustered; although the little *Morning*, with her bluff bows and weak engines, could scarcely expect to hold her own against such a powerful competitor. By half-past ten those on shore could see the splintering of the ice as the ships crashed into the floes, and the shouts of the men as with wild excitement they cheered each fresh success, could be distinctly heard.

Scarcely half a mile of ice remained and the contest became keener and keener. On came the *Terra Nova*, but in spite of all her mighty efforts the persistent little *Morning*, dodging right and left and seizing every chance opening, kept doggedly at her side, and still seemed to have a chance of winning the race.

Meanwhile the spectators, in their nondescript tattered garments, stood breathlessly watching this wonderful scene.

'For long intervals we remained almost spell-bound, and then a burst of frenzied cheering broke out. It Page 188 seemed to us almost too good to be real. By eleven o'clock all the thick ice had vanished, and there remained only the thin area of decayed floe which has lately made the approach to the ships so dangerous; a few minutes later the *Terra Nova* forged ahead and came crashing into the open, to be followed almost immediately by her stout little companion, and soon both ships were firmly anchored to all that remains of the *Discovery's* prison, the wedge that still holds in our small bay....

'And so to-night the ships of our small fleet are lying almost side by side; a rope from the *Terra Nova* is actually secured to the *Discovery*. Who could have thought it possible? Certainly not we who have lived through the trying scenes of the last month.'

The small wedge of sea-ice that still remained in the bay was cracked in many places, and would doubtless have departed of its own accord in a few days; but Scott, naturally impatient to get away, decided to hasten matters by explosions. Consequently at 1 A.M. on February 16 there was an explosion which shook the whole bay, and rudely disturbed not only the ice but also the slumbers of those who were not members of the explosion party.

A few hours later another explosive charge was borne out, and when all was ready Scott pressed the firing key. 'There was a thunderous report which shook the ship throughout, and then all was calm again. For a brief moment one might have imagined that nothing had happened, but then one saw that each Page 189 crack was slowly widening; presently there came the gurgle of water as it was sucked into our opening ice-bed, and in another minute there was a creaking aft and our stern rose with a jump as the keel was freed from the ice which had held it down. Then, as the great mass of ice on our port hand slowly glided out to sea, our good ship swung gently round and lay peacefully riding to her anchors with the blue water lapping against her sides.... Thus it was that the *Discovery* came to her own again—the right to ride the high seas.'

On that day it would have been impossible to find a prouder or happier ship's company, but with all their feelings of elation they did not imagine that everything would run smoothly after such a long period of disuse, and they knew also that much hard work lay in front of them if they were to carry out the remainder of their program. If the *Discovery* was free before the navigable season closed Scott had resolved to spend the remaining time in exploring the region to the westward of Cape North, but now after two years' imprisonment coal was lacking for such a scheme. Directly the relief ships had arrived he had asked them for as great a quantity as possible, but although the replies had at first been satisfactory, a long month's fight with wind and ice had sadly reduced the amount they could afford to give. The only thing to do was to get without any delay what could be spared, and on the afternoon of the 16th the *Terra Nova* came alongside to hand over her supply. 'The afternoon,' Scott says, 'was beautifully calm and Page 190 bright, and the weather seemed to smile peacefully on the termination of our long and successful struggle with the ice.... We little guessed what lay before us.'

On the 15th a large wooden cross, bearing a simply carved inscription to the memory of poor Vince, was erected on the summit of Hut Point, and on the following day the small company landed together and stood bareheaded round this memorial, while Scott read some short prayers.

The water was oily calm and the sky threatening as they pulled back to the ship after paying this last tribute of homage to their shipmate, but weather of this kind had been too common to attract attention. On that night Captain MacKay was dining in the *Discovery* for the first time, and a great effort had been made to show him how good an Antarctic feast could be. In the middle of dinner, however, word came down to Scott that the wind had sprung up, and although he expected nothing serious he went up to see what was happening. Then he saw they were in for a stiff blow, and reluctantly had to inform his guests of the fact. One glance at the sky satisfied MacKay, who was over the rail like a shot, and in a few minutes the *Terra Nova* was steaming for the open and lost in the drift.'

THE 'TERRA NOVA' LEAVING THE ANTARCTIC.
Photo by F. Debenham.

Very soon both wind and sea had risen, but although Scott did not altogether like the look of things and determined to get up steam as soon as possible, he did not want to hurry those in the engine-room after such a long period of disuse. But early in the morning Page 191 of the 17th the situation became really dangerous, and the *Discovery* began to jerk at her cables in the most alarming manner.

'I knew,' he wrote on the night of that eventful day, 'that in spite of our heavy anchor the holding ground was poor, and I watched anxiously to see if the ship dragged.

'It came at last, just as Skelton sent a promise of steam in half an hour. The sea was again breaking heavily on the ice-foot astern and I walked up and down wondering which was coming first, the steam or this wave-beaten cliff. It was not a pleasant situation, as the distance grew shorter every minute, until the spray of the breaking waves fell on our poop, and this was soon followed by a tremendous blow as our stern struck the ice. We rebounded and struck again, and our head was just beginning to falloff and the ship to get broadside on (heaven knows what would have happened then) when steam was announced.'

Then the ship just held her own and only just; the engines alone would not send her to windward in the teeth of the gale. Once around Hut Point, Scott knew that they would be safe with open sea before them; and the end of the Point was only a quarter of a mile out, though off the end there was a shallow patch which had to be cleared before safety could be reached. So finding that no headway was being made he began to edge out towards the Point, and all seemed well until, nearly opposite to the Point itself, he saw to his alarm that a strong current was sweeping past.

Page 192 'Nothing remained but to make a dash for it, and I swung the helm over and steered for the open. But the moment our bows entered the fast-running stream we were swung round like a top, and the instant after we crashed head foremost onto the shoal and stopped dead with our masts shivering. We were in the worst possible position, dead to windward of the bank with wind, sea, and current all tending to set us faster ashore.

'We took the shore thus at about 11 A.M., and the hours that followed were truly the most dreadful I have ever spent. Each moment the ship came down with a sickening thud which shook her from stem to stern, and each thud seemed to show more plainly that, strong as was her build, she could not long survive such awful blows.'

Hour after hour passed while the ship quivered and trembled and crashed again and again into her rocky bed. Nothing more could be done for her until the gale abated, but seeing the impossibility of doing anything at the time, Scott recognized that the next best thing was to be prepared to act promptly when the weather moderated. Then he discovered once more how absolutely he could rely on the support and intelligence of his companions. Skelton already had made a list of weights by the removal of which the ship could be lightened, and when the boatswain was summoned to discuss the manner in which the anchors could be laid out he also had his scheme cut and dried.

The first sign of a lull came at 7 P.M., and soon after Page 193 they assembled to the dreariest dinner ever remembered in the *Discovery*. But when they were half-way through this silent meal Mulock, the officer of the watch, suddenly burst in and said, 'The ship's working astern, sir.'

In record time Scott reached the bridge, and found that both wind and sea had dropped in the most extraordinary manner. But what surprised him even more was that the current, which had been running strongly to the north, had turned and was running with equal speed to the south. Each time that the ship lifted on a wave she worked two or three inches astern, and though she was still grinding heavily she no longer struck the bottom with such terrific force. Scarcely, however, had these facts been observed when Skelton rushed up to say that the inlets were free again.

'Every soul was on deck and in a moment they were massed together and running from side to side in measured time. The telegraphs were put full speed astern; soon the engines began to revolve, and the water foamed and frothed along the side. For a minute or two the ship seemed to hesitate, but then there came a steady grating under the bottom, which gradually traveled forward, and ceased as the ship, rolling heavily, slid gently into deep water.... Rarely, if ever, can a ship have appeared in such an uncomfortable plight as ours to find herself free and safe within the space of an hour.... To be in ten feet of water in a ship that draws fourteen feet cannot be a pleasant position—nor can there be a doubt Page 194 that the shocks which the *Discovery* sustained would have very seriously damaged a less stoutly built vessel.'

None too soon were they clear of the shoal, for in a very short time the wind was again blowing from the south; but as, on the 18th, the wind though still blowing strong had gone round to the southeast and brought smoother water in the Sound, it was decided to make for the inlets of the glacier tongue to the north, and complete the coaling operations.

On occasions when haste was necessary there was, by mutual consent, no distinction between officers and men. And Scott mentions 'as a sight for the gods' the scene of biologists, vertebrate zoologists, lieutenants, and A.B.'s with grimed faces and chafed hands working with all their might on the coaling whips.

The *Morning* handed over twenty-five tons of coal, and this was all the more a generous gift since it reduced Colbeck to the narrowest margin, and compelled him to return directly homeward without joining in any attempt at further exploration. 'His practical common sense told him he could be of little use to us, and with his usual loyalty he never hesitated to act for the best, at whatever sacrifice to his own hopes and wishes.'

Before they left the glacier in McMurdo Sound it was arranged that the three ships should journey up the coast together and then separate, the *Morning* proceeding to the north, while the *Discovery* and the *Terra Nova* turned west. The companies of both relief Page 195 ships, however, expressed a strong desire to be with the *Discovery* when she entered her first civilized port; so Scott fixed upon Port Ross, in the Auckland Islands, as a spot at which they might meet before the final return to New Zealand.

February 20 saw the *Discovery* speeding along a stretch of coast that had been quite unknown until she had two years previously made her way south along it, and at that time she had been obliged to keep a long distance out on account of the pack-ice. But now gaps which had been missed could be filled in; and even more than this was done, for Mulock remained on deck night and day taking innumerable angles to peaks and headlands, while Wilson, equally indefatigable, transferred this long panorama of mountain scenery to his sketch-book.

Two days later the pumps refused to act, and the whole of the engine-room staff were on duty for twenty-four hours on end; and on the 24th the carpenter called attention to the rudder. On inspection Scott saw that the solid oak rudder-head was completely shattered, and was held together by little more than its weight; as the tiller was moved right or left the rudder followed it, but with a lag of many degrees, so that the connection between the two was evidently insecure. In such a condition it was obvious that they could not hope to weather a gale without losing all control over the ship, and that no time was to be lost in shipping their spare rudder in place of the damaged one. So Scott determined to seek shelter in Robertson Page 196 Bay, and by night the damaged rudder had been hoisted on deck and the spare one prepared for lowering into its place. Since the *Discovery* had left winter quarters an almost incredible amount of work had been done to bring her into sea trim.

Difficulty after difficulty had arisen, but the energy of the company had never slackened, and by February 25 Scott was able to say that everything was once more in order, though he was a little doubtful about the steering power of their spare rudder.

At this time it was all the more important that the ship should give no further trouble, because according to their program they were about to penetrate a new region, and expected to find quite enough to do without considering internal difficulties. With high hopes that steam power would enable them to pass beyond the point reached by Sir James Ross in his sailing ships they turned to the west, and at first all went well with them. Pack-ice, however, was destined to be an insuperable obstacle to their advance, and on the 26th they decided to turn to the north-east and try to find a way around this formidable barrier. 'It is grievously disappointing to find the pack so far to the east; Ross carried the open water almost to Cape North.' And again on March 1, Scott sounds a note of lamentation: 'There can be no doubt that since leaving Victoria Land we have been skirting a continuous mass of pack, which must cover the whole sea south of the Balleny Islands. That it should have lain so far to the eastward this year is very annoying; Page 197 however, if we can push on upon this course we ought to strike the islands.'

Early in the morning of the following day land was reported, and by noon they were abreast of it; but what this island, and others that were dimly to be seen to the north, could be, puzzled them considerably, and not until some time later was the problem solved. In 1839 Balleny discovered a group of islands in this region, and three years later Ross saw land which he imagined was to the southward of Balleny's discoveries, and believing it to be divided into three distinct masses named it the Russell Islands. Consequently Scott arrived expecting to see two groups of islands, and was naturally perplexed when only one group was to be seen. After, however, studying the accounts of these islands and comparing them with what he could actually see, he recognized that they had just passed Balleny's Sturge Island, which Balleny had seen from the north, and so could have had no idea of its length in a north-and-south line. Later Ross must have seen this same island, and, as Scott saw to be quite possible, from a great distance must have thought that it was divided into three, and hence made the mistake of naming it as a separate group. Fortunately Mulock was able to obtain sufficient bearings to fix accurately the position of each island.

Now that the knotty question as to the geography of the Balleny Islands was settled, they went on to look for the land that Wilkes claimed to have discovered in 1840, but not a glimpse nor a vestige of it could they Page 198 see; and, on March 4, they had to conclude that Wilkes Land was once and for all definitely disposed of. With this negative, but nevertheless important, result, the exploring work ended, and although a lack of coal had prevented their cherished plan of rounding Cape North, they had at least the satisfaction of clearing up some geographical misconceptions in a more northerly latitude.

From the 6th to the 14th continuous gales brought conditions of greater physical discomfort than had ever been experienced on board the *Discovery*, for she was in very light trim and tossed about the mountainous seas like a cork. It was, therefore, the greatest relief to furl their sails off the entrance of Ross Harbour on the 15th, and to steam into the calm waters of the Bay.

Neither the *Terra Nova* nor the *Morning* had yet arrived, and the days of waiting were spent in making their ship as smart as possible before the eyes of the multitude gazed upon her. Thus, in a few days, the *Discovery* looked as though she had spent her adventurous years in some peaceful harbor.

On March 19 the *Terra Nova* hove in sight, and was followed on the next day by the *Morning*. Both ships had experienced the most terrible weather, and everyone on board the little *Morning* declared that she had only been saved from disaster by the consummate seamanship of Captain Colbeck.

A few days later the small fleet again set sail, and after a most favorable voyage was at daybreak on April 1 Page 199 off the Heads of Lyttelton Harbor; and before noon they were safely berthed alongside the jetty, from which they had sailed with such hearty wishes more than two years before.

'New Zealand,' Scott said, 'welcomed us as its own, and showered on us a wealth of hospitality and kindness which assuredly we can never forget, however difficult we may have found it to express our thanks. In these delightful conditions, with everything that could make for perfect rest and comfort, we abode for two full months before we set out on our last long voyage.'

June 8, however, found them at sea again, and a month or so later they anchored in Port Stanley (Falkland Islands), where they replenished their stock of coal and took the last series of magnetic observations in connection with their Southern Survey. And from the Falkland Islands, Scott wrote a letter which is yet another testimony of the admiration he felt for his companions. 'The praise,' he wrote, 'for whatever success we have had is really due to the ship's company as a whole rather than to individuals. That is not very clear, perhaps; what I mean is that the combination of individual effort for the common good has achieved our results, and the absence of any spirit of self-seeking. The motto throughout has been "share and share alike," and its most practical form lies, perhaps, in the fact that throughout our three years there has been no distinction between the food served to officers and men.

Page 200 'Under these circumstances I naturally feel that I can claim no greater share of achievement than those who have stood by me so loyally, and so I regard myself merely as the lucky figure-head.

'But it is good news to hear that the Admiralty are sympathetic, for I feel that no effort should be spared to gain their recognition of the splendid qualities displayed by officers and men.'

Early on the morning of September 9 the homeland was sighted, and for those who gazed longingly over the bulwarks and waited to welcome and be welcomed, there was only one cloud to dim the joy of their return. For with the happiness came also the sad thought that the end had come to those ties, which had held together the small band of the *Discovery* in the closest companionship and most unswerving loyalty.

Page 201 THE LAST EXPEDITION

Page 203 PREFACE TO 'SCOTT'S LAST EXPEDITION'

By Sir CLEMENTS R. MARKHAM, K.C.B.

Fourteen years ago Robert Falcon Scott was a rising naval officer, able, accomplished, popular, highly thought of by his superiors, and devoted to his noble profession. It was a serious responsibility to induce him to take up the work of an explorer; yet no man living could be found who was so well fitted to command a great Antarctic Expedition. The undertaking was new and unprecedented. The object was to explore the unknown Antarctic Continent by land. Captain Scott entered upon the enterprise with enthusiasm tempered by prudence and sound sense. All had to be learnt by a thorough study of the history of Arctic traveling, combined with experience of different conditions in the Antarctic Regions. Scott was the initiator and founder of Antarctic sledge-traveling.

His discoveries were of great importance. The survey and soundings along the Barrier cliffs, the discovery of King Edward Land, the discovery of Ross Island and the other volcanic islets, the examination of the Barrier surface, the discovery of the Victoria Mountains—a range of great height and many hundreds Page 204 of miles in length, which had only before been seen from a distance out at sea—and above all the discovery of the great ice cap on which the South Pole is situated, by one of the most remarkable Polar journeys on record. His small but excellent scientific staff worked hard and with trained intelligence, their results being recorded in twelve large quarto volumes.

The great discoverer had no intention of losing touch with his beloved profession though resolved to complete his Antarctic work. The exigencies of the naval service called him to the command of battleships and to confidential work of the Admiralty; so that five years elapsed before he could resume his Antarctic labours.

The object of Captain Scott's second expedition was mainly scientific, to complete and extend his former work in all branches of science. It was his ambition that in his ship there should be the most completely equipped expedition for scientific purposes connected with the Polar regions, both as regards men and material, that ever left these shores. In this he succeeded. He had on board a fuller complement of geologists, one of them especially trained for the study, of physiography, biologists, physicists, and surveyors than ever before composed the staff of a Polar expedition. Thus Captain Scott's objects were strictly scientific, including the completion and extension of his former discoveries. The results will be explained in the second volume of this work. They will be found to be extensive and important. Never before, in the Page 205 Polar regions, have meteorological, magnetic and tidal observations been taken, in one locality, during five years. It was also part of Captain Scott's plan to reach the South Pole by a long and most arduous journey, but here again his intention was, if possible, to achieve scientific results on the way, especially hoping to discover fossils which would throw light on the former history of the great range of mountains which he had made known to science.

The principal aim of this great man — for he rightly has his niche among the Polar *Dii Majores* — was the advancement of knowledge. From all aspects Scott was among the most remarkable men of our time, and the vast number of readers of his journal will be deeply impressed with the beauty of his character. The chief traits which shone forth through his life were conspicuous in the hour of death. There are few events in history to be compared, for grandeur and pathos, with the last closing scene in that silent wilderness of snow. The great leader, with the bodies of his dearest friends beside him, wrote and wrote until the pencil dropped from his dying grasp. There was no thought of himself, only the earnest desire to give comfort and consolation to others in their sorrow. His very last lines were written lest he who induced him to enter upon Antarctic work should now feel regret for what he had done.

'If I cannot write to Sir Clements, tell him I thought much of him, and never regretted his putting me in command of the *Discovery*.'

Page 206 The following appointments were held in the Royal Navy by Captain Scott between 1905 and 1910:

January to July, 1906	Admiralty (Assistant Director of Naval Intelligence.)

Aug. 21, 1906, to Jan. 1, 1907	*Victorious* (Flag Captain to Rear-Admiral Egerton, Rear-Admiral in the Atlantic Fleet).
Jan. 2, 1907, to Aug. 24, 1907	*Albermarle* (Flag Captain to Rear-Admiral Egerton, Rear-Admiral in the Atlantic Fleet).
Aug. 25, 1907, to Jan. 24, 1908	Not actively employed afloat between these dates.
Jan. 25, 1908, to May 29, 1908	*Essex* (Captain).
May 30, 1908, to March 23, 1909	*Bulwark* (Flag Captain to Rear-Admiral Colville, Rear-Admiral the Nore Division, Home Fleet).

Then Naval Assistant to Second Sea Lord of the Admiralty. Appointed to H.M.S. *President* for British Antarctic Expedition June 1, 1910.

Page 207 On September 2, 1908, at Hampton Court Palace, Captain Scott was married to Kathleen, daughter of the late Canon Lloyd Bruce. Peter Markham Scott was born on September 14, 1909.

On September 13, 1909, Captain Scott published his plans for the British Antarctic Expedition of the following year, and his appeal resulted in £10,000 being collected as a nucleus fund. Then the Government made a grant of £20,000, and grants followed from the Governments of Australia, New Zealand, and South Africa.

Nine days after the plans were published arrangements were made to purchase the steamship *Terra Nova*, the largest and strongest of the old Scottish whalers. The original date chosen for sailing was August 1, 1910, but owing to the united efforts of those engaged upon the fitting out and stowing of the ship, she was able to leave Cardiff on June 15. Business, however, prevented Captain Scott from leaving England until a later date, and in consequence he sailed in the *Saxon* to South Africa, and there awaited the arrival of the *Terra Nova*.

Page 208 BRITISH ANTARCTIC EXPEDITION, 1910

SHORE PARTIES

Officers

Name	Rank, &c.
Robert Falcon Scott	*Captain, C.V.O., R.N.*
Edward R. G. R. Evans	*Lieutenant, R.N.*
Victor L. A. Campbell	*Lieutenant, R.N. (Emergency List)*
Henry R. Bowers	*Lieutenant, R.I.M.*
Lawrence E. G. Oates	*Captain 6th Inniskilling Dragoons.*
G. Murray Levick	*Surgeon, R.N.*
Edward L. Atkinson	*Surgeon, R.N., Parasitologist.*

Scientific Staff

Edward Adrian Wilson	*B.A., M.B. (Cantab), Chief of the Scientific Staff, and Zoologist.*
George C. Simpson	*D.Sc., Meteorologist.*
T. Griffith Taylor	*B.A., B.Sc., B.E., Geologist.*
Edward W. Nelson	*Biologist.*
Frank Debenham	*B.A., B.Sc., Geologist.*
Charles S. Wright	*B.A., Physicist.*
Raymond E. Priestley	*Geologist.*
Herbert G. Ponting	*F.R.G.S, Camera Artist.*
Cecil H. Meares	*In Charge of Dogs.*
Bernard C. Day	*Motor Engineer.*

Apsley Cherry-Garrard	*B.A., Asst. Zoologist.*
Tryggve Gran	*Sub-Lieutenant, Norwegian N.R., B.A., Ski Expert.*

Page 209*Men*

W. Lashly	*Chief Stoker, R.N.*
W. W. Archer	*Chief Steward, late R.N.*
Thomas Clissold	*Cook, late R.N.*
Edgar Evans	*Petty Officer, R.N.*
Robert Forde	*Petty Officer, R.N.*
Thomas Crean	*Petty Officer, R.N.*
Thomas S. Williamson	*Petty Officer, R.N.*
Patrick Keohane	*Petty Officer, R.N.*
George P. Abbott	*Petty Officer, R.N.*
Frank V. Browning	*Petty Officer, 2nd class, R.N.*
Harry Dickason	*Able Seaman, R.N.*
F. J. Hooper	*Steward, late R.N.*
Anton Omelchenko	*Groom.*
Demetri Gerof	*Dog Driver.*

SHIP'S PARTY

Officers, &c.

Harry L. L. Pennell	*Lieutenant, R.N.*
Henry E. de P.	*Lieutenant, R.N.*

Rennick	
Wilfred M. Bruce	*Lieutenant, R.N.R.*
Francis R. H. Drake	*Asst. Paymaster, R.N. (Retired), Secretary and Meteorologist in Ship.*
Denis G. Lillie	*M.A., Biologist in Ship.*
James R. Dennistoun	*In Charge of Mules in Ship.*
Alfred B. Cheetham	*R.N.R., Boatswain.*
William Williams	*Chief Engine-room Artificer, R.N., 2nd Engineer.*
William A. Horton	*Eng. Rm. Art. 3rd Class, R.N. 2nd Engineer.*
Francis E. C. Davies	*Leading Shipwright, R.N.*
Frederick Parsons	*Petty Officer, R.N.*
William L. Heald	*Late P.O., R.N.*Page 210
Arthur S. Bailey	*Petty Officer, 2nd Class, R.N.*
Albert Balson	*Leading Seaman, R.N.*
Joseph Leese	*Able Seaman, R.N.*
John Hugh Mather	*Petty Officer, R.N.V.R.*
Robert Oliphant	*Able Seaman.*
Thomas F. McLeod	*Able Seaman.*
Mortimer McCarthy	*Able Seaman.*
William Knowles	*Able Seaman.*
Charles Williams	*Able Seaman.*
James Skelton	*Able Seaman.*
William McDonald	*Able Seaman.*
James Paton	*Able Seaman.*

Robert Brissenden	*Leading Stoker, R.N.*
Edward A. McKenzie	*Leading Stoker, R.N.*
William Burton	*Leading Stoker, R.N.*
Bernard J. Stone	*Leading Stoker, R.N.*
Angus McDonald	*Fireman.*
Thomas McGillon	*Fireman.*
Charles Lammas	*Fireman.*
W. H. Neale	*Steward.*

Page 211 CHAPTER I

THROUGH STORMY SEAS

> The ice was here, the ice was there,
> The ice was all around:
> It cracked and growled, and roared and howled,
> Like noises in a swound. — COLERIDGE.

No sooner was it known that Scott intended to lead another Antarctic expedition than he was besieged by men anxious to go with him. The selection of a small company from some eight thousand volunteers was both a difficult and a delicate task, but the fact that the applications were so numerous was at once a convincing proof of the interest shown in the expedition, and a decisive answer to the dismal cry that the spirit of romance and adventure no longer exists in the British race.

On June 15, 1910, the *Terra Nova* left Cardiff upon her great mission, and after a successful voyage arrived, on October 28, at Lyttelton. There an enormous amount of work had to be done before she could be ready to leave civilization, but as usual the kindness received in New Zealand was 'beyond words.'

A month of strenuous labour followed, and then, on Page 212 November 26, they said farewell to Lyttelton, and after calling at Port Chalmers set out on Tuesday, the 29th, upon the last stage of their voyage. Two days later they encountered a stiff wind from the N. W. and a confused sea.

'The ship a queer and not altogether cheerful sight under the circumstances.

'Below one knows all space is packed as tight as human skill can devise—and on deck! Under the forecastle fifteen ponies close side by side, seven one side, eight the other, heads together and groom between—swaying, swaying continually to the plunging, irregular motion.'

Outside the forecastle and to leeward of the fore hatch were four more ponies, and on either side of the main hatch were two very large packing-cases containing motor sledges, each 16 X 5 X 4. A third sledge stood across the break of the poop in the space hitherto occupied by the after winch, and all these cases were so heavily lashed with heavy chain and rope lashings that they were thought to be quite secure. The petrol for the sledges was contained in tins and drums protected in stout wooden packing-cases, which were ranged across the deck immediately in front of the poop and abreast the motor sledges.

Round and about these packing-cases, stretching from the galley forward to the wheel aft, coal bags containing the deck cargo of coal were stacked; and upon the coal sacks, and upon and between the motor sledges, and upon the ice-house were the thirty-three dogs. Perforce they had to be chained up, and although Page 213 they were given as much protection as possible, their position was far from pleasant. 'The group formed,' in Scott's opinion, 'a picture of wretched dejection: such a life is truly hard for these poor creatures.'

The wind freshened with great rapidity on Thursday evening, and very soon the ship was plunging heavily and taking much water over the lee rail. Cases of all descriptions began to break loose on the upper deck, the principal trouble being caused by the loose coal bags, which were lifted bodily by the seas and swung against the lashed cases. These bags acted like battering rams, no lashings could possibly have withstood them, and so the only remedy was to set to work and heave coal sacks overboard and re-lash the cases. During this difficult and dangerous task seas continually broke over the men, and at such times they had to cling for dear life to some fixture to prevent themselves from being washed overboard. No sooner was some appearance of order restored than another unusually heavy wave tore away the lashings, and the work had to be done allover again.

As the night wore on the sea and wind continued to rise, and the ship to plunge more and more. 'We shortened sail to main topsail and staysail, stopped engines and hove to, but to little purpose.'

From Oates and Atkinson, who worked through the entire night, reports came that it was impossible to keep the ponies on their legs. But worse news was to follow, for in the early morning news came from the engine-room that the pumps had choked, and that the water had risen over the gratings.

Page 214 From that moment, about 4 A.M., the engine-room became the center of interest, but in spite of every effort the water still gained. Lashly and Williams, up to their necks in rushing water, stuck gamely to the work of clearing suctions, and for a time, with donkey engine and bilge pump sucking, it looked as if the water might be got under. But the hope was short-lived; five minutes of pumping invariably led to the same result—a general choking of the pumps.

The ship was very deeply-laden and was in considerable danger of becoming waterlogged, in which condition anything might have happened. The hand pump produced nothing more than a dribble and its suction could not be reached, for as the water crept higher it got in contact with the boiler and eventually became so hot that no one could work at the suctions. A great struggle to conquer these misfortunes followed, but Williams had at last to confess that he was beaten and must draw fires.

'What was to be done? Things for the moment appeared very black. The sea seemed higher than ever; it came over lee rail and poop, a rush of green water; the ship wallowed in it; a great piece of the bulwark carried clean away. The bilge pump is dependent on the main engine. To use the pump it was necessary to go ahead. It was at such times that the heaviest seas swept in over the lee rail; over and over again the rail, from the forerigging to the main, was covered by a solid sheet of curling water which swept aft and high on the poop. On one Page 215 occasion I was waist deep when standing on the rail of the poop.'

All that could be done for the time being was to organize the afterguard to work buckets, and to keep the men steadily going on the choked hand-pumps, which practically amounted to an attempt to bale out the ship! For a day and a night the string of buckets was passed up a line from the engine-room; and while this arduous work was going on the officers and men sang chanteys, and never for a moment lost their good spirits.

In the meantime an effort was made to get at the suction of the pumps; and by 10 P.M. on Friday evening a hole in the engine-room bulkhead had been completed. Then E. R. Evans, wriggling over the coal, found his way to the pump shaft and down it, and cleared the suction of the coal balls (a mixture of coal and oil) which were choking it. Soon afterwards a good stream of water came from the pump, and it was evident that the main difficulty had been overcome. Slowly the water began to decrease in the engine-room, and by 4 A.M. on Saturday morning the bucket-parties were able to stop their labours.

The losses caused by this gale were serious enough, but they might easily have been worse. Besides the damage to the bulwarks of the ship, two ponies, one dog, ten tons of coal, sixty-five gallons of petrol, and a case of biologists' spirit were lost. Another dog was washed away with such force that his chain broke and he disappeared, but the next wave miraculously Page 216 washed him back on board. In a few hours everyone was hopeful again, but anxiety on account of the ponies remained. With the ship pitching heavily to a south-westerly swell, at least two of these long-suffering animals looked sadly in need of a spell of rest, and Scott's earnest prayer was that there might be no more gales. 'December ought to be a fine month in the Ross Sea; it always has been, and just now conditions point to fine weather. Well, we must be prepared for anything, but I'm anxious, anxious about these animals of ours.'

Meanwhile Bowers and Campbell had worked untiringly to put things straight on deck, and with the coal removed from the upper deck and the petrol re-stored, the ship was in much better condition to fight the gales. 'Another day,' Scott wrote on Tuesday, December 6, 'ought to put us beyond the reach of westerly gales'; but two days later the ship was once more plunging against a stiff breeze and moderate sea, and his anxiety about the ponies was greater than ever. The dogs, however, had recovered wonderfully from the effects of the great gale, their greatest discomfort being that they were almost constantly wet.

During Friday, December 9, some very beautiful bergs were passed, the heights of which varied from sixty to eighty feet. Good progress was made during this day, but the ice streams thickened as they advanced, and on either side of them fields of pack began to appear. Yet, after the rough weather they had Page 217 been having, the calm sea was a blessing even if the ice had arrived before it was expected. 'One can only imagine the relief and comfort afforded to the ponies, but the dogs are visibly cheered and the human element is full of gaiety. The voyage seems full of promise in spite of the imminence of delay.'

Already Scott was being worried by the pace at which the coal was going, and he determined if the pack became thick to put out the fires and wait for the ice to open. Very carefully all the evidence of former voyages had been examined so that the best meridian to go south on might be chosen, and the conclusion arrived at was that the 178 W. was the best. They entered the pack more or less on this meridian, and were rewarded by meeting worse conditions than any ship had ever experienced — worse, indeed, than Scott imagined to be possible on any meridian which they might have chosen. But as very little was known about the movements of the pack the difficulties of making a choice may very easily be imagined, and, in spite of disappointments, Scott's opinion that the 178 W. was the best meridian did not change. 'The situation of the main bodies of pack,' he says, 'and the closeness with which the floes are packed depend almost entirely on the prevailing winds. One cannot tell what winds have prevailed before one's arrival; therefore one cannot know much about the situation or density. Within limits the density is changing from day to day and even from hour to hour; such changes depend on the wind, but it may not necessarily be a local wind, Page 218 so that at times they seem almost mysterious. One sees the floes pressing closely against one another at a given time, and an hour or two afterwards a gap of a foot or more may be seen between each. When the floes are pressed together it is difficult and sometimes impossible to force a way through, but when there is release of pressure the sum of many little gaps allows one to take a zigzag path.'

During Sunday they lay tight in the pack, and after service at 10 A.M. all hands exercised themselves on ski over the floes and got some delightful exercise. 'I have never thought of anything as good as this life. The novelty, interest, colour, animal life, and good fellowship go to make up an almost ideal picnic just at present,' one of the company wrote on that same day — an abundant proof that if delays came they brought their compensations with them.

With rapid and complete changes of prospect they managed to progress — on the Monday — with much bumping and occasional stoppages, but on the following day they were again firmly and tightly wedged in the pack. To most of them, however, the novelty of the experience prevented any sense of impatience, though to Scott the strain of waiting and wondering what he ought to do as regards the question of coal was bound to be heavy.

This time of waiting was by no means wasted, for Gran gave hours of instruction in the use of ski, and Meares took out some of the fattest dogs and exercised them with a sledge. Observations were also constantly Page 219 taken, while Wilson painted some delightful pictures and Ponting took a number of beautiful photographs of the pack and bergs. But as day followed day and hopes of progress were not realized, Scott, anxious to be free, decided on Monday, December 19, to push west. 'Anything to get out of these terribly heavy floes. Great patience is the only panacea for our ill case. It is bad luck.'

Over and over again when the end of their troubles seemed to be reached, they found that the thick pack was once more around them. And what to do under the circumstances called for most difficult decisions. If the fires were let out it meant a dead loss of two tons of coal when the boilers were again heated. But these two tons only covered a day under banked fires, so that for anything longer than twenty-four hours it was a saving to put out the fires. Thus at each stoppage Scott was called upon to decide how long it was likely to last.

Christmas Day came with the ice still surrounding the ship, but although the scene was 'altogether too Christmassy,' a most merry evening was spent. For five hours the officers sat round the table and sang lustily, each one of them having to contribute two songs to the entertainment. 'It is rather a surprising circumstance,' Scott remarks, 'that such an unmusical party should be so keen on singing.'

Christmas, however, came and went without any immediate prospect of release, the only bright side of this exasperating delay being that everyone was Page 220 prepared to exert himself to the utmost, quite regardless of the results of his labours. But on Wednesday, December 28, the ponies, despite the unremitting care and attention that Oates gave to them, were the cause of the gravest anxiety. 'These animals are now the great consideration, balanced as they are against the coal expenditure.'

By this time, although the ice was still all around them, many of the floes were quite thin, and even the heavier ice appeared to be breakable. So, after a consultation with Wilson, Scott decided to raise steam, and two days later the ship was once more in the open sea.

From the 9th to the 30th they had been in the pack, and during this time 370 miles had been covered in a direct line. Sixty-one tons[1] of coal had been used, an average of six miles to the ton, and although these were not pleasant figures to contemplate, Scott considered that under the exceptional conditions they might easily have been worse. For the ship herself he had nothing but praise to give. 'No other ship, not even the *Discovery*, would have come through so well.... As a result I have grown strangely attached to the *Terra Nova*. As she bumped the floes with mighty shocks, crushing and grinding her way through some, twisting and turning to avoid others, she seemed like a living thing fighting a great fight. If only she had more economical engines she would be suitable in all respects.'

[Footnote 1: When the *Terra Nova* left Lyttelton she had 460 tons of coal on board.]

Page 221 Scientifically as much as was possible had been done, but many of the experts had of necessity been idle in regard to their own specialties, though none of them were really idle; for those who had no special work to do were magnificently eager to find any kind of work that required to be done. 'Everyone strives to help everyone else, and not a word of complaint or anger has been heard on board. The inner life of our small community is very pleasant to think upon, and very wonderful considering the extremely small space in which we are confined. The attitude of the men is equally worthy of admiration. In the forecastle as in the wardroom there is a rush to be first when work is to be done, and the same desire to sacrifice selfish consideration to the success of the expedition. It is very good to be able to write in such high praise of one's companions, and I feel that the possession of such support ought to ensure success. Fortune would be in a hard mood indeed if it allowed such a combination of knowledge, experience, ability, and enthusiasm to achieve nothing.'

Fortune's wheel, however, was not yet prepared to turn in their favor, for after a very few hours of the open sea a southern blizzard met them. In the morning watch of December 31, the wind and sea increased and the outlook was very distressing, but at 6 A.M. ice was sighted ahead. Under ordinary conditions the safe course would have been to go about and stand to the east, but on this occasion Page 222 Scott was prepared to run the risk of trouble if he could get the ponies into smoother water. Soon they passed a stream of ice over which the sea was breaking heavily, and the danger of being among loose floes in such a sea was acutely realized. But presently they came to a more compact body of floes, and running behind this they were agreeably surprised to find themselves in comparatively smooth water. There they lay to in a sort of ice bay, and from a dangerous position had achieved one that was safe as long as their temporary shelter lasted.

As the day passed their protection, though still saving them from the heavy swell, gradually diminished, but 1910 did not mean to depart without giving them an Old Year's gift and surprise. 'At 10 P.M. to-night as the clouds lifted to the west a distant but splendid view of the great mountains was obtained. All were in sunshine; Sabine and Whewell were most conspicuous—the latter from this view is a beautiful sharp peak, as remarkable a landmark as Sabine itself. Mount Sabine was 110 miles away when we saw it. I believe we could have seen it at a distance of thirty or forty miles farther — such is the wonderful clearness of the atmosphere.'

The New Year brought better weather with it, and such good progress was made that by mid-day on Tuesday, January 3, the ship reached the Barrier five miles east of Cape Crozier. During the voyage they had often discussed the idea of making their winter station at this Cape, and the prospect had Page 223 seemed to become increasingly fascinating the more they talked of it.

But a great disappointment awaited them, for after one of the whale boats had been lowered and Scott, Wilson, Griffith Taylor, Priestley, and E. R. Evans had been pulled towards the shore, they discovered that the swell made it impossible for them to land.

'No good!! Alas! Cape Crozier with all its attractions is denied us.'

On the top of a floe they could see an old Emperor penguin molting and a young one shedding its down. This was an age and stage of development of the Emperor chick of which they were ignorant, but fortune decreed that this chick should be undisturbed. Of this incident Wilson wrote in his Journal: 'A landing was out of the question.... But I assure you it was tantalizing to me, for there, about 6 feet above us on a small dirty piece of the old bay ice about ten feet square, one living Emperor penguin chick was standing disconsolately stranded, and close by stood one faithful old Emperor parent asleep. This young Emperor was still in the down, a most interesting fact in the bird's life history at which we had rightly guessed, but which no one had actually observed before.... This bird would have been a treasure to me, but we could not risk life for it, so it had to remain where it was.'

Sadly and reluctantly they had to give up hopes of making their station at Cape Crozier, and this Page 224 was all the harder to bear because every detail of the shore promised well for a wintering party. There were comfortable quarters for the hut, ice for water snow for the animals, good slopes for skiing, proximity to the Barrier and to the rookeries of two types of penguins, good ground for biological work, a fairly easy approach to the Southern Road with no chance of being cut off, and so forth. 'It is a thousand pities to have to abandon such a spot.'

The *Discovery's* post-office was still standing as erect as when it had been planted, and comparisons between what was before their eyes and old photographs showed that no change at all seemed to

165

have occurred anywhere—a result that in the case of the Barrier caused very great surprise.

In the meantime all hands were employed in making a running survey, the program of which was:

Bruce continually checking speed with hand log.

Bowers taking altitudes of objects as they come abeam.
Nelson noting results.
Pennell taking verge plate bearings on bow and quarter.
Cherry-Garrard noting results.
Evans taking verge plate bearings abeam.
Atkinson noting results.
Campbell taking distances abeam with range finder.
Wright noting results.
Rennick sounding with Thomson machine.
Drake noting results.

Page 225 'We plotted the Barrier edge from the point at which we met it to the Crozier cliffs; to the eye it seems scarcely to have changed since *Discovery* days, and Wilson thinks it meets the cliff in the same place.'

Very early on Wednesday morning they rounded Cape Bird and came in sight of Mount Discovery and the Western Mountains. 'It was good to see them again, and perhaps after all we are better this side of the Island. It gives one a homely feeling to see such a familiar scene.' Scott's great wish now was to find a place for winter quarters that would not easily be cut off from the Barrier, and a cape, which in the *Discovery* days had been called 'the Skuary,' was chosen. 'It was separated from old *Discovery* quarters by two deep bays on either side of the Glacier Tongue, and I thought that these bays would remain frozen until late in the season, and that when they froze over again the ice would soon become firm.'

There Scott, Wilson, and E. R. Evans landed, and at a glance saw, as they expected, that the place was ideal for their wintering station. A spot for the hut was chosen on a beach facing northwest and well protected behind by numerous small hills; but the most favorable circumstance of all in connection with this cape, which was re-christened Cape Evans, was the strong chance of communication being established at an early date with Cape Armitage.[1] Not a moment was wasted, and while Scott was Page 226 on shore Campbell took the first steps towards landing the stores.

[Footnote 1: The extreme south point of the Island, 12 miles further, on one of whose minor headlands, Hut Point, stood the *Discovery* hut.]

Fortunately the weather was gloriously calm and fine, and the landing began under the happiest conditions. Two of the motors were soon hoisted out, and in spite of all the bad weather and the tons of sea-water that had washed over them the sledges and all the accessories appeared to be in perfect condition. Then came the turn of the ponies, and although it was difficult to make some of them enter the horse box, Oates rose to the occasion and got most of them in by persuasion, while the ones which refused to be persuaded were simply lifted in by the sailors. 'Though all are thin and some few looked pulled down I was agreeably surprised at the evident vitality which they still possessed — some were even skittish. I cannot express the relief when the whole seventeen were safely picketed on the floe.'

Meares and the dogs were out early on the Wednesday morning, and ran to and fro during most of the day with light loads. The chief trouble with the dogs was due to the fatuous conduct of the penguins, the latter showing a devouring curiosity in the proceedings and a total disregard for their own safety, with the result that a number of them were killed in spite of innumerable efforts to teach the penguins to keep out of reach, they only squawked and ducked as much as to say, 'What's it got to do with you, you silly ass? Let us alone.' These incidents naturally demoralized the dogs and annoyed Meares, who Page 227 while trying to stop one sledge, fell into the middle of the dogs and was carried along until they reached the penguins of their desire.

The motor sledges were running by the afternoon, Day managing one and Nelson the other. 'It is early to call them a success, but they are certainly extremely promising.' Before night the site for the hut was leveled, and the erecting party was encamped on shore in a large tent with a supply of food for eight days. Nearly all the timber, &c., for the hut and a supply of food for both ponies and dogs had also been landed.

Despite this most strenuous day's labour, all hands were up again at 5 A.M. on Thursday.

'Words cannot express the splendid way in which everyone works and gradually the work gets organized. I was a little late on the scene this morning, and thereby witnessed a most extraordinary scene. Some six or seven killer whales, old and young, were skirting the fast floe edge ahead of the ship; they seemed excited and dived rapidly, almost touching the floe. As we watched, they suddenly appeared astern, raising their snouts out of water. I had heard weird stories of these beasts, but had never associated serious danger with them. Close to the water's edge lay the wire stern rope of the ship, and our two Esquimaux dogs were tethered to this. I did not think of connecting the movements of the whales with this fact, and seeing them so close I shouted to Ponting, who was standing abreast of the ship. He seized his camera and ran Page 228 towards the floe edge to get a close picture of the beasts, which had momentarily disappeared. The next moment the whole floe under him and the dogs heaved up and split into fragments. One could hear the "booming" noise as the whales rose under the ice and struck it with their backs. Whale after whale rose under the ice, setting it rocking fiercely; luckily Ponting kept his feet and was able to fly to security; by an extraordinary chance also, the splits had been made around and between the dogs, so that neither of them fell into the water. Then it was clear that the whales shared our astonishment, for one after another their huge hideous heads shot vertically into the air through the cracks which they had made... There cannot be a doubt that they looked up to see what had happened to Ponting and the dogs....

'Of course, we have known well that killer whales continually skirt the edge of the floes and that they would undoubtedly snap up anyone who was unfortunate enough to fall into the water; but the facts that they could display such deliberate cunning, that they were able to break ice of such thickness (at least 2-1/2 feet), and that they could act in unison, were a revelation to us. It is clear that they are endowed with singular intelligence, and in future we shall treat that intelligence with every respect.'

On Thursday the motor sledges did good work, and hopes that they might prove to be reliable began to increase. Infinite trouble had been taken to obtain Page 229 the most suitable material for Polar work, and the three motor sledge tractors were the outcome of experiments made at Lantaret in France and at Lillehammer and Fefor in Norway, with sledges built by the Wolseley Motor Company from suggestions offered principally by B. T. Hamilton, R. W. Skelton, and Scott himself. With his rooted objection to cruelty in any shape or form, Scott had an intense, and almost pathetic, desire that these sledges should be successful; over and over again he expressed his hopes and fears of them.

With ponies, motor sledges, dogs, and men parties working hard, the transportation progressed rapidly on the next two days, the only drawback being that the ice was beginning to get thin in the cracks and on some of the floes. Under these circumstances the necessity for wasting no time was evident, and so on the Sunday the third motor was got out and placed on the ice, and Scott, leaving Campbell to find the best crossing for the motor, started for the shore with a single man load.

Soon after the motor had been brought out Campbell ordered that it should be towed on to the firm ice, because the ice near the ship was breaking up. And then, as they were trying to rush the machine over the weak place, Williamson suddenly went through; and while he was being hauled out the ice under the motor was seen to give, and slowly the machine went right through and disappeared. The men made strenuous efforts to keep hold of the rope, but it cut through the ice towards them with an increasing strain, Page 230 and one after another they were obliged to let go. Half a minute later nothing remained but a big hole, and one of the two best motors was lying at the bottom of the sea.

The ice, too, was hourly becoming more dangerous, and it was clear that those who were on shore were practically cut off from the ship. So in the evening Scott went to the ice-edge farther to the north, and found a place where the ship could come and be near ice heavy enough for sledding. Then he semaphored directions to Pennell, and on the following morning the ship worked her way along the ice-edge to the spot that had been chosen.

A good solid road was formed right up to the ship, and again the work of transportation went on with the greatest energy. In this Bowers proved 'a perfect treasure,' there was not a single case he did not know nor a single article on which he could not at once place his hand, and every case as it came on shore was checked by him.

On Tuesday night, January 10, after six days in McMurdo Sound, the landing was almost completed, and early in the afternoon of Thursday a message was sent from the ship that nothing remained on board except mutton, books, pictures, and the pianola. 'So at last we really are a self-contained party ready for all emergencies. We are LANDED eight days after our arrival—a very good record.'

Page 231 CHAPTER II

DEPÔT LAYING TO ONE TON CAMP

> And the deed of high endeavour
> Was no more to the favoured few.
> But brain and heart were the measure
> Of what every man might do.
> RENNELL RODD.

While the landing was being carried out, the building party had worked so rapidly that, if necessity had arisen, the hut could have been inhabited by the 12th; at the same time another small party had been engaged in making a cave in the ice which was to serve as a larder, and this strenuous work continued until the cave was large enough to hold all the mutton, and a considerable quantity of seal and penguin. Close to this larder Simpson and Wright were busy in excavating for the differential magnetic hut.

In every way indeed such good progress had been made that Scott could begin to think about the depôt journey. The arrangements of this he discussed with Bowers, to whose grasp of the situation he gives the highest praise. 'He enters into one's idea's at once, and evidently thoroughly understands the principles of the game.'

Of these arrangements Wilson wrote in his journal:

Page 232 'He (Scott) wants me to be a driver with himself, Meares, and Teddie Evans, and this is what I would have chosen had I had a free choice of all. The dogs run in two teams and each team wants two men. It means a lot of running as they are being driven now, but it is the fastest and most interesting work of all, and we go ahead of the whole caravan with lighter loads and at a faster rate.... About this time next year may I be there or thereabouts! With so many young bloods in the heyday of youth and strength beyond my own I feel there will be a most difficult task in making choice towards the end and a most keen competition — *and* a universal lack of selfishness and self-seeking, with a complete absence of any jealous feeling in any single one of any of the comparatively large number who at present stand a chance of being on the last piece next summer.... I have never been thrown in with a more unselfish lot of men — each one doing his utmost fair and square in the most cheery manner possible.'

Sunday, January 15, was observed as a 'day of rest,' and at 10 A.M. the men and officers streamed over from the ship, and Scott read Divine Service on the beach. Then he had a necessary but unpalatable task to perform, because some of the ponies had not fulfilled expectations, and Campbell had to be told that the two allotted to him must be exchanged for a pair of inferior animals. At this time the party to be led by Campbell was known as the Eastern Party, but, owing to the impossibility of landing on King Page 233 Edward's Land, they were eventually taken to the north part of Victoria Land, and thus came to be known as the Northern Party. Scott's reluctance to make the alteration in ponies is evident, but in writing of it he says: 'He (Campbell) took it like the gentleman he is, thoroughly appreciating the reason.'

On that same afternoon Scott and Meares took a sledge and nine dogs, some provisions, a cooker and sleeping-bags, and started to Hut Point; but, on their arrival at the old *Discovery* hut, a most unpleasant surprise awaited them, for to their chagrin they found that some of Shackleton's party, who had used the hut for shelter, had left it in an uninhabitable state.

'There was something too depressing in finding the old hut in such a desolate condition.... To camp outside and feel that all the old comfort and cheer had departed, was dreadfully heartrending. I went to bed thoroughly depressed. It seems a fundamental expression of civilized human sentiment that men who come to such places as this should leave what comfort they can to welcome those who follow, and finding that such a simple duty had been neglected by our immediate predecessors oppressed me horribly.'

After a bad night they went up the hills, and there Scott found much less snow than he had ever seen. The ski run was completely cut through in two places, the Gap and Observation Hill were almost bare, on the side of Arrival Heights was a great bare slope, and on the top of Crater Heights was an immense bare Page 234 table-land. The paint was so fresh and the inscription so legible on the cross put up to the memory of Vince that it looked as if it had just been erected, and although the old flagstaff was down it could with very little trouble have been put up again. Late in the afternoon of Monday Scott and Meares returned to Cape Evans, and on the following day the party took up their abode in the hut.

'The word "hut,"' Scott wrote, 'is misleading. Our residence is really a house of considerable size, in every respect the finest that has ever been erected in the Polar regions. The walls and roof have double thickness of boarding and seaweed insulation on both sides of the frames. The roof with all its coverings weighs six tons. The outer shell is wonderfully solid therefore and the result is extraordinary comfort and warmth inside, whilst the total weight is comparatively small. It amply repays the time and attention given to its planning.

'On the south side Bowers has built a long annex, to contain spare clothing and ready provisions, on the north there is a solid stable to hold our fifteen ponies in the winter. At present these animals are picketed on long lines laid on a patch of snow close by, above them, on a patch of black sand and rock, the dogs extend in other long lines. Behind them again is a most convenient slab of hard ice in which we have dug two caverns. The first is a larder now fully stocked with seals, penguins, mutton, and beef. The other is devoted to science in the shape of differential magnetic Page 235 instruments which will keep a constant photographic record of magnetic changes. Outside these caverns is another little hut for absolute magnetic observations, and above them on a small hill, the dominant miniature peak of the immediate neighborhood, stand the meteorological instruments and a flagstaff carrying the Union Jack.

'If you can picture our house nestling below this small hill on a long stretch of black sand, with many tons of provision cases ranged in neat blocks in front of it and the sea lapping the ice-foot below, you will have some idea of our immediate vicinity. As for our wider surroundings it would be difficult to describe their beauty in sufficiently glowing terms. Cape Evans is one of the many spurs of Erebus and the one that stands closest under the mountain, so that always towering above us we have the grand snowy peak with its smoking summit. North and south of us are deep bays, beyond which great glaciers come rippling over the lower slopes to thrust high blue-walled snouts into the sea. The sea is blue before us, dotted with shining bergs or ice floes, whilst far over the Sound, yet so bold and magnificent as to appear near, stand the beautiful Western Mountains with their numerous lofty peaks, their deep glacial valley and clear-cut scarps, a vision of mountain scenery that can have few rivals.

'Ponting is the most delighted of men; he declares this is the most beautiful spot he has ever seen, and spends all day and most of the night Page 236 in what he calls "gathering it in" with camera and cinematograph.

'I have told you of the surroundings of our house but nothing of its internal arrangements. They are in keeping with the dignity of the mansion.

'The officers (16) have two-thirds of the interior, the men (9) the remaining third; the dividing line is fixed by a wall of cases containing things which suffer from being frozen.

'In the officers' quarters there is an immense dark room, and next it on one side a space devoted to the physicist and his instruments, and on the other a space devoted to charts, chronometers and instruments generally.

'I have a tiny half cabin of my own, next this Wilson and Evans have their beds. On the other side is a space set apart for five beds, which are occupied by Meares, Oates, Atkinson, Garrard and Bowers. Taylor, Debenham and Gran have another proportional space opposite. Nelson and Day have a little cabin of their own with a bench. Lastly Simpson and Wright occupy beds bordering the space set apart for their instruments and work. In the center is a 12-foot table with plenty of room for passing behind its chairs....

'To sum up, the arrangements are such that everyone is completely comfortable and conveniently placed for his work—in fact we could not be better housed. Of course a good many of us will have a small enough chance of enjoying the comforts of our home. We shall be away sledding late this year and off again Page 237 early next season, but even for us it will be pleasant to feel that such comfort awaits our return.'

So in less than a fortnight after the arrival in McMurdo Sound they had absolutely settled down, and were anxious to start upon their depôt journey as soon as the ponies had recovered thoroughly from the effects of the voyage. These autumn journeys, however, required much thought and preparation, mainly because the prospect of the parties being cut off from their winter quarters necessitated a great deal of food being taken both for men and animals. Sledding gear and wintering boots were served out to the selected travelers, sledges were prepared by P.O. Evans and Crean, and most of the stores were tested and found to be most excellent in quality. 'Our clothing is as good as good. In fact first and last, running through the whole extent of our outfit, I can say with pride that there is not a single arrangement which I would have had altered.... Everything looks hopeful for the depôt journey if only we can get our stores and ponies past the Glacier Tongue.'

Thus Scott wrote on the 20th, but the following day brought a serious suspense with it; for during the afternoon came a report that the *Terra Nova* was ashore, and Scott, hastening to the Cape, saw at once that she was firmly fixed and in a very uncomfortable position.

Visions of the ship being unable to return to New Zealand arose in his mind 'with sickening pertinacity,' and it was characteristic of him that at the moment when there was every prospect of a complete disarrangement of well-laid plans, he found his one Page 238 consolation in determining that, whatever happened, nothing should interfere with the southern work.

The only possible remedy seemed to be an extensive lightening of the ship with boats, as the tide had evidently been high when she struck. Scott, with two or three companions, watched anxiously from the shore while the men on board shifted cargo aft, but no ray of hope came until the ship was seen to be turning very slowly, and then they saw the men running from side to side and knew that an attempt was being made to roll her off. At first the rolling produced a more rapid turning movement, and then she seemed again to hang though only for a short time. Meanwhile the engines had been going astern and presently a slight movement became apparent, but those who were watching the ship did not know that she was getting clear until they heard the cheers on board. Then she gathered stern way and was clear.

'The relief was enormous. The wind dropped as she came off, and she is now securely moored off the northern ice-edge, where I hope the greater number of her people are finding rest. For here and now I must record the splendid manner in which these men are working. I find it difficult to express my admiration for the manner in which the ship is handled and worked under these very trying circumstances... Pennell has been over to tell me about it to-night; I think I like him more every day.'

On that same day Meares and Oates went to the Glacier Tongue and satisfied themselves that the ice Page 239 was good; and with the 25th fixed for the date of departure it was not too much to hope that the ice would remain for three or four more days. The ponies for Campbell's party were put on board on the 22nd, but when Scott got up at 5 A.M. on the following morning he saw, to his astonishment, that the ice was going out of the bay in a solid mass. Then everything was rushed on at top speed, and a wonderful day's work resulted. All the forage, food, sledges and equipment were got off to the ship at once, the dogs followed; in short everything to do with the depôt party was hurriedly put on board except the ponies, which were to cross the Cape and try to get over the Southern Road on the morning of the 24th.

The Southern Road was the one feasible line of communication between the new station at Cape Evans and the *Discovery* hut, for the rugged mountains and crevassed ice-slopes of Ross Island prevented a passage by land. The Road provided level going below the cliffs of the ice-foot except where disturbed by the descending glacier; and there it was necessary to cross the body of the glacier itself. It consisted of the more enduring ice in the bays and the sea-ice along the coast, which only stayed fast for the season. Thus it was most important to get safely over the dangerous part of this Road before the seasonal going-out of the sea-ice. To wait until after the ice went out and the ship could sail to Hut Point would have meant both uncertainty and delay. Scott knew well enough that the Road might not hold for many more hours, Page 240 and it actually broke up on the very day after the party had passed.

Early on Tuesday, January 24, a boat from the ship fetched Scott and the Western Party; and at the same time the ponies were led out of the camp, Wilson and Meares going ahead of them to test the track. No sooner was Scott on board than he was taken to inspect Lillie's catch of sea animals. 'It was wonderful, quantities of sponges, isopods, pentapods, large shrimps, corals, &c. &c.; but the *pièce de résistance* was the capture of several bucketsful of cephalodiscus of which only seven pieces had been previously caught. Lillie is immensely pleased, feeling that it alone repays the whole enterprise.' In the forenoon the ship skirted the Island, and with a telescope those on board could watch the string of ponies steadily progressing over the sea-ice past the Razor Back Islands; and, as soon as they were seen to be well advanced, the ship steamed on to the Glacier Tongue, and made fast in the narrow angle made by the sea-ice with the glacier.

Then, while Campbell investigated a broad crack in the sea ice on the Southern Road, Scott went to meet the ponies, which, without much difficulty, were got on to the Tongue, across the glacier, and then were picketed on the sea-ice close to the ship. But when Campbell returned with the news that the big crack was 30 feet across, it was evident that they must get past it on the glacier, and Scott asked him to peg out a road clear of cracks.

Page 241 Soon afterwards Oates reported that the ponies were ready to start again, and they were led along; Campbell's road, their loads having already been taken on the floe. At first all went well, but when the animals got down on the floe level and Oates led across an old snowed-up crack, the third pony made a jump at the edge and sank to its stomach in the middle. Gradually it sank deeper and deeper until only its head and forelegs showed above the slush. With some trouble ropes were attached to these, and the poor animal, looking very weak and miserable, was eventually pulled out.

After this experience the other five ponies were led farther round to the west and were got safely out on the floe; a small feed was given to them, and then they were started off with their loads.

The dogs in the meantime were causing some excitement for, starting on hard ice with a light load, they obviously preferred speed to security. Happily, however, no accident happened, and Scott, writing from Glacier Tongue on January 24, was able to say: 'All have arrived safely, and this evening we start our sledges south. I expect we shall have to make three relays to get all our stores on to the Barrier some fifteen miles away. The ship is to land a geologising party on the west side of the Sound, and then to proceed to King Edward's Land to put the Eastern party on short.'

The geologising party consisted of Griffith Taylor, Debenham, Wright, and P.O. Evans, and for reasons Page 242 already mentioned the Eastern party were eventually known as the Northern party.

On the night of the 24th Scott camped six miles from the glacier and two miles from Hut Point, he and Wilson having driven one team of dogs, while Meares and E. Evans drove the other. But on the following day Scott drove his team to the ship, and when the men had been summoned aft he thanked them for their splendid work.

'They have behaved like bricks and a finer lot of fellows never sailed in a ship.... It was a little sad to say farewell to all these good fellows and Campbell and his men. I do most heartily trust that all will be successful in their ventures, for indeed their unselfishness and their generous high spirit deserves reward. God bless them.'

How completely Scott's hopes were realized in the case of Campbell's party is now well known. Nothing more miraculous than the story of their adventures has ever been told. The party consisted of Campbell, Levick, Priestley, Abbott, Browning, and Dickason, and the courage shown by the leader and his companions in facing endless difficulties and privations has met with the unstinted admiration that it most thoroughly deserved.

For the depôt laying journey Scott's party consisted of 12 men (Wilson, Bowers, Oates, Atkinson, Cherry-Garrard, E. Evans, Gran, Meares, Forde, Page 243 Keohane, Crean, and himself), 8 ponies and 26 dogs. Of the dogs he felt at this time more than a little doubtful, but the ponies were in his opinion bound to be a success. 'They work with such extraordinary steadiness, stepping out briskly and cheerfully, following in each other's tracks. The great drawback is the ease with which they sink in soft snow: they go through in lots of places where the men scarcely make an impression — they struggle pluckily when they sink, but it is trying to watch them.'

In three days he hoped that all the loads would be transported to complete safety, and on Friday, the 27th, only one load remained to be brought from Hut Point. The strenuous labour of this day tired out the dogs, but the ponies worked splendidly. On the next day, however, both Keohane's and Bowers' ponies showed signs of breaking down, and Oates began to take a gloomy view of the situation. In compensation for these misfortunes the dogs, as they got into better condition, began to do excellent work. During Sunday they ran two loads for over a mile past the stores on the Barrier to the spot chosen for 'Safety Camp,' the big home depôt. 'I don't think that any part of the Barrier is likely to go, but it's just as well to be prepared for everything, and our camp must deserve its distinctive title of "Safety."'

By this time the control of the second dog team had been definitely handed over to Wilson, and in his journal he gives an admirable account of his experiences. 'The seals have been giving a lot of Page 244 trouble, that is just to Meares and myself with our dogs.... Occasionally when one pictures oneself quite away from trouble of that kind, an old seal will pop his head up at a blowhole a few yards ahead of the team, and they are all on top of him before one can say "knife"! Then one has to rush in with the whip — and everyone of the team of eleven jumps over the harness of the dog next to him, and the harnesses become a muddle that takes much patience to unravel, not to mention care lest the whole team should get away with the sledge and its load, and leave one behind.... I never did get left the whole of this depôt journey, but I was often very near it, and several times had only time to seize a strap or a part of the sledge, and be dragged along helter-skelter over everything that came in the way, till the team got sick of galloping and one could struggle to one's feet again. One gets very wary and wide-awake when one has to manage a team of eleven dogs and a sledge load by oneself, but it was a most interesting experience, and I had a delightful leader, "Stareek" by name — Russian for "Old Man," and he was the most wise old man.... Dog driving like this in the orthodox manner is a very different thing from the beastly dog driving we perpetrated in the *Discovery* days.... I got to love all my team and they got to know me well.... Stareek is quite a ridiculous "old man" and quite the nicest, quietest, cleverest old dog I have ever come across. He looks in face as if he knew all the wickedness of all the world Page 245 and all its cares, and as if he were bored to death by them.'

When Safety Camp was reached there was no need for haste until they started upon their journey. 'It is only when we start that we must travel fast.' Work, however, on the Monday was more strenuous than successful, for the ponies sank very deep and had great difficulty in bringing up their loads. During the afternoon Scott disclosed his plan of campaign, which was to go forward with five weeks' food for men and animals, then to depôt a fortnight's supply after twelve or thirteen days and return to Safety Camp. The loads for ponies under this arrangement worked out at a little over 600 lbs., and for the dog teams at 700 lbs., both apart from sledges. Whether the ponies could manage these loads depended on the surface, and there was a great possibility that the dogs would have to be lightened, but under the circumstances it was the best plan they could hope to carry out.

On Tuesday when everything was ready for the start the one pair of snow-shoes was tried on 'Weary Willy' with magical effect. In places where he had floundered woefully without the shoes he strolled round as if he was walking on hard ground. Immediately after this experiment Scott decided that an attempt must be made to get more snow-shoes, and within half an hour Meares and Wilson had started, on the chance that the ice had not yet gone out, to the station twenty miles away. But on the next day they returned with the news that there was no Page 246 possibility of reaching Cape Evans, and an additional stroke of bad fortune fell when Atkinson's foot, which had been troublesome for some time, was examined and found to be so bad that he had to be left behind with Crean as a companion.

Writing on Wednesday, February 1, from 'Safety Camp, Great Barrier,' Scott said: 'I told you that we should be cut off from our winter station, and that I had to get a good weight of stores on to the Barrier to provide for that contingency. We are safely here with all requisite stores, though it has taken nearly a week. But we find the surface very soft and the ponies flounder in it. I sent a dog team back yesterday to try and get snow-shoes for ponies, but they found the ice broken south of Cape Evans and returned this morning. Everyone is doing splendidly and gaining the right sort of experience for next year. Every mile we advance this year is a help for next.'

PONY CAMP ON THE BARRIER.
Photo by Capt. R. F. Scott.

At last the start was made on Thursday, February 2, but when, after marching five miles, Scott asked for their one pair of snow-shoes, he found that they had been left behind, and Gran—whose expertness on ski was most useful—immediately volunteered to go back and get them. While he was away the party rested, for at Scott's suggestion they had decided to take to night marching. And so at 12.30 A.M. they started off once more on a surface that was bad at first but gradually improved, until just before camping time Bowers, who was leading, suddenly plunged into soft snow. Several of the others, following close behind Page 247 him, shared the same fate, and soon three ponies were plunging and struggling in a drift, and had to be unharnessed and led round from patch to patch until firmer ground was reached.

Then came another triumph for the snow-shoes, which were put on Bowers' pony, with the result that after a few minutes he settled down, was harnessed to his load, and brought in not only that but also another over places into which he had previously been plunging. Again Scott expressed his regret that such a great help to their work had been left behind at the station, and it was all the more trying for him to see the ponies half engulfed in the snow, and panting and heaving from the strain, when the remedies for his state of affairs were so near and yet so impossible to reach.

During the next march ten miles were covered, and the ponies, on a better surface, easily dragged their loads, but signs of bad weather began to appear in the morning, and by 4 P.M. on Saturday a blizzard arrived and held up the party in Corner Camp for three days. 'No fun to be out of the tent—but there are no shirkers with us. Oates has been out regularly to feed the ponies; Meares and Wilson to attend to the dogs; the rest of us as occasion required.'

The ponies looked fairly comfortable during the blizzard, but when it ceased and another march was made on Tuesday night, the effects of the storm were too clearly seen. All of them finished the march listlessly, and two or three were visibly thinner.

Page 248 But by far the worst sufferer was Forde's 'Blucher' whose load was reduced to 200 lbs., and finally Forde pulled this in and led his pony. Extra food was given in the hope that they would soon improve again; but at all costs most of them had got to be kept alive, and Scott began to fear that very possibly the journey would have to be curtailed.

During the next two marches, however, the ponies seemed to be stronger. 'Surface very good and animals did splendidly,' Scott wrote on Friday, February 10, and then gave in his diary for the day an account of their nightly routine. 'We turn out of our sleeping-bags about 9 P.M. Somewhere about 11.30 I shout to the Soldier[1] "How are things?" There is a response suggesting readiness, and soon after figures are busy amongst sledges and ponies. It is chilling work for the fingers and not too warm for the feet. The rugs come off the animals, the harness is put on, tents and camp equipment are loaded on the sledges, nosebags filled for the next halt; one by one the animals are taken off the picketing rope and yoked to the sledge. Oates watches his animal warily, reluctant to keep such a nervous creature standing in the traces. If one is prompt one feels impatient and fretful whilst watching one's more tardy fellows. Wilson and Meares hang about ready to help with odds and ends.

[Footnote 1: Oates.]

'Still we wait: the picketing lines must be gathered up, a few pony putties need adjustment, a party has been slow striking their tent. With numbed fingers on Page 249 our horse's bridle and the animal striving to turn its head from the wind one feels resentful. At last all is ready. One says "All right, Bowers, go ahead," and Birdie leads his big animal forward, starting, as he continues, at a steady pace. The horses have got cold and at the word they are off, the Soldier's and one or two others with a rush. Finnesko give poor foothold on the slippery sastrugi,[1] and for a minute or two drivers have some difficulty in maintaining the pace on their feet. Movement is warming, and in ten minutes the column has settled itself to steady marching.

[Footnote 1: Irregularities formed by the wind on a snow-plain.]

'The pace is still brisk, the light bad, and at intervals one or another of us suddenly steps on a slippery patch and falls prone. These are the only real incidents of the march—for the rest it passes with a steady tramp and slight variation of formation. The weaker ponies drop a bit but not far, so that they are soon up in line again when the first halt is made. We have come to a single halt in each half march. Last night it was too cold to stop long and a very few minutes found us on the go again.

'As the end of the half march approaches I get out my whistle. Then at a shrill blast Bowers wheels slightly to the left, his tent mates lead still farther out to get the distance for the picket lines; Oates and I stop behind Bowers and Evans, the two other sledges of our squad behind the two other of Bowers'. So we are drawn up in camp formation. The picket Page 250 lines are run across at right angles to the line of advance and secured to the two sledges at each end. It a few minutes ponies are on the lines covered, tents up again and cookers going.

'Meanwhile the dog drivers, after a long cold wait at the old camp, have packed the last sledge and come trotting along our tracks. They try to time their arrival in the new camp immediately after our own, and generally succeed well. The mid-march halt runs into an hour to an hour and a half, and at the end we pack up and tramp forth again. We generally make our final camp about 8 o'clock, and within an hour and a half most of us are in our sleeping-bags.... At the long halt we do our best for our animals by building snow walls and improving their rugs, &c.

A softer surface on the 11th made the work much more difficult, and even the dogs, who had been pulling consistently well, showed signs of exhaustion before the march was over. Early on Sunday morning they were near the 79th parallel, and exact bearings had to be taken, since this camp, called Bluff Camp, was expected to play an important part in the future. By this time three of the ponies, Blossom, James Pigg, and Blucher, were so weak that Scott decided to send E. Evans, Forde and Keohane back with them.

Progress on the next march was interrupted by a short blizzard, and Scott, not by any means for the first time, was struck by Bowers' imperviousness to Page 251 cold. 'Bowers,' he wrote, 'is wonderful. Throughout the night he has worn no head-gear but a common green felt hat kept on with a chin-stay and affording no cover whatever for the ears. His face and ears remain bright red. The rest of us were glad to have thick Balaclavas and wind helmets. I have never seen anyone so unaffected by the cold. To-night he remained outside a full hour after the rest of us had got into the tent. He was simply pottering about the camp doing small jobs to the sledges, &c. Cherry-Garrard is remarkable because of his eyes. He can only see through glasses and has to wrestle with all sorts of inconveniences in consequence. Yet one could never guess it—for he manages somehow to do more than his share of the work.'

Another disappointing day followed, on which the surface was so bad that the ponies frequently sank lower than their hocks, and the soft patches of snow left by the blizzard lay in sandy heaps and made great friction for the runners. Still, however, they struggled on; but Gran with Weary Willy could not go the pace, and when they were three-quarters of a mile behind the others the dog teams (which always left the camp after the others) overtook them. Then the dogs got out of hand and attacked Weary Willy, who put up a sterling fight but was bitten rather badly before Meares and Gran could drive off the dogs. Afterwards it was discovered that Weary Willy's load was much heavier than that of the other ponies, and an attempt to continue the march had quickly Page 252 to be abandoned owing to his weak condition. As some compensation for his misfortunes he was given a hot feed, a large snow wall, and some extra sacking, and on the following day he showed appreciation of these favors by a marked improvement. Bowers' pony, however, refused work for the first time, and Oates was more despondent than ever; 'But,' Scott says, 'I've come to see that this is a characteristic of him. In spite of it he pays every attention to the weaker horses.'

No doubt remained on the Thursday that both Weary Willy and Bowers' pony could stand very little more, and so it was decided to turn back on the following day. During the last march out the temperature fell to -21° with a brisk south-west breeze, and frost-bites were frequent. Bowers with his ears still uncovered suffered severely, but while Scott and Cherry-Garrard nursed them back he seemed to feel nothing but surprise and disgust at the mere fact of possessing such unruly organs. 'It seems as though some of our party will find spring journeys pretty trying. Oates' nose is always on the point of being frost-bitten; Meares has a refractory toe which gives him much trouble—this is the worse prospect for summit work. I have been wondering how I shall stick the summit again, this cold spell gives ideas. I think I shall be all right, but one must be prepared for a pretty good doing.'

The depôt was built during the next day, February 17, Lat. 79° 29' S, and considerably over a ton of stuff was landed.

Page 253 Stores left in depôt:

lbs.

245 7 weeks' full provision bags for 1 unit

  12 2 days' provision bags for 1 unit

   8 8 weeks' tea

  31 6 weeks' extra butter

176 lbs. biscuit (7 weeks' full biscuit)

  85 8-1/2 gallons oil (12 weeks' oil for 1 unit)

850 5 sacks of oats

424 4 bales of fodder

250 Tank of dog biscuit

100 2 cases of biscuit
_____

2181

1 skein white line

1 set breast harness

2 12 ft. sledges

2 pair ski, 1 pair ski sticks

1 *Minimum Thermometer*[1]

1 tin Rowntree cocoa

1 tin matches

[Footnote 1: See page 337.]

Sorry as Scott was not to reach 80°, he was satisfied that they had 'a good leg up' for next year, and could at least feed the ponies thoroughly up to this point. In addition to a flagstaff and black flag, One Ton Camp was marked with piled biscuit boxes to act as reflectors, and tea-tins were tied on the top of the sledges, which were planted upright in the snow. The depôt cairn was more than six feet above the surface, and so the party had the satisfaction of knowing that it could scarcely fail to show up for many miles.

Page 254 CHAPTER III

PERILS

> ...Yet I argue not
> Against Heaven's hand or will, nor bate a jot
> Of heart or hope; but still bear up and steer
> Right onward.
> MILTON.

On the return journey Scott, Wilson, Meares and Cherry-Garrard went back at top speed with the dog teams, leaving Bowers, Oates and Gran to follow with the ponies. For three days excellent marches were made, the dogs pulling splendidly, and anxious as Scott was to get back to Safety Camp and find out what had happened to the other parties and the ponies, he was more than satisfied with the daily records. But on Tuesday, February 21, a check came in their rapid journey, a check, moreover, which might have been a most serious disaster.

The light though good when they started about 10 P.M. on Monday night quickly became so bad that but little of the surface could be seen, and the dogs began to show signs of fatigue. About an hour and a half after the start they came upon mistily outlined Page 255 pressure ridges and were running by the sledges when, as the teams were trotting side by side, the middle dogs of the teams driven by Scott and Meares began to disappear. 'We turned,' Cherry-Garrard says, 'and saw their dogs disappearing one after another, like dogs going down a hole after a rat.'

In a moment the whole team were sinking; two by two they vanished from sight, each pair struggling for foothold. Osman, the leader, put forth all his strength and most wonderfully kept a foothold. The sledge stopped on the brink of the crevasse, and Scott and Meares jumped aside.

In another moment the situation was realized. They had actually been traveling along the bridge of a crevasse, the sledge had stopped on it, while the dogs hung in their harness in the abyss. 'Why the sledge and ourselves didn't follow the dogs we shall never know. I think a fraction of a pound of added weight must have taken us down.' Directly the sledge had been hauled clear of the bridge and anchored, they peered into the depths of the cracks. The dogs, suspended in all sorts of fantastic positions, were howling dismally and almost frantic with terror. Two of them had dropped out of their harness and, far below, could be seen indistinctly on a snow-bridge. The rope at either end of the chain had bitten deep into the snow at the side of the crevasse and with the weight below could not possibly be moved.

By this time assistance was forthcoming from Wilson and Cherry-Garrard, the latter hurriedly Page 256 bringing the Alpine rope, the exact position of which on the sledge he most fortunately knew. The prospect, however, of rescuing the team was not by any means bright, and for some minutes every attempt failed. In spite of their determined efforts they could get not an inch on the main trace of the sledge or on the leading rope, which with a throttling pressure was binding poor Osman to the snow.

Then, as their thoughts became clearer, they set to work on a definite plan of action. The sledge was unloaded, and the tent, cooker, and sleeping-bags were carried to a safe place; then Scott, seizing the lashing off Meares' sleeping-bag, passed the tent-poles across the crevasse, and with Meares managed to get a few inches on the leading line. This freed Osman, whose harness was immediately cut. The next step was to secure the leading rope to the main trace and haul up together. By this means one dog was rescued and unlashed, but the rope already had cut so far back at the edge that efforts to get more of it were useless.

SNOWED-UP TENT AFTER THREE DAYS' BLIZZARD.
Photo by Lieut. T. Gran.

'We could now unbend the sledge and do that for which we should have aimed from the first, namely, run the sledge across the gap and work from it.' So the sledge was put over the crevasse and pegged down on both sides, Wilson holding on to the anchored trace while the others worked at the leader end. The leading rope, however, was so very small that Scott was afraid of its breaking, and Meares was lowered down to secure the Alpine rope to the leading end of Page 257 the trace; when this had been done the chance of rescuing the dogs at once began to improve.

Two by two the dogs were hauled up until eleven out of the thirteen were again in safety. Then Scott began to wonder if the two other dogs could not be saved, and the Alpine rope was paid down to see if it was long enough to reach the bridge on which they were coiled. The rope was 90 feet, and as the amount remaining showed that the depth of the bridge was about 65 feet, Scott made a bowline and insisted upon being lowered down. The bridge turned out to be firm, and he quickly got hold of the dogs and saw them hauled to the surface. But before he could be brought up terrific howls arose above, and he had to be left while the rope-tenders hastened to stop a fight between the dogs of the two teams.

'We then hauled Scott up,' Cherry-Garrard says; 'it was all three of us could do, my fingers a good deal frost-bitten in the end. That was all the dogs, Scott has just said that at one time he never hoped to get back with the thirteen, or even half of them. When he was down in the crevasse he wanted to go off exploring, but we dissuaded him.... He kept on saying, "I wonder why this is running the way it is, you expect to find them at right angles."'

For over two hours the work of rescue had continued, and after it was finished the party camped and had a meal, and congratulated themselves on a miraculous escape. Had the sledge gone down Scott and Meares must have been badly injured, if not killed Page 258 outright, but as things had turned out even the dogs showed wonderful signs of recovery after their terrible experience.

On the following day Safety Camp was reached, but the dogs were as thin as rakes and so ravenously hungry that Scott expressed a very strong opinion that they were underfed. 'One thing is certain, the dogs will never continue to drag heavy loads with men sitting on the sledges; we must all learn to run with the teams and the Russian custom must be dropped.'

At Safety Camp E. Evans, Forde and Keohane were found, but to Scott's great sorrow two of their ponies had died on the return journey. Forde had spent hour after hour in nursing poor Blucher, and although the greatest care had also been given to Blossom, both of them were left on the Southern Road. The remaining one of the three, James Pigg, had managed not only to survive but actually to thrive, and, severe as the loss of the two ponies was, some small consolation could be gained from the fact that they were the oldest of the team, and the two which Oates considered to be the least useful.

After a few hours' sleep Scott, Wilson, Meares, Cherry-Garrard and Evans started off to Hut Point, and on arrival were astonished to find that, although the hut had been cleared and made habitable, no one was there. A pencil line on the wall stated that a bag containing a mail was inside, but no bag was to be found. But presently what turned out to be the true Page 259 solution of this curious state of affairs was guessed, namely, that Atkinson and Crean had been on their way from the hut to Safety Camp as the others had come from the camp to the hut, and later on Scott saw their sledge track leading round on the sea-ice.

Feeling terribly anxious that some disaster might have happened to Atkinson and Crean owing to the weakness of the ice round Cape Armitage, Scott and his party soon started back to Safety Camp, but it was not until they were within a couple of hundred yards of their destination that they saw three tents instead of two, and knew that Atkinson and Crean were safe. No sooner, however, had Scott received his letters than his feelings of relief were succeeded by sheer astonishment.

'Every incident of the day pales before the startling contents of the mail bag which Atkinson gave me—a letter from Campbell setting out his doings and the finding of *Amundsen* established in the Bay of Whales.

'One thing only fixes itself definitely in my mind. The proper, as well as the wiser, course for us is to proceed exactly as though this had not happened. To go forward and do our best for the honour of the country without fear or panic.

'There is no doubt that Amundsen's plan is a very serious menace to ours. He has a shorter distance to the Pole by 60 miles—I never thought he could have got so many dogs [116] safely to the ice. His Page 260 plan for running them seems excellent. But above and beyond all he can start his journey early in the season—an impossible condition with ponies.'

The ship, to which Scott had said good-by a month before, had, after landing the Western Geological Party at Butter Point, proceeded along the Barrier, and on February 5 had come across Amundsen camped in the Bay of Whales. No landing place, however, for Campbell's party could be found. 'This,' Campbell says, 'was a great disappointment to us all, but there was nothing for it but to return to McMurdo Sound to communicate with the main party, and then try to effect a landing in the vicinity of Smith's Inlet or as far to the westward as possible on the north coast of Victoria Land, and if possible to explore the unknown coast west of Cape North. We therefore made the best of our way to Cape Evans, and arrived on the evening of the 8th. Here I decided to land the two ponies, as they would be very little use to us on the mountainous coast of Victoria Land, and in view of the Norwegian expedition I felt the Southern Party would require all the transport available. After landing the ponies we steamed up to the sea-ice by Glacier Tongue, and from there, taking Priestley and Abbott, I went with letters to Hut Point, where the depôt party would call on their way back.'

Thus Scott came on Wednesday, February 22, to receive the news which was bound to occupy his thoughts, however resolutely he refused to allow it to interfere in any way with his plans.

Page 261 Thursday was spent preparing sledges to meet Bowers, Oates and Gran at Corner Camp, and on the following day Scott, Crean and Cherry-Garrard with one sledge and tent, E. Evans, Atkinson and Forde with second sledge and tent, and Keohane leading James Pigg, started their march. At 3 P.M. on Saturday Scott turned out and saw a short black line on the horizon towards White Island. Presently he made certain that it was Bowers and his companions, but they were traveling fast and failed to see Scott's camp; so when the latter reached Corner Camp he did not find Bowers, but was glad to see five pony walls and consequently to know that all the animals were still alive.

Having depôted six full weeks' provisions, Scott, Cherry-Garrard and Crean started for home, leaving the others to bring James Pigg by easier stages. The next day, however, had to be spent in the tent owing to a howling blizzard, and not until the Tuesday did Scott reach Safety Camp, where he found that the ponies were without exception terribly thin, and that Weary Willy was especially in a pitiable condition.

As no advantage was to be gained by staying at Safety Camp, arrangements were made immediately for a general shift to Hut Point, and about four o'clock the two dog teams driven by Wilson and Meares got safely away. Then the ponies were got ready to start, the plan being for them to follow in the tracks of the dogs; the route was over about six miles of sea-ice, which, owing to the spread of water holes, caused Scott to feel gravely anxious.

Page 262 At the very start, however, Weary Willy fell down, and his plight was so critical that Bowers, Cherry-Garrard and Crean were sent on with Punch, Cuts, Uncle Bill and Nobby to Hut Point, while Scott, with Oates and Gran, decided to stay behind and attend to the sick pony. But despite all the attempts to save him, Weary Willy died during the Tuesday night. 'It makes a late start *necessary for next year*,' Scott wrote in his diary on Wednesday, March 1, but on the following day he had to add to this, 'The events of the past 48 hours bid fair to wreck the expedition, and the only one comfort is the miraculous avoidance of loss of life.'

Early on the morning following Weary Willy's death, Scott, Oates and Gran started out and pulled towards the forage depôt, which was at a point on the Barrier half a mile from the edge, in a S.S.E. direction from Hut Point. On their approach the sky looked black and lowering, and mirage effects of huge broken floes loomed out ahead. At first Scott thought that this was one of the strange optical illusions common in the Antarctic, but as he drew close to the depôt all doubt was dispelled. The sea was full of broken pieces of Barrier edge, and at once his thoughts flew to the ponies and dogs.

They turned to follow the sea-edge, and suddenly discovering a working crack, dashed over it and hastened on until they were in line between Safety Camp and Castle Rock. Meanwhile Scott's first thought was to warn E. Evans' party which was traveling Page 263 back from Corner Camp with James Pigg. 'We set up tent, and Gran went to the depôt with a note as Oates and I disconsolately thought out the situation. I thought to myself that if either party had reached safety either on the Barrier or at Hut Point they would immediately have sent a warning messenger to Safety Camp. By this time the messenger should have been with us. Some half-hour passed, and suddenly with a "Thank God!" I made certain that two specks in the direction of Pram Point were human beings.'

When, however, Scott hastened in their direction he discovered them to be Wilson and Meares, who were astonished to see him, because they had left Safety Camp before the breakdown of Weary Willy had upset the original program. From them Scott heard alarming reports that the ponies were adrift on the sea-ice.

The startling incidents that had led to this state of affairs began very soon after Bowers, Crean and Cherry-Garrard had left Safety Camp with the ponies. 'I caught Bowers up at the edge of the Barrier,' Cherry-Garrard wrote in his diary, 'the dogs were on ahead and we saw them turn and make right round Cape Armitage. "Uncle Bill" got done, and I took up the dog tracks which we followed over the tide crack and well on towards Cape Armitage.

'The sea-ice was very weak, and we came to fresh crack after fresh crack, and at last to a big crack with water squelching through for many feet on both Page 264 sides. We all thought it impossible to proceed and turned back.... The ponies began to get very done, and Bowers decided to get back over the tide crack, find a snowy place, and camp.

'This had been considered with Scott as a possibility and agreed to. Of course according to arrangements then Scott would have been with the ponies.

'We camped about 11 P.M. and made walls for the ponies. Bowers cooked with a primus of which the top is lost, and it took a long time. He mistook curry powder for cocoa, and we all felt very bad for a short time after trying it. Crean swallowed all his. Otherwise we had a good meal.

'While we were eating a sound as though ice had fallen outside down the tent made us wonder. At 2 A.M. we turned in, Bowers went out, and all was quiet. At 4.30 A.M. Bowers was wakened by a grinding sound, jumped up, and found the situation as follows: —

'The whole sea-ice had broken up into small floes, from ten to thirty or forty yards across. We were on a small floe, I think about twenty yards across, two sledges were on the next floe, and "Cuts" had disappeared down the opening. Bowers shouted to us all and hauled the two sledges on to our floe in his socks. We packed anyhow, I don't suppose a camp was ever struck quicker. It seemed to me impossible to go on with the ponies and I said so, but Bowers decided to try.

'We decided that to go towards White Island Page 265 looked best, and for five hours traveled in the following way: — we jumped the ponies over floe to floe as the cracks joined.... We then manhauled the sledges after them, then according to the size of the floe sometimes harnessed the ponies in again, sometimes man-hauled the sledge to the next crack, waited our chance, sometimes I should think five or ten minutes, and repeated the process.'

At length they worked their way to heavier floes lying near the Barrier edge, and at one time thought that it was possible to get up; but very soon they discovered that there were gaps everywhere off the high Barrier face. In this dilemma Crean volunteered to try and reach Scott, and after traveling a great distance and leaping from floe to floe, he found a thick floe from which with the help of his ski stick he could climb the Barrier face. 'It was a desperate venture, but luckily successful.'

And so while Scott, Oates, Wilson, Meares and Gran were discussing the critical situation, a man, who proved to be Crean, was seen rapidly making for the depôt from the west.

As soon as Scott had considered the latest development of the situation he sent Gran back to Hut Point with Wilson and Meares, and started with Oates, Crean, and a sledge for the scene of the mishap. A halt was made at Safety Camp to get some provisions and oil, and then, marching carefully round, they approached the ice-edge, and to their joy caught sight of Bowers and Cherry-Garrard. With the help Page 266 of the Alpine rope both the men were dragged to the surface, and after camp had been pitched at a safe distance from the edge all hands started upon salvage work. The ice at this time lay close and quiet against the Barrier edge, and some ten hours after Bowers and Cherry-Garrard had been hauled up, the sledges and their contents were safely on the Barrier. But then, just as the last loads were saved, the ice began to drift again, and so, for the time, nothing could be done for the ponies except to leave them well-fed upon their floes.

'None of our party had had sleep the previous night and all were dog tired. I decided we must rest, but turned everyone out at 8.30 yesterday morning [after three or four hours]. Before breakfast we discovered the ponies had drifted away. We had tried to anchor their floes with the Alpine rope, but the anchors had drawn. It was a sad moment.'

Presently, however, Bowers, who had taken the binoculars, announced that he could see the ponies about a mile to the N. W. 'We packed and went on at once. We found it easy enough to get down to the poor animals and decided to rush them for a last chance of life. Then there was an unfortunate mistake: I went along the Barrier edge and discovered what I thought and what proved to be a practicable way to land a pony, but the others meanwhile, a little overwrought, tried to leap Punch across a gap. The poor beast fell in; eventually we had to kill him — it was awful. I recalled all hands and pointed out my Page 267 road. Bowers and Oates went out on it with a sledge and worked their way to the remaining ponies, and started back with them on the same track.... We saved one pony; for a time I thought we should get both, but Bowers' poor animal slipped at a jump and plunged into the water: we dragged him out on some brash ice — killer whales all about us in an intense state of excitement. The poor animal couldn't rise, and the only merciful thing was to kill it. These incidents were too terrible. At 5 P.M. (Thursday, March 2), we sadly broke our temporary camp and marched back to the one I had just pitched.... So here we are ready to start our sad journey to Hut Point. Everything out of joint with the loss of our ponies, but mercifully with all the party alive and well.'

At the start on the march back the surface was so bad that only three miles were covered in four hours, and in addition to this physical strain Scott was also deeply anxious to know that E. Evans and his party were safe; but while they were camping that night on Pram Point ridges, Evans' party, all of whom were well, came in.

Then it was decided that Atkinson should go on to Hut Point in the morning to take news to Wilson, Meares and Gran, who were looking after the dogs, and having a wretched time in trying to make two sleeping-bags do the work of three.

On March 2 Wilson wrote in his journal: 'A very bitter wind blowing and it was a cheerless job waiting for six hours to get a sleep in the bag.... As the ice had all gone out of the strait we were cut off from Page 268 any return to Cape Evans until the sea should again freeze over, and this was not likely until the end of April. We rigged up a small fireplace in the hut and found some wood and made a fire for an hour or so at each meal, but as there was no coal and not much wood we felt we must be economical with the fuel, and so also with matches and everything else, in case Bowers should lose his sledge loads, which had most of the supplies for the whole party to last twelve men for two months.... There was literally nothing in the hut that one could cover oneself with to keep warm, and we couldn't run to keeping the fire going. It was very cold work. There were heaps of biscuit cases here which we had left in *Discovery* days, and with these we built up a small inner hut to live in.'

On Saturday Scott and some of his party reached the hut, and on Sunday he was able to write: 'Turned in with much relief to have all hands and the animals safely housed.' Only two ponies, James Pigg and Nobby, remained out of the eight that had started on the depôt journey, but disastrous as this was to the expedition there was reason to be thankful that even greater disasters had not happened.

Page 269 CHAPTER IV

A HAPPY FAMILY

By mutual confidence and mutual aid
Great deeds are done and great discoveries made.
ANON.

With the certainty of having to stay in the *Discovery* hut for some time, the party set to work at once to make it as comfortable as possible. With packing-cases a large *L*-shaped inner apartment was made, the intervals being stopped with felt, and an empty kerosene tin and some firebricks were made into an excellent little stove which was connected to the old stove-pipe.

As regards food almost an unlimited supply of biscuit was available, and during a walk to Pram Point on Monday, March 6, Scott and Wilson found that the sea-ice in Pram Point Bay had not gone out and was crowded with seals, a happy find that guaranteed the party as much meat as they wanted. 'We really have everything necessary for our comfort and only need a little more experience to make the best of our resources.... It is splendid to see the way in which everyone is learning the ropes, and the resource which Page 270 is being shown. Wilson as usual leads in the making of useful suggestions and in generally providing for our wants. He is a tower of strength in checking the ill-usage of clothes — what I have come to regard as the greatest danger with Englishmen.'

On Saturday night a blizzard sprang up and gradually increased in force until it reminded Scott and Wilson of the gale which drove the *Discovery* ashore. The blizzard continued until noon on Tuesday, on which day the Western Geological Party (Griffith Taylor, Wright, Debenham and P.O. Evans) returned to the hut after a successful trip.

Two days later another depôt party started to Corner Camp, E. Evans, Wright, Crean and Forde in one team; Bowers, Oates, Cherry-Garrard and Atkinson in the other. 'It was very sporting of Wright to join in after only a day's rest. He is evidently a splendid puller.'

During the absence of this party the comforts of the hut were constantly being increased, but continuous bad weather was both depressing to the men and very serious for the dogs. Every effort had been made to make the dogs comfortable, but the changes of wind made it impossible to give them shelter in all directions. At least five of them were in a sorry plight, and half a dozen others were by no means strong, but whether because they were constitutionally harder or whether better fitted by nature to protect themselves the other ten or a dozen animals were as fit as they could be. As it was found to be impossible to keep the dogs comfortable in the traces, the majority Page 271 of them were allowed to run loose; for although Scott feared that this freedom would mean that there would be some fights to the death, he thought it preferable to the risk of losing the animals by keeping them on the leash. The main difficulty with them was that when the ice once got thoroughly into the coats their hind legs became half paralyzed with cold, but by allowing them to run loose it was hoped that they would be able to free themselves of this serious trouble. 'Well, well, fortune is not being very kind to us. This month will have sad memories. Still I suppose things might be worse; the ponies are well housed and are doing exceedingly well....'

The depôt party returned to the hut on March 23, but though the sea by this time showed symptoms of *wanting* to freeze, there was no real sign that the ice would hold for many a long day. Stock therefore was taken of their resources, and arrangements were made for a much longer stay than had been anticipated. A week later the ice, though not thickening rapidly, held south of Hut Point, but the stretch from Hut Point to Turtle Back Island still refused to freeze even in calm weather, and Scott began to think that they might not be able to get back to Cape Evans before May. Soon afterwards, however, the sea began to freeze over completely, and on Thursday evening, April 6, a program, subject to the continuance of good weather, was arranged for a shift to Cape Evans. 'It feels good,' Cherry-Garrard wrote, 'to have something doing in the air.' But the weather prevented them from starting on the appointed day, and although Page 272 Scott was most anxious to get back and see that all was well at Cape Evans, the comfort achieved in the old hut was so great that he confessed himself half-sorry to leave it.

Describing their life at Hut Point he says, 'We gather around the fire seated on packing-cases, with a hunk of bread and butter and a steaming pannikin of tea, and life is well worth living. After lunch we are out and about again; there is little to tempt a long stay indoors, and exercise keeps us all the fitter.

'The failing light and approach of supper drives us home again with good appetites about 5 or 6 o'clock, and then the cooks rival one another in preparing succulent dishes of fried seal liver.... Exclamations of satisfaction can be heard every night—or nearly every night; for two nights ago (April 4) Wilson, who has proved a genius in the invention of "plats," almost ruined his reputation. He proposed to fry the seal liver in penguin blubber, suggesting that the latter could be freed from all rankness.... The "fry" proved redolent of penguin, a concentrated essence of that peculiar flavour which faintly lingers in the meat and should not be emphasized. Three heroes got through their pannikins, but the rest of us decided to be contented with cocoa and biscuit after tasting the first mouthful.[1]

[Footnote 1: Wilson, referring to this incident in his Journal, showed no signs of contrition. 'Fun over a fry I made in my new penguin lard. It was quite a success and tasted like very bad sardine oil.']

'After supper we have an hour or so of smoking Page 273 and conversation — a cheering, pleasant hour — in which reminiscences are exchanged by a company which has very literally had world-wide experience. There is scarce a country under the sun which one or another of us has not traveled in, so diverse are our origins and occupations.

'An hour or so after supper we tail off one by one.... Everyone can manage eight or nine hours' sleep without a break, and not a few would have little difficulty in sleeping the clock round, which goes to show that our exceedingly simple life is an exceedingly healthy one, though with faces and hands blackened with smoke, appearances might not lead an outsider to suppose it.'

On Tuesday, April 11, a start could be made for Cape Evans, the party consisting of Scott, Bowers, P.O. Evans and Taylor in one tent; E. Evans, Gran, Crean, Debenham and Wright in another; Wilson being left in charge at Hut Point, with Meares, Forde, Keohane, Oates, Atkinson and Cherry-Garrard.

In fine weather they marched past Castle Rock, and it soon became evident that they must go well along the ridge before descending, and that the difficulty would be to get down over the cliffs. Seven and a half miles from the start they reached Hutton Rocks, a very icy and wind-swept spot, and as the wind rose and the light became bad at the critical moment they camped for a short time. Half an hour later the weather cleared and a possible descent to the ice cliffs could be seen, but between Hutton Rock Page 274 and Erebus all the slope was much cracked and crevassed. A clear track to the edge of the cliffs was chosen, but on arriving there no low place could be found (the lowest part being 24 feet sheer drop), and as the wind was increasing and the snow beginning to drift off the ridge a quick decision had to be made.

Then Scott went to the edge, and having made standing places to work the Alpine rope, Bowers., E. Evans and Taylor were lowered. Next the sledges went down fully packed and then the remainder of the party, Scott being the last to go down. It was a neat and speedy piece of work, and completed in twenty minutes without serious frost-bites.

The surface of ice covered with salt crystals made pulling very heavy to Glacier Tongue, which they reached about 5.30 P.M. A stiff incline on a hard surface followed, but as the light was failing and cracks were innumerable, several of the party fell in with considerable risk of damage. The north side, however, was well snow-covered, with a good valley leading to a low ice cliff in which a broken piece provided an easy descent. Under the circumstances Scott decided to push on to Cape Evans, but darkness suddenly fell upon them, and after very heavy pulling for many hours they were so totally unable to see anything ahead, that at 10 P.M. they were compelled to pitch their camp under little Razor Back Island. During the night the wind began to rise, and in the morning a roaring blizzard was blowing, and obviously the ice on which they had pitched their camp was Page 275 none too safe. For hours they waited vainly for a lull, until at 3 P.M. Scott and Bowers went round the Island, with the result that they resolved to shift their camp to a little platform under the weather side. This operation lasted for two very cold hours, but splendid shelter was gained, the cliffs rising almost sheer from the tents. 'Only now and again a whirling wind current eddied down on the tents, which were well secured, but the noise of the wind sweeping over the rocky ridge above our heads was deafening; we could scarcely hear ourselves speak.' Provisions for only one more meal were left, but sleep all the same was easier to get than on the previous night, because they knew that they were no longer in danger of being swept out to sea.

The wind moderated during the night, and early in the morning the party in a desperately cold and stiff breeze and with frozen clothes were again under weigh. The distance, however, was only two miles, and after some very hard pulling they arrived off the point and found that the sea-ice continued around it. 'It was a very great relief to see the hut on rounding it and to hear that all was well.'

In choosing the site of the hut Scott had thought of the possibility of northerly winds bringing a swell, but had argued, first, that no heavy northerly swell had ever been recorded in the Sound; secondly, that a strong northerly wind was bound to bring pack which would damp the swell; thirdly, that the locality was well protected by the Barne Glacier; and, lastly, Page 276 that the beach itself showed no signs of having been swept by the sea. When, however, the hut had been erected and he found that its foundation was only eleven feet above the level of the sea-ice, he could not rid himself entirely of misgivings.

As events turned out the hut was safe and sound enough, but not until Scott reached it, on April 13, did he realize how anxious he had been. 'In a normal season no thoughts of its having been in danger would have occurred to me, but since the loss of the ponies and the breaking of Glacier Tongue, I could not rid myself of the fear that misfortune was in the air and that some abnormal swell had swept the beach.' So when he and his party turned the small headland and saw that the hut was intact, a real fear was mercifully removed. Very soon afterwards the travelers were seen by two men at work near the stables, and then the nine occupants (Simpson, Day, Nelson, Ponting, Lashly, Clissold, Hooper, Anton and Demetri) came rapidly to meet and welcome them. In a minute the most important events of the quiet station life were told, the worst news being that one pony, named Hacken-schmidt, and one dog had died. For the rest the hut arrangements had worked admirably, and the scientific routine of observations was in full swing.

After their primitive life at the *Discovery* hut the interior space of the home at Cape Evans seemed palatial, and the comfort luxurious. 'It was very good to eat in civilized fashion, to enjoy the first bath for three months, and have contact with clean, dry Page 277 clothing. Such fleeting hours of comfort (for custom soon banished their delight) are the treasured remembrance of every Polar traveler.' Not for many hours or even minutes, however, was Scott in the hut before he was taken round to see in detail the transformation that had taken place in his absence, and in which a very proper pride was taken by those who had created it.

First of all a visit was paid to Simpson's Corner, where numerous shelves laden with a profusion of self-recording instruments, electric batteries and switchboards were to be seen, and the tickings of many clocks, the gentle whir of a motor and occasionally the trembling note of an electric bell could be heard. 'It took me days and even months to realize fully the aims of our meteorologist and the scientific accuracy with which he was achieving them.'

From Simpson's Corner Scott was taken on his tour of inspection into Ponting's dark room, and found that the art of photography had never been so well housed within the Polar regions and rarely without them. 'Such a palatial chamber for the development of negatives and prints can only be justified by the quality of the work produced in it, and is only justified in our case by such an artist as Ponting.'

From the dark room he went on to the biologists' cubicle, shared, to their mutual satisfaction, by Day and Nelson. There the prevailing note was neatness, and to Day's mechanical skill everyone paid tribute. The heating, lighting and ventilating arrangements Page 278 of the hut had been left entirely in his charge, and had been carried out with admirable success. The cook's corner was visited next, and Scott was very surprised to see the mechanical ingenuity shown by Clissold. 'Later,' he says, 'when I found that Clissold was called in to consult on the ailments of Simpson's motor, and that he was capable of constructing a dog sledge out of packing-cases, I was less surprised, because I knew by this time that he had had considerable training in mechanical work before he turned his attention to pots and pans.'

The tour ended with an inspection of the shelters for the animals, and when Scott saw the stables he could not help regretting that some of the stalls would have to remain empty, though he appreciated fully the fact that there was ample and safe harborage for the ten remaining ponies. With Lashly's help, Anton had completed the furnishing of the stables in a way that was both neat and effective.

Only five or six dogs had been left in Demetri's charge, and it was at once evident that every care had been taken of them; not only had shelters been made, but a small 'lean to' had also been built to serve as a hospital for any sick animal. The impressions, in short, that Scott received on his return to Cape Evans were almost wholly pleasant, and in happy contrast with the fears that had assailed him on the homeward route.

Not for long, however, did he, Bowers and Crean stay to enjoy the comforts of Cape Evans, as on Page 279 Monday, April 17, they were off again to Hut Point with two 10-foot sledges, a week's provisions of sledding food, and butter, oatmeal, &c., for the hut. Scott, Lashly, Day and Demetri took the first sledge; Bowers, Nelson, Crean and Hooper the second; and after a rather adventurous journey, in which 'Lashly was splendid at camp work as of old,' they reached Hut Point at 1 P.M. on the following day, and found everyone well and in good spirits. The party left at the hut were, however, very short of seal-meat, a cause of anxiety, because until the sea froze over there was no possibility of getting the ponies back to Cape Evans. But three seals were reported on the Wednesday and promptly killed, and so Scott, satisfied that this stock was enough for twelve days, resolved to go back as soon as the weather would allow him.

Leaving Meares in charge of the station with Demetri to help with the dogs, Lashly and Keohane to look after the ponies, and Nelson, Day and Forde to get some idea of the life and experience, the homeward party started on Friday morning. On this journey Scott, Wilson, Atkinson and Crean pulled one sledge, and Bowers, Oates, Cherry-Garrard and Hooper the other. Scott's party were the leaders, and their sledge dragged so fearfully that the men with the second sledge had a very easy time in keeping up. Then Crean declared that although the loads were equal there was a great difference in the sledges. 'Bowers,' Scott says, 'politely assented when I voiced this sentiment, but I am sure he and his party thought it the Page 280 plea of tired men. However, there was nothing like proof, and he readily assented to change sledges. The difference was really extraordinary; we felt the new sledge a featherweight compared with the old, and set up a great pace for the home quarters regardless of how much we perspired.'

All of them arrived at Cape Evans with their garments soaked through, and as they took off their wind clothes showers of ice fell upon the floor. The accumulation was almost beyond belief and showed the whole trouble of sledding in cold weather. Clissold, however, was at hand with 'just the right meal,' an enormous dish of rice and figs, and cocoa in a bucket. The sledding season was at an end, and Scott admitted that in spite of all the losses they had sustained it was good to be home again, while Wilson, Oates, Atkinson and Cherry-Garrard, who had not seen the hut since it had been fitted out, were astonished at its comfort.

On Sunday, April 23, two days after the return from Hut Point, the sun made it's last appearance and the winter work was begun. Ponies for exercise were allotted to Bowers, Cherry-Garrard, Hooper, Clissold, P.O. Evans and Crean, besides Oates and Anton, but in making this allotment Scott was obliged to add a warning that those who exercised the ponies would not necessarily lead them in the spring.

Wilson at once began busily to paint, and Atkinson was equally busy unpacking and setting up his sterilizers and incubators. Wright began to wrestle with the electrical instruments; Oates started to make bigger stalls in the stables; Cherry-Garrard employed himself Page 281 in building a stone house for taxidermy and with a view to getting hints for a shelter at Cape Crozier during the winter, while Taylor and Debenham took advantage of the last of the light to examine the topography of the peninsula. E. Evans surveyed the Cape and its neighborhood, and Simpson and Bowers, in addition to their other work, spent hours over balloon experiments. In fact everyone was overflowing with energy.

On Friday, April 28, Scott, eager to get the party safely back from Hut Point, hoped that the sea had at last frozen over for good, but a gale on the following day played havoc with the ice; and although the strait rapidly froze again, the possibility of every gale clearing the sea was too great to be pleasant. Obviously, however, it was useless to worry over a state of affairs that could not be helped, and the arrangements for passing the winter steadily progressed.

At Scott's request Cherry-Garrard undertook the editorship of the *South Polar Times* and the following notice was issued:

The first number of the *South Polar Times* will be published on Midwinter Day.

All are asked to send in contributions, signed anonymously, and to place these contributions in this box as soon as possible. No contributions for this number will be accepted after May 31.

A selection of these will be made for publication. It is not intended that the paper shall be too scientific.

Page 282 Contributions may take the form of prose, poetry or drawing. Contributors whose writings will lend themselves to illustration are asked to consult with the Editor as soon as possible.

The Editor,
S. P. T.

The editor, warned by Scott that the work was not easy and required a lot of tact, at once placed great hopes in the assistance he would receive from Wilson, and how abundantly these hopes were fulfilled has been widely recognized not only by students of Polar literature, but also by those who admire art merely for art's sake.

On the evening of Tuesday, May 2, Wilson opened the series of winter lectures with a paper on 'Antarctic Flying Birds,' and in turn Simpson, Taylor, Ponting, Debenham and others lectured on their special subjects. But still the *Discovery* hut party did not appear, although the strait (by May 9) had been frozen over for nearly a week; and repeatedly Scott expressed a wish that they would return. In the meantime there was work and to spare for everyone, and as the days went by Scott was also given ample opportunities to get a thorough knowledge of his companions.

'I do not think,' he wrote, 'there can be any life quite so demonstrative of character as that which we had on these expeditions. One sees a remarkable reassortment of values. Under ordinary conditions it is so easy to carry a point with a little bounce; self-assertion is a mask which covers many a weakness....

Page 283 Here the outward show is nothing, it is the inward purpose that counts. So the "gods" dwindle and the humble supplant them. Pretence is useless.

'One sees Wilson busy with pencil and colour box, rapidly and steadily adding to his portfolio of charming sketches and at intervals filling the gaps in his zoological work of *Discovery* times; withal ready and willing to give advice and assistance to others at all times; his sound judgment appreciated and therefore a constant referee.

'Simpson, master of his craft... doing the work of two observers at least... So the current meteorological and magnetic observations are taken as never before on Polar expeditions.'

'Wright, good-hearted, strong, keen, striving to saturate his mind with the ice problems of this wonderful region...'

And then after referring in terms of praise to the industry of E. Evans, the versatile intellect of Taylor, and the thoroughness and conscientiousness of Debenham, Scott goes on to praise unreservedly the man to whom the whole expedition owed an immense debt of gratitude.

'To Bowers' practical genius is owed much of the smooth working of our station. He has a natural method in line with which all arrangements fall, so that expenditure is easily and exactly adjusted to supply, and I have the inestimable advantage of knowing the length of time which each of our possessions will last us and the assurance that there can be no waste.

Page 284 Active mind and active body were never more happily blended. It is a restless activity admitting no idle moments and ever budding into new forms.

'So we see the balloon ascending under his guidance and anon he is away over the floe tracking the silk thread which held it. Such a task completed, he is away to exercise his pony, and later out again with the dogs, the last typically self-suggested, because for the moment there is no one else to care for these animals.... He is for the open air, seemingly incapable of realizing any discomfort from it, and yet his hours within doors spent with equal profit. For he is intent on tracking the problems of sledding food and clothes to their innermost bearings and is becoming an authority on past records. This will be no small help to me and one which others never could have given.

'Adjacent to the physicists' corner of the hut Atkinson is quietly pursuing the subject of parasites. Already he is in a new world. The laying out of the fish trap was his action and the catches are his field of labour.... His bench with its array of microscopes, etc., is next the dark room in which Ponting spends the greater part of his life. I would describe him as sustained by artistic enthusiasm....

'Cherry-Garrard is another of the open-air, self-effacing, quiet workers; his whole heart is in the life, with profound eagerness to help everyone. One has caught glimpses of him in tight places; sound all through and pretty hard also....

'Oates' whole heart is in the ponies. He is really Page 285 devoted to their care, and I believe will produce them in the best possible form for the sledding season. Opening out the stores, installing a blubber stove, etc., has kept him busy, whilst his satellite, Anton, is ever at work in the stables — an excellent little man.

'P.O. Evans and Crean are repairing sleeping-bags, covering felt boots, and generally working on sledding kit. In fact there is no one idle, and no one who has the least prospect of idleness.

On May 8 as one of the series of lectures Scott gave an outline of his plans for next season, and hinted that in his opinion the problem of reaching the Pole could best be solved by relying on the ponies and man haulage. With this opinion there was general agreement, for as regards glacier and summit work everyone seemed to distrust the dogs. At the end of the lecture he asked that the problem should be thought over and freely discussed, and that any suggestions should be brought to his notice. 'It's going to be a tough job; that is better realized the more one dives into it.'

At last, on May 13, Atkinson brought news that the dogs were returning, and soon afterwards Meares and his team arrived, and reported that the ponies were not far behind. For more than three weeks the weather at Hut Point had been exceptionally calm and fine, and with joy Scott saw that all of the dogs were looking remarkably well, and that the two ponies also seemed to have improved. 'It is a great comfort to have the men and dogs back, and a greater to Page 286 contemplate all the ten ponies comfortably stabled for the winter. Everything seems to depend on these animals.'

With their various occupations, lectures in the evening, and games of football—when it was not unusual for the goal-keepers to get their toes frost-bitten—in the afternoons, the winter passed steadily on its way; the only stroke of misfortune being that one of the dogs died suddenly and that a post-mortem did not reveal any sufficient cause of death. This was the third animal that had died without apparent reason at winter-quarters, and Scott became more than ever convinced that to place any confidence in the dog teams would be a mistake.

On Monday, May 22, Scott, Wilson, Bowers, Atkinson, P.O. Evans and Clissold went off to Cape Royds with a go-cart which consisted of a framework of steel tubing supported on four bicycle wheels— and sleeping-bags, a cooker and a small quantity of provisions. The night was spent in Shackleton's hut, where a good quantity of provisions was found; but the most useful articles that the party discovered were five hymn-books, for hitherto the Sunday services had not been fully choral because seven hymn-books were all that could be mustered.

"BIRDIE" BOWERS READING THE THERMOMETER ON THE
RAMP, JUNE 6TH, 1911.

June 6 was Scott's birthday, a fact which his small company did not forget. At lunch an immense birthday cake appeared, the top of which had been decorated by Clissold with various devices in chocolate and crystallized fruit, a flag and photographs of Scott.

Page 287 A special dinner followed, and to this sumptuous meal they sat down with their sledge banners hung around them. 'After this luxurious meal everyone was very festive and amiably argumentative. As I write there is a group in the dark room discussing political progress with large discussions, another at one corner of the dinner table airing its views on the origin of matter and the probability of its ultimate discovery, and yet another debating military problems.... Perhaps these arguments are practically unprofitable, but they give a great deal of pleasure to the participants.... They are boys, all of them, but such excellent good-natured ones; there has been no sign of sharpness or anger, no jarring note, in all these wordy contests; all end with a laugh. Nelson has offered Taylor a pair of socks to teach him some geology! This lulls me to sleep!'

On Monday evening, June 12, E. Evans gave a lecture on surveying, and Scott took the opportunity to note a few points to which he wanted especial attention to be directed. The essential points were:

1. Every officer who takes part in the Southern journey ought to have in his memory the approximate variation of the compass at various stages of the journey and to know how to apply it to obtain a true course from the compass....
2. He ought to know what the true course is to reach one depôt from another.
3. He should be able to take an observation with the theodolite.
4. He should be able to work out a meridian altitude observation. Page 288
5. He could advantageously add to his knowledge the ability to work out a longitude observation or an ex-meridian altitude.
6. He should know how to read the sledgemeter.

7. He should note and remember the error of the watch he carries and the rate which is ascertained for it from time to time.
8. He should assist the surveyor by noting the coincidences of objects, the opening out of valleys, the observation of new peaks, &c.

That these hints upon Polar surveying did not fall upon deaf ears is proved by a letter Scott wrote home some four months later. In it he says '"Cherry" has just come to me with a very anxious face to say that I must not count on his navigating powers. For the moment I didn't know what he was driving at, but then I remembered that some months ago I said that it would be a good thing for all the officers going South to have some knowledge of navigation so that in emergency they would know how to steer a sledge home. It appears that "Cherry" thereupon commenced a serious and arduous course of abstruse navigational problems which he found exceedingly tough and now despaired mastering. Of course there is not one chance in a hundred that he will ever have to consider navigation on our journey and in that one chance the problem must be of the simplest nature, but it makes it much easier for me to have men who Page 289 take the details of one's work so seriously and who strive so simply and honestly to make it successful.'

In Wilson's diary there is also this significant entry: 'Working at latitude sights — mathematics which I hate — till bedtime. It will be wiser to know a little navigation on the Southern sledge journey.'

Some time before Scott's suggestions stimulated his companions to master subjects which they found rather difficult and irksome, a regular daily routine had begun. About 7 A.M. Clissold began to prepare breakfast, and half an hour later Hooper started to sweep the floor and lay the table. Between 8 and 8.30 the men were out and about doing odd jobs, Anton going off to feed the ponies, Demetri to see to the dogs. Repeatedly Hooper burst upon the slumberers with announcements of the time, and presently Wilson and Bowers met in a state of nature beside a washing basin filled with snow and proceeded to rub glistening limbs with this chilly substance. A little later others with less hardiness could be seen making the most of a meager allowance of water. A few laggards invariably ran the nine o'clock rule very close, and a little pressure had to be applied so that they should not delay the day's work.

By 9.20 breakfast was finished, and in ten minutes the table was cleared. Then for four hours the men were steadily employed on a program of preparation for sledding. About 1.30 a cheerful half-hour was spent over the mid-day meal, and afterwards, if the weather permitted, the ponies were exercised, and those who were not employed in this way generally exercised themselves in some way or other. After this the officers went steadily on with their special work until 6.30, when dinner was served and finished within the hour. Then came reading, writing, games, and usually the gramophone, but three nights of the week were given up to lectures. At 11 P.M. the acetylene lights were put out, and those who wished to stay up had to depend on candle-light. The majority of candles, however, were extinguished by midnight, and the night watchman alone remained awake to keep his vigil by the light of an oil lamp.

Extra bathing took place either on Saturday afternoon or Sunday morning; chins were shaven, and possibly clean clothes put on. 'Such signs, with the regular service on Sunday, mark the passage of the weeks. It is not a very active life, perhaps, but certainly not an idle one. Few of us sleep more than eight hours of the twenty-four.'

On June 19, Day gave a lecture on his motor sledge and was very hopeful of success, but Scott again expressed his doubts and fears. 'I fear he is rather more sanguine in temperament than his sledge is reliable in action. I wish I could have more confidence in his preparations, as he is certainly a delightful companion.' Three days later Midwinter was celebrated with great festivities, and after lunch the Editor handed over the first number of the *S. P. T.* to Scott. Everyone at once gathered at the top of the table; 'It was like a lot of schoolgirls round a teacher' is the editor's description of the scene, and Scott read aloud most of the contents. An article called 'Valhalla,' written by Taylor, some verses called 'The Sleeping Bag,' and Wilson's illustrations to 'Antarctic Archives' were the popular favorites; indeed the editor attributed the success of the paper mainly to Wilson, though Day's delightful cover of carved venesta wood and sealskin was also 'a great help.' As all the contributions were anonymous great fun was provided by attempts to guess the various authors, and some of the denials made by the contributors were perhaps more modest than strictly truthful.

These festive proceedings, however, were almost solemn when compared with the celebrations of the evening. In preparation for dinner the 'Union Jacks' and sledge flags were hung about the large table, and at seven o'clock everyone sat down to a really good dinner.

Scott spoke first, and drew attention to the nature of the celebration as a half-way mark not only in the winter but in the plans of the expedition. Fearing in his heart of hearts that some of the company did not realize how rapidly the weeks were passing, and that in consequence work which ought to have been in full swing had barely been begun, he went on to say that it was time they knew how they stood in every respect, and especially thanked the officer in charge of the stores and those who looked after the Page 292 animals, for knowing the exact position as regards provision and transport. Then he said that in respect to the future chance must play a great part, but that experience showed him that no more fitting men could have been chosen to support him on the journey to the South than those who were to start in that direction in the following spring. Finally he thanked all of his companions for having put their shoulders to the wheel and given him so much confidence.

Thereupon they drank to the Success of the Expedition, and afterwards everyone was called to speak in turn.

'Needless to say, all were entirely modest and brief; unexpectedly, all had exceedingly kind things to say of me – in fact I was obliged to request the omissions of compliments at an early stage. Nevertheless it was gratifying to have a really genuine recognition of my attitude towards the scientific workers of the expedition, and I felt very warmly towards all these kind, good fellows for expressing it. If good will and fellowship count towards success, very surely shall we deserve to succeed. It was matter for comment, much applauded, that there had not been a single disagreement between any two members of our party from the beginning. By the end of dinner a very cheerful spirit prevailed.'

The table having been cleared and upended and the chairs arranged in rows, Ponting displayed a series of slides from his own local negatives, and then, after the healths of Campbell's party and of those on board Page 293 the *Terra Nova* had been drunk, a set of lancers was formed. In the midst of this scene of revelry Bowers suddenly appeared, followed by satellites bearing an enormous Christmas tree, the branches of which bore flaming candles, gaudy crackers, and little presents for everyone; the distribution of which caused infinite amusement. Thus the high festival of Midwinter was celebrated in the most convivial way, but that it was so reminiscent of a Christmas spent in England was partly, at any rate, due to those kind people who had anticipated the celebration by providing presents and other tokens of their interest in the expedition.

'Few,' Scott says, 'could take great exception to so rare an outburst in a long run of quiet days. After all we celebrated the birth of a season, which for weal or woe must be numbered amongst the greatest in our lives.'

Page 294 CHAPTER V

WINTER

Come what may
Time and the hour runs through the darkest day.
SHAKESPEARE.

During the latter part of June the Cape Crozier Party were busy in making preparations for their departure. The object of their journey to the Emperor penguin rookery in the cold and darkness of an Antarctic winter was to secure eggs at such a stage as could furnish a series of early embryos, by means of which alone the particular points of interest in the development of the bird could be worked out. As the Emperor is peculiar in nesting at the coldest season of the year, this journey entailed the risk of sledge traveling in midwinter, and the travelers had also to traverse about a hundred miles of the Barrier surface, and to cross a chaos of crevasses which had previously taken a party as much as two hours to cross by daylight.

PITCHING THE DOUBLE TENT ON THE SUMMIT.
Photo by Lieut. H. R. Bowers.

Such was the enterprise for which Wilson, Bowers and Cherry-Garrard were with the help of others making preparations, and apart from the Page 295 extraordinarily adventurous side of this journey, it was most interesting because the travelers were to make several experiments. Each man was to go on a different food scale, eiderdown sleeping-bags were to be carried inside the reindeer ones, and a new kind of crampon and a double tent were to be tried. 'I came across a hint as to the value of a double tent in Sverdrup's book, "New Land,"' Scott wrote on June 20, 'and P.O. Evans has made a lining for one of the tents, it is secured on the inner side of the poles and provides an air space inside the tent. I think it is going to be a great success.'

By the 26th preparations for the party to start from Cape Evans were completed, their heavy load when they set out on the following morning being distributed on two 9-foot sledges, 'This winter travel is a new and bold venture, but the right men have gone to attempt it. All good luck go with them!'

While the winter travelers were pursuing their strenuous way work went steadily on at Cape Evans, with no exciting nor alarming incident until July 4. On the morning of that day the wind blew furiously, but it moderated a little in the afternoon when Atkinson and Gran, without Scott's knowledge, decided to start over the floe for the North and South Bay thermometers respectively. This happened at 5.30 P.M., and Gran had returned by 6.45, but not until later did Scott hear that he had only gone two or three hundred yards from the land, and that it had taken him nearly an hour to find his way back.

Page 296 Atkinson's continued absence passed unnoticed until dinner was nearly finished, but Scott did not feel seriously alarmed until the wind sprang up again and still the wanderer did not return. At 9.30, P.O. Evans, Crean and Keohane, who had been out looking for him, returned without any news, and the possibility of a serious accident had to be faced. Organized search parties were at once dispatched, Scott and Clissold alone remaining in the hut. And as the minutes slipped slowly by Scott's fears naturally increased, as Atkinson had started for a point not much more than a mile off and had been away more than five hours. From that fact only one conclusion could be drawn, and there was but small comfort to be got from the knowledge that every spot which was likely to be the scene of an accident would be thoroughly searched.

Thus 11 o'clock came, then 11.30 with its six hours of absence; and the strain of waiting became almost unbearable. But a quarter of an hour later Scott heard voices from the Cape, and presently, to his extreme relief, Meares and Debenham appeared with Atkinson, who was badly frost-bitten in the hand, and, as was to be expected after such an adventure, very confused.

At 2 A.M. Scott wrote in his diary, 'The search parties have returned and all is well again, but we must have no more of these very unnecessary escapades. Yet it is impossible not to realize that this bit of experience has done more than all the talking I could have Page 297 ever accomplished to bring home to our people the dangers of a blizzard.'

On investigation it was obvious that Atkinson had been in great danger. First of all he had hit Inaccessible Island, and not until he arrived in its lee did he discover that his hand was frost-bitten. Having waited there for some time he groped his way to the western end, and then wandering away in a swirl of drift to clear some irregularities at the ice-foot, he completely lost the island when he could only have been a few yards from it. In this predicament he clung to the old idea of walking up wind, and it must be considered wholly providential that on this course he next struck Tent Island. Round this island he walked under the impression that it was Inaccessible Island, and at last dug himself a shelter on its lee side. When the moon appeared he judged its bearing well, and as he traveled homeward was vastly surprised to see the real Inaccessible Island appear on his left. 'There can be no doubt that in a blizzard a man has not only to safeguard the circulation in his limbs, but must struggle with a sluggishness of brain and an absence of reasoning power which is far more likely to undo him.'

About mid-day on Friday, July 7, the worst gale that Scott had ever known in Antarctic regions began, and went on for a week. The force of the wind, although exceptional, had been equaled earlier in the year, but the extraordinary feature of this gale was the long continuance of a very cold temperature. On Page 298 Friday night the thermometer registered -39°, and throughout Saturday and the greater part of Sunday it did not rise above -35°. It was Scott's turn for duty on Saturday night, and whenever he had to go out of doors the impossibility of enduring such conditions for any length of time was impressed forcibly upon him. The fine snow beat in behind his wind guard, the gusts took away his breath, and ten paces against the wind were enough to cause real danger of a frost-bitten face. To clear the anemometer vane he had to go to the other end of the hut and climb a ladder; and twice while engaged in this task he had literally to lean against the wind with head bent and face averted, and so stagger crab-like on his course.

By Tuesday the temperature had risen to +5° or +7°, but the gale still continued and the air was thick with snow. The knowledge, however, that the dogs were comfortable was a great consolation to Scott, and he also found both amusement and pleasure in observing the customs of the people in charge of the stores. The policy of every storekeeper was to have something up his sleeve for a rainy day, and an excellent policy Scott thought it. 'Tools, metal material, leather, straps, and dozens of items are administered with the same spirit of jealous guardianship by Day, Lashly, Oates and Meares, while our main storekeeper Bowers even affects to bemoan imaginary shortages. Such parsimony is the best guarantee that we are prepared to face any serious call.'

For an hour on Wednesday afternoon the wind Page 299 moderated, and the ponies were able to get a short walk over the floe, but this was only a temporary lull, for the gale was soon blowing as furiously as ever. And the following night brought not only a continuance of the bad weather but also bad news. At mid-day one of the best ponies, Bones, suddenly went off his feed, and in spite of Oates' and Anton's most careful attention he soon became critically ill. Oates gave him an opium pill and later on a second, and sacks were heated and placed on the suffering animal, but hour after hour passed without any improvement. As the evening wore on Scott again and again visited the stable, only to hear the same tale from Oates and Crean,[1] who never left their patient. 'Towards midnight,' Scott says, 'I felt very downcast. It is so certain that we cannot afford to lose a single pony — the margin of safety has already been overstepped, we are reduced to face the circumstance that we must keep all the animals alive or greatly risk failure.'

[Footnote 1: Bones was the pony which had been allotted to Crean.]

Shortly after midnight, however, there were signs of an improvement, and two or three hours afterwards the pony was out of danger and proceeded to make a rapid and complete recovery. So far, since the return to Cape Evans, the ponies had given practically no cause for anxiety, and in consequence Scott's hopes that all would continue to be well with them had steadily grown; but this shock shattered his sense of security, and although various alterations were made in the arrangements of the stables and extra Page 300 precautions were taken as regards food, he was never again without alarms for the safety of the precious ponies.

Another raging blizzard swept over Cape Evans on July 22 and 23, but the spirit of good comradeship still survived in spite of the atrocious weather and the rather monotonous life. 'There is no longer room for doubt that we shall come to our work with a unity of purpose and a disposition for mutual support which have never been equaled in these paths of activity. Such a spirit should tide us over all minor difficulties.'

By the end of the month Scott was beginning to wonder why the Crozier Party did not return, but on Tuesday, August 1, they came back looking terribly weather-worn and 'after enduring for five weeks the hardest conditions on record.' Their faces were scarred and wrinkled, their eyes dull, and their hands whitened and creased with the constant exposure to damp and cold. Quite obviously the main part of their afflictions arose from sheer lack of sleep, and after a night's rest they were very different people both in mind and body.

Writing on August 2, Scott says, 'Wilson is very thin, but this morning very much his keen, wiry self — Bowers is quite himself to-day. Cherry-Garrard is slightly puffy in the face and still looks worn. It is evident that he has suffered most severely — but Wilson tells me that his spirit never wavered for a moment. Bowers has come through best, all things Page 301 considered, and I believe that he is the hardest traveler that ever undertook a Polar journey, as well as one of the most undaunted; more by hint than direct statement I gather his value to the party, his untiring energy and the astonishing physique which enables him to continue to work under conditions which are absolutely paralyzing to others. Never was such a sturdy, active, undefeatable little man.'

Gradually Scott gathered an account of this wonderful journey from the three travelers who had made it. For more than a week the thermometer fell below -60°, and on one night the minimum showed -71°, and on the next -77°. Although in this fearful cold the air was comparatively still, occasional little puffs of wind eddied across the snow plain with blighting effect. 'No civilized being has ever encountered such conditions before with only a tent of thin canvas to rely on for shelter.' Records show that Amundsen when journeying to the N. magnetic pole met temperatures of a similar degree, but he was with Esquimaux who built him an igloo shelter nightly, he had also a good measure of daylight, and finally he turned homeward and regained his ship after five days' absence, while this party went outward and were absent for five weeks.

Nearly a fortnight was spent in crossing the coldest region, and then rounding C. Mackay they entered the wind-swept area. Blizzard followed blizzard, but in a light that was little better than complete darkness they staggered on. Sometimes they found Page 302 themselves high on the slopes of Terror on the left of the track, sometimes diving on the right amid crevasses and confused ice disturbance. Having reached the foothills near Cape Crozier they ascended 800 feet, packed their belongings over a moraine ridge, and began to build a hut. Three days were spent in building the stone walls and completing the roof with the canvas brought for the purpose, and then at last they could attend to the main object of their journey.

The scant twilight at mid-day was so short that a start had to be made in the dark, and consequently they ran the risk of missing their way in returning without light. At their first attempt they failed to reach the penguin rookery, but undismayed they started again on the following day, and wound their way through frightful ice disturbances under the high basalt cliffs. In places the rock over-hung, and at one spot they had to creep through a small channel hollowed in the ice. At last the sea-ice was reached, but by that time the light was so far spent that everything had to be rushed. Instead of the 2,000 or 3,000 nesting birds that had been seen at this rookery in *Discovery* days, they could only count about a hundred. As a reason for this a suggestion was made that possibly the date was too early, and that if the birds had not permanently deserted the rookery only the first arrivals had been seen.

With no delay they killed and skinned three penguins to get blubber for their stove, and with six eggs, only three of which were saved, made a hasty dash Page 303 for their camp, which by good luck they regained.

On that same night a blizzard began, and from moment to moment increased in fury. Very soon they found that the place where they had, with the hope of shelter, built their hut, was unfortunately chosen, for the wind instead of striking them directly was deflected on to them in furious, whirling gusts. Heavy blocks of snow and rock placed on the roof were hurled away and the canvas ballooned up, its disappearance being merely a question of time.

Close to the hut they had erected their tent and had left several valuable articles inside it; the tent had been well spread and amply secured with snow and boulders, but one terrific gust tore it up and whirred it away. Inside the hut they waited for the roof to vanish, and wondered, while they vainly tried to make it secure, what they could do if it went. After fourteen hours it disappeared, as they were trying to pin down one corner. Thereupon the smother of snow swept over them, and all they could do was to dive immediately for their sleeping-bags. Once Bowers put out his head and said, 'We're all right,' in as ordinary tones as he could manage, whereupon Wilson and Cherry-Garrard replied, 'Yes, we're all right'; then all of them were silent for a night and half a day, while the wind howled and howled, and the snow entered every chink and crevice of their sleeping-bags.

'This gale,' Scott says, 'was the same (July 23) in which we registered our maximum wind force, and Page 304 it seems probable that it fell on Cape Crozier even more violently than on us.'

The wind fell at noon on the following day, and the wretched travelers then crept from their icy nests, spread the floorcloth over their heads, and lit their primus. For the first time in forty-eight hours they tasted food, and having eaten their meal under these extraordinary conditions they began to talk of plans to build shelters on the homeward route. Every night, they decided, they must dig a large pit and cover it as best they could with their floorcloth.

Fortune, however, was now to befriend them, as about half a mile from the hut Bowers discovered their tent practically uninjured. But on the following day when they started homeward another blizzard fell upon them, and kept them prisoners for two more days.

By this time the miserable condition of their effects was beyond description. The sleeping-bags could not be rolled up, in fact they were so thoroughly frozen that attempts to bend them actually broke the skins. All socks, finnesko, and mitts had long been coated with ice, and when placed in breast-pockets or inside vests at night they did not even show signs of thawing. Indeed it is scarcely possible to realize the horrible discomforts of these three forlorn travelers, as they plodded back across the Barrier in a temperature constantly below -60°.

ADÉLIE PENGUIN ON NEST.
Photo by C. S. Wright.

EMPEROR PENGUINS ON SEA-ICE.
Photo by C. S. Wright.

'Wilson,' Scott wrote, 'is disappointed at seeing so little of the penguins, but to me and to everyone Page 305 who has remained here the result of this effort is the appeal it makes to our imagination as one of the most gallant stories of Polar history. That men should wander forth in the depth of a Polar night to face the most dismal cold and the fiercest gales in darkness is something new; that they should have persisted in this effort in spite of every adversity for five full weeks is heroic. It makes a tale for our generation which I hope may not be lost in the telling.

'Moreover the material results are by no means despicable. We shall know now when that extraordinary bird the Emperor penguin lays its eggs, and under what conditions; but even if our information remains meager concerning its embryology, our party has shown the nature of the conditions which exist on the Great Barrier in winter. Hitherto we have only imagined their severity; now we have proof, and a positive light is thrown on the local climatology of our Strait.'

Of the indomitable spirit shown by his companions on this journey Cherry-Garrard gives wonderful and convincing proof in his diary. Bowers, with his capacity for sleeping under the most distressing conditions, was 'absolutely magnificent'; and the story of how he arranged a line by which he fastened the cap of the tent to himself, so that if it went away a second time it should not be unaccompanied, is only one of the many tales of his resource and determination.

In addition to the eggs that the party had brought back and the knowledge of the winter conditions on Page 306 the Barrier that they had gained, their journey settled several points in connection with future sledding work. They had traveled on a very simple food ration in different and extreme proportions, for the only provisions they took were pemmican, butter, biscuit and tea. After a short experience they found that Wilson, who had arranged for the greatest quantity of fat, had too much of it, while Cherry-Garrard, who had declared for biscuit, had more than he could eat. Then a middle course was struck which gave a proportion agreeable to all of them, and which at the same time suited the total quantities of their various articles of food. The only change that was suggested was the addition of cocoa for the evening meal, because the travelers, thinking that tea robbed them of their slender chance of sleep, had contented themselves with hot water. 'In this way,' Scott decided, 'we have arrived at a simple and suitable ration for the inland plateau.'

Of the sleeping-bags there was little to be said, for although the eiderdown bag might be useful for a short spring trip, it became iced up too quickly to be much good on a long journey. Bowers never used his eiderdown bag,[1] and in some miraculous manner he managed more than once to turn his reindeer bag. The weights of the sleeping-bags before and after the journey give some idea of the ice collected.

[Footnote 1: He insisted upon giving it to Cherry-Garrard. 'It was,' the latter says, 'wonderfully self-sacrificing of him, more than I can write. I felt a brute to take it, but I was getting useless unless I got some sleep, which my big bag would not allow.']

Starting   Final
Weight   Weight Page 307

Wilson, reindeer and eiderdown.	17 lbs.	40 lbs.
Bowers, reindeer only.	17 "	33 "
C.-Garrard, reindeer and eiderdown.	18 "	45 "

The double tent was considered a great success, and the new crampons were much praised except by Bowers, whose fondness for the older form was not to be shaken. 'We have discovered,' Scott stated in summing up the results of the journey, 'a hundred details of clothes, mitts, and footwear: there seems no solution to the difficulties which attach to these articles in extreme cold; all Wilson can say, speaking broadly, is "The gear is excellent, excellent." One continues to wonder as to the possibilities of fur clothing as made by the Esquimaux, with a sneaking feeling that it may outclass our more civilized garb. For us this can only be a matter of speculation, as it would have been quite impossible to have obtained such articles. With the exception of this radically different alternative, I feel sure we are as near perfection as experience can direct. At any rate we can now hold that our system of clothing has come through a severer test than any other, fur included.'

With the return of the Cape Crozier Party lectures were resumed, and apart from one or two gales the weather was so good and the returning light so stimulating both to man and beast, that the spirits of the former rose apace while those of the latter became almost riotous when exercised. On August 10, Scott Page 308 and the new masters were to take charge on September 1, so that they could exercise their respective animals and get to know them as well as possible. The new arrangement was:

Bowers	Victor
Wilson	Nobby
Atkinson	Jehu
Wright	Chinaman
Cherry-Garrard	Michael
Evans (P.O.)	Snatcher
Crean	Bones
Keohane	Jimmy Pigg

On the same day Oates gave his second excellent lecture on 'Horse Management,' and afterwards the problem of snow-shoes was seriously discussed. Besides the problem of the form of the shoes was also the question of the means of attachment, and as to both points all sorts of suggestions were made. At that time Scott's opinion was that the pony snow-shoes they had, which were made on the grating or racquet principle, would probably be the best, the only alternative seeming to be to perfect the principle of the lawn mowing shoe. 'Perhaps,' he adds, 'we shall come to both kinds: the first for the quiet animals and the last for the more excitable. I am confident the matter is of first importance.'

Page 309 Ten days later Scott had to admit that the ponies were becoming a handful, and for the time being they would have been quite unmanageable if they had been given any oats. As it was, Christopher, Snippets and Victor were suffering from such high spirits that all three of them bolted on the 21st.

A prolonged gale arrived just as the return of the sun was due, and for three days everyone was more or less shut up in the hut. Although the temperature was not especially low anyone who went outside for even the briefest moment had to dress in wind clothes, because exposed woolen or cloth materials became so instantaneously covered with powdery crystals, that when they were brought back into the warmth they were soon wringing wet. When, however, there was no drift it was quicker and easier to slip on an overcoat, and for his own garment of this description Scott admits a sentimental attachment. 'I must confess,' he says, 'an affection for my veteran uniform overcoat, inspired by its persistent utility. I find that it is twenty-three years of age and can testify to its strenuous existence. It has been spared neither rain, wind, nor salt sea spray, tropic heat nor Arctic cold; it has outlived many sets of buttons, from their glittering gilded youth to green old age, and it supports its four-stripe shoulder straps as gaily as the single lace ring of the early days which proclaimed it the possession of a humble sub-lieutenant. Withal it is still a very long way from the fate of the "one-horse shay."'

Page 310 Not until August 26 did the sun appear, and everyone was at once out and about and in the most cheerful frame of mind. The shouts and songs of men could be heard for miles, and the outlook on life of every member of the expedition seemed suddenly to have changed. For if there is little that is new to be said about the return of the sun in Polar regions, it must always be a very real and important event to those who have lived without it for so many months, and who have almost forgotten the sensation of standing in brilliant sunshine.

Page 311 CHAPTER VI

GOOD-BYE TO CAPE EVANS

So far as I can venture to offer an opinion on such a matter, the purpose of our being in existence, the highest object that human beings can set before themselves, is not the pursuit of any such chimera as the annihilating of the unknown; but it is simply the unwearied endeavour to remove its boundaries a little further from our little sphere of action.—HUXLEY.

With the return of the sun preparations for the summer campaign continued more zealously and industriously than ever, and what seemed like a real start was made when Meares and Demetri went off to Hut Point on September 1 with the dog teams. For such an early departure there was no real reason unless Meares hoped to train the dogs better when he had got them to himself; but he chose to start, and Scott, after setting out the work he had to do, left him to come and go between the two huts as he pleased.

Meanwhile with Bowers' able assistance Scott set to work at sledding figures, and although he felt as the scheme developed that their organization would not be found wanting, he was also a little troubled by the immense amount of detail, and by the fact that every arrangement had to be more than usually elastic, so that both the complete success and the utter failure of Page 312 the motors could be taken fully into account. 'I think,' he says, 'that our plan will carry us through without the motors (though in that case nothing else must fail), and will take full advantage of such help as the motors may give.'

The spring traveling could not be extensive, because of necessity the majority of the company had to stay at home and exercise the ponies, which was not likely to be a light task when the food of these enterprising animals was increased. E. Evans, Gran and Forde, however, were to go and re-mark Corner Camp, and then Meares with his dogs was to carry as much fodder there as possible, while Bowers, Simpson, P.O. Evans and Scott were to 'stretch their legs' across the Western Mountains.

DOG PARTY STARTING FROM HUT POINT.
Photo by F. Debenham.

DOG LINES.
Photo by F. Debenham.

During the whole of the week ending on September 10, Scott was occupied with making detailed plans for the Southern journey, every figure being checked by Bowers, 'who has been an enormous help.' And later on, in speaking of the transport department, Scott says, 'In spite of all the care I have taken to make the details of my plan clear by lucid explanation, I find that Bowers is the only man on whom I can thoroughly rely to carry out the work without mistakes.' The result of this week's work and study was that Scott came to the conclusion that there would be no difficulty in getting to the Glacier if the motors were successful, and that even if the motors failed they still ought to get there with any ordinary degree of good fortune. To work three units of four men from that point onward

Page 313 would, he admitted, take a large amount of provisions, but with the proper division he thought that they ought to attain their object. 'I have tried,' he said, 'to take every reasonable possibility of misfortune into consideration;... I fear to be too sanguine, yet taking everything into consideration I feel that our chances ought to be good. The animals are in splendid form. Day by day the ponies get fitter as their exercise increases.... But we cannot spare any of the ten, and so there must always be anxiety of the disablement of one or more before their work is done.'

Apart from the great help he would obtain if the motors were successful, Scott was very eager that they should be of some use so that all the time, money and thought which had been given to their construction should not be entirely wasted. But whatever the outcome of these motors, his belief in the possibility of motor traction for Polar work remained, though while it was in an untried and evolutionary state he was too cautious and wise a leader to place any definite reliance upon it.

If, however, Scott was more than a little doubtful about the motors, he was absolutely confident about the men who were chosen for the Southern advance. 'All are now experienced sledge travelers, knit together with a bond of friendship that has never been equaled under such circumstances. Thanks to these people, and more especially to Bowers and Petty Officer Evans, there is not a single detail of our equipment Page 314 which is not arranged with the utmost care and in accordance with the tests of experience.'

On Saturday, September 9, E. R. Evans, Forde and Gran left for Corner Camp, and then for a few days Scott was busy finishing up the Southern plans, getting instruction in photography, and preparing for his journey to the west. On the Southern trip he had determined to make a better show of photographic work than had yet been accomplished, and with Ponting as eager to help others as he was to produce good work himself an invaluable instructor was at hand.

With the main objects of having another look at the Ferrar Glacier and of measuring the stakes put out by Wright in the previous year, of bringing their sledge impressions up to date, and of practicing with their cameras, Scott and his party started off to the west on the

15th, without having decided precisely where they were going or how long they would stay away.

Two and a half days were spent in reaching Butter Point, and then they proceeded up the Ferrar Glacier and reached the Cathedral Rocks on the 19th. There they found the stakes placed by Wright across the glacier, and spent the remainder of that day and the whole of the next in plotting accurately their position. 'Very cold wind down glacier increasing. In spite of this Bowers wrestled with theodolite. He is really wonderful. I have never seen anyone who could go on so long with bare fingers. My own fingers went every few moments.'

After plotting out the figures it turned out that the Page 315 movement varied from 24 to 32 feet, an extremely important observation, and the first made on the movements of the coastal glaciers. Though a greater movement than Scott expected to find, it was small enough to show that the idea of comparative stagnation was correct. On the next day they came down the Glacier, and then went slowly up the coast, dipping into New Harbor, where they climbed the moraine, took angles and collected rock specimens. At Cape Bernacchi a quantity of pure quartz was found, and in it veins of copper ore—an interesting discovery, for it was the first find of minerals suggestive of the possibility of working.

On the next day they sighted a long, low ice wall, and at a distance mistook it for a long glacier tongue stretching seaward from the land. But as they approached it they saw a dark mark, and it suddenly dawned upon them that the tongue was detached from the land. Half recognizing familiar features they turned towards it, and as they got close they saw that it was very like their old Erebus Glacier Tongue. Then they sighted a flag upon it, and realized that it was the piece broken off from the Erebus Tongue. Near the outer end they camped, and climbing on to it soon found the depôt of fodder left by Campbell, and the line of stakes planted to guide the ponies in the autumn. So there, firmly anchored, was the piece broken from the Glacier Tongue in the previous March, a huge tract about two miles long which had turned through half a circle, so that the old western end was towards Page 316 the east. 'Considering the many cracks in the ice mass it is most astonishing that it should have remained intact throughout its sea voyage. At one time it was suggested that the hut should be placed on this Tongue. What an adventurous voyage the occupants would have had! The Tongue which was 5 miles south of Cape Evans is now 4° miles W.N.W. of it.[1]

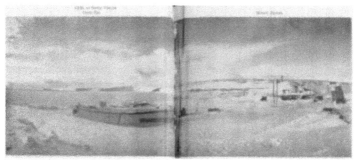

PANORAMA AT CAPE EVANS.
Photo by F. Debenham.

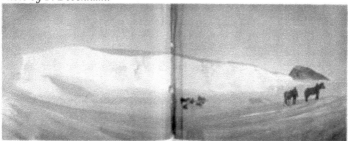

BERG IN SOUTH BAY.
Photo by F. Debenham.

From the Glacier Tongue they still pushed north, and on the 24th, just before the fog descended upon them, they got a view along the stretch of coast to the north. So far the journey had been more pleasant than Scott had anticipated, but two days after they had turned back a heavy blizzard descended upon them, and although an attempt was made to continue marching, they were soon compelled to camp. After being held up completely on the 27th they started again on the following day in a very frost-biting wind. From time to time they were obliged to halt so that their frozen features could be brought round, Simpson suffering more than the rest of the party; and with drift coming on again they were weather-bound in their tent during the early part of the afternoon. At 3 P.M., however, the drift ceased, and they started off once more in a wind as biting as ever. Then Scott saw an ominous yellow fuzzy appearance on the southern ridges of Erebus, and knew that another snowstorm was approaching; but hoping that this storm would miss them, he kept on until Inaccessible Island was suddenly blotted out. Thereupon a rush was made for a camp site, but the blizzard swept upon Page 317 them, and in the driving snow they found it utterly impossible to set up their inner tent, and could only just manage to set up the outer one. A few hours later the weather again cleared, and as they were more or less snowed up, they decided to push for Cape Evans in spite of the wind. 'We arrived in at 1.15 A.M., pretty well done. The wind never let up for an instant; the temperature remained about -16°, and the 21 statute miles which we marched in the day must be remembered amongst the most strenuous in my memory.... The objects of our little journey were satisfactorily accomplished, but the greatest source of pleasure to me is to realize that I have such men as Bowers and P.O. Evans for the Southern journey. I do not think that harder men or better sledge travelers ever took the trail. Bowers is a little wonder. I realize all that he must have done for the C. Crozier Party in their far severer experience.'

Late as the hour was when the travelers appeared at Cape Evans, everyone was soon up and telling Scott what had happened during his absence. E. Evans, Gran and Forde had reached Corner Camp and found that it showed up well, and consequently all anxiety as to the chance of finding One Ton Camp was removed. Forde, however, had got his hand so badly frost-bitten that he was bound to be incapacitated for some time, and this meant that the arrangements that had already been made for a geological party to go to the west would in all probability have to be altered.

Page 318 All of the ponies were reported to be very well, but Scott's joy at this news vanished on October 3 when Atkinson reported that Jehu was still too weak to pull a load. Oates also was having great trouble with Christopher, who did not appreciate being harnessed and generally bolted at the mere sight of a sledge. 'He is going,' Scott, in referring to this most intractable pony, wrote, 'to be a trial, but he is a good strong pony and should do yeoman service. Day is increasingly hopeful about the motors. He is an ingenious person and has been turning up new rollers out of a baulk of oak supplied by Meares, and with Simpson's small motor as a lathe. The motors may save the situation.'

On the 5th Scott made a thorough inspection of Jehu and became convinced that he was useless. Chinaman and James Pigg were also no towers of strength. 'But the other seven are in fine form and must bear the brunt of the work somehow. If we suffer more loss we shall depend on the motor, and then!... well, one must face the bad as well as the good.'

During the following day, after Christopher had given his usual exhibition at the start, Wilson, Oates, Cherry-Garrard and Crean went over to Hut Point with their ponies; and late on the same afternoon the Hut Point telephone bell suddenly rang. The line had been laid by Meares some time before, but hitherto there had been no communication. Now, however, Scott heard a voice and found himself able to hold long Page 319 conversations with Meares and Oates. 'Not a very wonderful fact, perhaps, but it seems wonderful in this primitive land to be talking to one's fellow beings 15 miles away. Oates told me that the ponies had arrived in fine order, Christopher a little done, but carrying the heaviest load. If we can keep the telephone going it will be a great boon, especially to Meares later in the season.'

After service on Sunday morning Scott, continuing his course of photography under the excellent instruction of Ponting, went out to the Pressure Ridge, and thoroughly enjoyed himself. Worries, however, were in store, for later in the afternoon, by which time Scott had returned to the hut, a telephone message from Nelson's igloo brought the news that Clissold had fallen from a berg and hurt his back. In three minutes Bowers had organized a sledge party, and fortunately Atkinson was on the spot and able to join it. Scott himself at once hurried over the land, and found Ponting very distressed and Clissold practically insensible.

It appeared that Clissold had been acting as Ponting's 'model,' and that they had been climbing about the berg to get pictures. Ponting had lent his crampons and ice-axe to Clissold, but the latter nevertheless missed his footing after one of the 'poses,' and after sliding over a rounded surface of ice for some twelve feet, had dropped six feet on to a sharp angle in the wall of the berg. Unquestionably Clissold was badly hurt, and although neither Wilson nor Atkinson Page 320 thought that anything very serious had happened, there was no doubt that the accident would prevent him from taking the place allotted to him in the motor sledge party. Thus there were two men on the sick list, and after all the trouble that had been taken to get things ready for the summer journeys Scott naturally felt that these misfortunes were more than a little deplorable. On the other hand, all was going well with the ponies, though Christopher's dislike to sledges seemed rather to increase than to lessen. When once he was in the sledge he had always behaved himself until October 13, when he gave a really great exhibition of perversity. On this occasion a dog frightened him, and having twisted the rope from Oates' hands he bolted for all he was worth. When, however, he had obtained his freedom, he set about most systematically to get rid of his load. At first he gave sudden twists and thus dislodged two bales of hay, but when he caught sight of some other sledges a better idea at once struck him, and he dashed straight at them with the evident intention of getting free of his load at one fell swoop. Two or three times he ran for Bowers and then he turned his attention to Keohane, his plan being to charge from a short distance with teeth bared and heels flying. By this time his antics had brought a small group to the scene, and presently Oates, Bowers, Nelson and Atkinson managed to clamber on to the sledge. Undaunted, however, by this human burden, he tried to treat it as he had the bales of hay, and he did manage to Page 321 dispose of Atkinson with violence; but the others dug their heels into the snow and succeeded at last in tiring him out. 'I am exceedingly glad,' Scott says, 'there are not other ponies like him. These capers promise trouble, but I think a little soft snow on the Barrier may effectually cure them.'

On Tuesday, October 17, the motors were to be taken on to the floe, but the attempt was not successful, the axle casing (aluminum) splitting soon after the trial had begun. Once again Scott expressed his conviction that the motors would be of little assistance, though at the same time retaining his opinion that with more experience they might have been of the greatest service. 'The trouble is that if they fail, no one will ever believe this.'

The days at Cape Evans were now rapidly drawing to a close. Plans and preparations occupied the attention of everyone, and Scott's time was almost wholly occupied in preparing details and in writing. 'Words,' he said in a letter dated October, 1912, 'must always fail me when I talk of Bill Wilson. I believe he really is the finest character I ever met—the closer one gets to him the more there is to admire. Every quality is so solid and dependable; cannot you imagine how that counts down here? Whatever the matter, one knows Bill will be sound, shrewdly practical, intensely loyal, and quite unselfish. Add to this a wider knowledge of persons and things than is at first guessable, a quiet vein of humour and really consummate tact, and you have some idea of his values. I think Page 322 he is the most popular member of the party, and that is saying much.

'Bowers is all and more than I ever expected of him. He is a positive treasure, absolutely trustworthy, and prodigiously energetic. He is about the hardest man amongst us, and that is saying a good deal—nothing seems to hurt his tough little body, and certainly no hardship daunts his spirit. I shall have a hundred little tales to tell you of his indefatigable zeal, his unselfishness, and his inextinguishable good humor. He surprises always, for his intelligence is of quite a high order and his memory for details most exceptional. You can imagine him, as he is, an indispensable assistant to me in every detail concerning the management and organization of our sledding work and a delightful companion on the march.

'One of the greatest successes is Wright. He is very hard working, very thorough, and absolutely ready for anything. Like Bowers he has taken to sledding like a duck to water, and although he hasn't had such severe testing, I believe he would stand it pretty nearly as well. Nothing ever seems to worry him, and I can't imagine he ever complained of anything in his life.

'The Soldier is very popular with all—a delightfully humorous cheery old pessimist—striving with the ponies night and day and bringing woeful accounts of their small ailments into the hut.

'Atkinson will go far, I think; he has a positive passion for helping others. It is extraordinary what pains he will take to do a kind thing unobtrusively.

Page 323 'Cherry-Garrard is clean grit right through; one has caught glimpses of him in tight places.

'Day has the sweetest temper and all sorts of other nice characteristics. Moreover he has a very remarkable mechanical ability, and I believe is about as good a man as could have been selected for his job.

'I don't think I will give such long descriptions of the others, though most of them deserve equally high praise. Taken all round, they are a perfectly excellent lot.

'The men are equally fine. P.O. Evans looks after our sledges and sledge equipment with a care of management and a fertility of resource which is truly astonishing. On "trek" he is just as sound and hard as ever, and has an inexhaustible store of anecdote. Crean is perfectly happy, ready to do anything and go anywhere, the harder the work, the better. Evans and Crean are great friends. Lashly is his old self in every respect, hard working to the limit, quiet, abstemious and determined. You see altogether I have a good set of people with me, and it will go hard if we don't achieve something.

'The study of individual characters is a pleasant pastime in such a mixed community of thoroughly nice people... men of the most diverse upbringing and experience are really pals with one another, and the subjects which would be delicate ground of discussion between acquaintances are just those which are most freely used for jest.... I have never seen a temper lost in these discussions. So as I sit here I am Page 324 very satisfied with these things. I think that it would have been difficult to better the organization of the party — every man has his work and is especially adapted for it; there is no gap and no overlap. It is all that I desired, and the same might well be said of the men selected to do the work....

'I don't know what to think of Amundsen's chances. If he gets to the Pole, it must be before we do, as he is bound to travel fast with dogs and pretty certain to start early. On this account I decided at a very early date to act exactly as I should have done had he not existed. Any attempt to race must have wrecked my plan, besides which it doesn't appear the sort of thing one is out for.

'Possibly you will have heard something before this reaches you. Oh! and there are all sorts of possibilities. In any case you can rely on my not doing or saying anything foolish—only I'm afraid you must be prepared for the chance of finding our venture much belittled.

'After all, it is the work that counts, not the applause that follows.'

The transport of emergency stores to Hut Point was delayed by the weather until October 22, but on that day the most important stores—which were for the returning depôts and to provision the *Discovery* hut in case the *Terra Nova* did not arrive—were taken by Wilson, Bowers and P.O. Evans and their ponies to Glacier Tongue. Accidents, however, were still to happen, for while Bowers was holding the ponies so Page 325 that Wilson and Evans could unload them, Victor got the hook, which fastened the harness to the trace of another pony, into his nose. At that moment a lot of drift swept upon them, and immediately all three of the ponies stampeded, Snatcher making for home and Nobby for the Western Mountains, while Victor, with Bowers still hanging on to him, just bolted here, there and everywhere. Wilson and P.O. Evans at once started after their ponies, and the former by means of a biscuit as a bait managed to catch Nobby west of Tent Island, but Snatcher arrived, with a single trace and dangling sledge, by himself at Cape Evans. Half an hour after Wilson had returned Bowers brought in Victor, who had a gash in his nose, and was very much distressed. 'I don't know,' Scott says, 'how Bowers managed to hang on to the frightened animal; I don't believe anyone else would have done so.... Two lessons arise. First, however quiet the animals appear they must not be left by their drivers—no chance must be taken; secondly, the hooks on the hames of the harness must be altered in shape. I suppose such incidents as this were to be expected, one cannot have ponies very fresh and vigorous and expect them to behave like lambs, but I shall be glad when we are off and can know more definitely what resources we can count on.'

In addition to this mishap, a football match had been got up two days before, in which Debenham hurt his knee. Thus the Western

Party was again delayed, the only compensation for this accident Page 326 being that Forde's hand would have a better chance of recovery while Debenham's knee was given time to improve.

On the following day the motors seemed to be ready for the start, but various little defects again cropped up, and not until the next morning did they get away. At first there were frequent stops, but on the whole satisfactory progress was made, and as even a small measure of success would, in Scott's opinion, be enough to show their ability to revolutionize Polar transport, and so help to prevent the cruelty that is a necessary condition of animal transport, he was intensely anxious about the result of this trial trip. As this subject was one which was of the most supreme interest to Scott, it is well to quote the opinion of an expert upon these motor sledges. 'It has been said that Captain Scott's sledges failed, and without further consideration the design has been totally condemned, but this is quite unfair to the design; and it must be admitted by everyone who has had anything to do with the sledges, and has any sort of knowledge of mechanical principles, that it was *the engine* that failed, not the transmission gear at all. The engine used was a four-cylinder air-cooled one, and most unexpectedly in the cold climate of the Antarctic it over-heated and broke various parts, beyond possibility of repair under the severe conditions. The reason of the breakdown therefore applies to any and every form of motor sledge, and should a satisfactory engine be available for one form of sledge, it is equally Page 327 available for another. It therefore shows a lack of fair judgment to condemn the Scott sledge for a breakdown, which would have applied equally to every form of motor transport which could have been designed.'

Unquestionably the motor sledges did enough to make this unique experiment infinitely worth trying, and on Friday, October 27, Scott declared that the machines had already vindicated themselves. Even the seamen, who had been very doubtful about them, were profoundly impressed, and P.O. Evans admitted that, 'if them things can go on like that, I reckon you wouldn't want nothing else.'

As the days passed by, it was obvious that the Western Party — which consisted of Taylor, Debenham, Gran and Forde — would have to leave after the Southern Party. 'It is trying that they should be wasting the season in this way. All things considered, I shall be glad to get away and put our fortune to the test,' Scott wrote on the 28th. And two days later he added: 'Meares and Ponting are just off to Hut Point. Atkinson and Keohane will probably leave in an hour or so as arranged, and if the weather holds, we shall all get off tomorrow. So here end the entries in this diary with the first chapter of our History. The future is in the lap of the gods; I can think of nothing left undone to deserve success.'

Page 328 CHAPTER VII

THE SOUTHERN JOURNEY BEGINS

Free men freely work.
Whoever fears God, fears to sit at ease.
E. B. BROWNING.

'As we are just off on our Southern journey, with a good chance of missing the ship on our return,' Scott wrote before leaving Cape Evans on November 1, 'I send a word of greeting. We are going away with high hopes of success and for the moment everything smiles, but where risks must be taken the result must be dependent on chance to some extent.

'I am lucky in having with me the right men for the work; we have lived most happily together through the long winter, and now all are fit, ready, and eager to go forward, and, apart from the result, the work itself is extraordinarily fascinating.'

The march to Hut Point was begun in detachments, Scott leading Snippets and soon finding himself where he wished to be, at the tail of the team. After all Jehu had refuted predictions by being allowed to start, although so little confidence was still Page 329 placed in him that on the previous day he had been sent at his own pace to Hut Point. Chinaman was also 'an unknown quantity,' but the chief trouble on the opening march was caused by the persistently active Christopher, who kicked and bucked the whole way.

On this march, which reminded Scott of a regatta or a somewhat disorganized fleet with ships of very unequal speed, a good knowledge was obtained of the various paces of the ponies, and the plan of advance was, after some trouble, arranged. The start was to be made from Hut Point in three parties—the very slow ponies, the medium paced, and the fliers. The motors with Day, E. R. Evans, Lashly and Hooper (who had taken Clissold's place) were already on the way, and the dogs, with Meares and Demetri, were to follow the main detachments.

Night marching was decided upon, and after supper good-bye was said to Hut Point, and Atkinson, Wright and Keohane led off with Jehu, Chinaman and Jimmy Pigg. Two hours later Scott, Wilson and Cherry-Garrard left, their ponies marching steadily and well together on the sea-ice. At Safety Camp they found Atkinson, who reported that Chinaman and Jehu were already tired. Soon after Scott's party had camped for lunch, Ponting arrived with Demetri and a small dog team, and the cinematograph was up in time to catch the flying rearguard, which came along in fine form with Snatcher, 'a wonderful little beast,' leading. Christopher had given his customary exhibition when Page 330 harnessed, and although the Barrier surface had sobered him a little it was not thought advisable for him to stop, and so the party fled through in the wake of the advance guard, and were christened 'the through train.'

'After lunch,' Scott, writing from Camp 1 on November 3, says, 'we packed up and marched steadily on as before. I don't like these midnight lunches, but for man the march that follows is pleasant when, as today, the wind falls and the sun steadily increases its heat. The two parties in front of us camped five miles beyond Safety Camp, and we reached their camp some half or three-quarters of an hour later. All the ponies are tethered in good order, but most of them are tired—Chinaman and Jehu *very tired*.... A petrol tin is near the camp and a note stating that the motors passed at 9 P.M. 28th, going strong—they have from four to five days' lead and should surely keep it.'

On the next march they started in what for some time was to be the settled order—Atkinson's contingent at 8 P.M., Scott's at 10, Oates' an hour and a quarter later. Just after starting they picked up cheerful notices saying that all was well with both the motors, and Day wrote, 'Hope to meet in 80° 30' Lat.' But very soon afterwards a depôt of petrol was found; and worse was to follow, as some four miles out from Camp 1 they came across a tin bearing the sad announcement, 'Big end Day's motor No. 2 cylinder broken.' Half a mile beyond was the motor, its tracking sledges, &c.; and notes from E. Evans and Day to Page 331 tell the tale of the mishap. The only spare big end had been used for Lashly's machine, and as it would have taken a long time to strip Day's engine so that it could run on three cylinders, they had decided to abandon it and push on with the other alone. 'So the dream of help from the machines is at an end! The track of the remaining motor goes steadily forward, but now, of course, I shall expect to see it every hour of the march.'

On the second and third marches the ponies did fairly well on a bad surface, but as yet they had only light loads to pull; and not until they were tested was Scott prepared to express much confidence in them. At Camp 3 he found a troubled note from E. Evans saying that their maximum speed was about 7 miles a day. 'They have taken on nine bags of forage, but there are three black dots to the south which we can only imagine are the deserted motor with its loaded sledges. The men have gone on as a supporting party, as directed. It is a disappointment. I had hoped better of the machines once they got away on the Barrier Surface.'

From this camp they started in the usual order, having arranged that full loads should be carried if the black dots proved to be the motors, and very soon they found their fears confirmed. Another note from E. Evans stated a recurrence of the old trouble. The big end of No. 1 cylinder had cracked, otherwise the machine was in good order. 'Evidently,' Scott wrote in reference to this misfortune, 'the engines are not Page 332 fitted for working in this climate, a fact that should be certainly capable of correction. One thing is proved: the system of propulsion is altogether satisfactory. The motor party has proceeded as a man-hauling party as arranged.'

As they came to Camp 4 a blizzard threatened, and snow walls were at once built for the ponies. The last march, however, was more than a compensation for bad weather. Jehu and Chinaman with loads of over 450 lbs. had stepped out well and had finished as fit as they had started, while the better ponies had made nothing of their loads, Scott's Snippets having pulled over 700 lbs., sledge included. 'We are all much cheered by this performance. It shows a hardening up of ponies which have been well trained; even Oates is pleased!'

The blizzard only just gave them time to get everything done in the camp before it arrived. The ponies, however, in their new rugs and with sheltering walls as high as themselves could scarcely feel the wind, and as this protection was a direct result of experience gained in the previous year, Scott was glad to feel that some good had been obtained from that disastrous journey. But when the snow began to fall the ponies as usual suffered, because it was impossible to devise any means of keeping them comfortable in thick and driving snow. 'We men are snug and comfortable enough, but it is very evil to lie here and know that the weather is steadily sapping the strength of the beasts on which so Page 333 much depends. It requires much philosophy to be cheerful on such occasions.' In the midst of the drift during the forenoon of the 7th Meares and Demetri with the dogs arrived, and camped about a quarter of a mile away. In catching the main party up so soon Scott considered that Meares had played too much for safety, but at the same time it was encouraging to know that the dogs would pull the loads assigned to them, and that they could face such terrific winds.

The threatening weather continued until late on Tuesday night, and the question of starting was left open for a long time, several of the party thinking it unwise to march. At last, however, the decision was made to go, and the advance guard got away soon after midnight. Then, to Scott's surprise and delight, he discovered that his fears about the ponies were needless. Both Jehu and Chinaman took skittish little runs when their rugs were removed, and Chinaman even betrayed a not altogether irresistible desire to buck. In fact the only pony that gave any trouble was Christopher, and this not from any fatigue but from excessive spirit. Most of the ponies halted now and again to get a mouthful of snow, but Christopher had still to be sent through with a non-stop run, for his tricks and devices were as innumerable as ever. Oates had to cling like grim death to his bridle until the first freshness had worn off, and this was a long rather than a light task, as even after ten miles he was prepared to misbehave himself if he got the smallest chance.

Page 334 A few hundred yards from Camp 5 Bowers picked up a bale of forage and loaded it on his sledge, bringing the weight to nearly 800 lbs. Victor, however, went on as though nothing had happened, and although the surface was for the time wonderfully good, and it still remained a question how the ponies would get on under harder conditions, Scott admitted that so far the outlook was very encouraging. The cairns built in the previous year showed up very distinctly and were being picked up with the greatest ease, and this also was an additional cause for satisfaction because with pony walls, camp sites and cairns, the track on the homeward march seemed as if it must be easy to follow. Writing at Camp 5, Scott says, 'Everyone is as fit as can be. It was wonderfully warm as we camped this morning at 11 o'clock; the wind has dropped completely and the sun shines gloriously. Men and ponies revel in such weather. One devoutly hopes for a good spell of it as we recede from the windy Northern region. The dogs came up soon after we had camped, traveling easily.'

On the next march they remained faithful to their program of advancing a little over ten geographical miles nightly. But during the last two miles of this stage all of the ponies were together. 'It looked like a meet of the hounds, and Jehu ran away!!' was Cherry-Garrard's account of this scene in his diary. But in Scott's opinion it was clearly not advantageous to march in one detachment, because the slow advance-guard ponies were forced out of their pace by joining Page 335 with the others, while the fast rearguard had their speed reduced. This, however, was a great day for Jehu, whose attempt to bolt, though scarcely amounting to more than a sprawling canter, was freely acknowledged to be a creditable performance for a pony who at the start had been thought incapable of doing a single march.

The weather now began to change rapidly for the worse, and in consequence the pleasure of marching as rapidly vanished. In arriving at Camp 7 they had to struggle at first against a strong head wind, and afterwards in a snowstorm. Wright, who was leading, found it so impossible to see where he was going that he decided to camp some two miles short of the usual ten, but the ponies continued to do well and this was a compensation for the curtailed distance.

A worse surface was in store for them when they started from Camp 7, in fact Scott and Wilson described it as one of the worst they had ever seen. The snow that had fallen in the day remained soft, and added to this they had entered upon an area of soft crust between a few scattered hard sastrugi. In pits between these the snow lay in sandy heaps, making altogether the most difficult conditions for the ponies. Nevertheless the stronger ponies continued to pull excellently, and even the poor old crocks succeeded in covering 9-1/2 miles. 'Such a surface makes one anxious in spite of the rapidity with which changes take place. I expected these marches to be a little difficult, but not near so bad as to-day's.... In spite of the surface, the dogs ran up from the camp before last, Page 336 over 20 miles, in the night. They are working splendidly.'

The surface was still bad and the weather horrid on the following day, but 5 miles out the advance party came straight and true upon the last year's Bluff depôt. Here Scott found a note, from which he learned the cheering news that E. Evans and his party must be the best part of five days ahead. On the other hand, Atkinson had a very gloomy report to make of Chinaman, who could, he thought, only last a few more miles. Oates, however, much more optimistic than usual, considered that Chinaman would last for several days; and during another horrid march to Camp 10 all the ponies did well, Jehu especially distinguishing himself.

'We shall be,' Scott wrote from this camp on Monday, November 13, 'in a better position to know how we stand when we get to One Ton Camp, now only 17 or 18 miles, but I am anxious about these beasts—very anxious, they are not the ponies they ought to have been, and if they pull through well, all the thanks will be due to Oates. I trust the weather and surface conditions will improve; both are rank bad at present.' The next stage took them within 7 or 8 miles of One Ton Camp, and with a slightly improved surface and some sun the spirits of the party revived. But, although the ponies were working splendidly, it was painful work for them to struggle on through the snow, and Christopher's antics when harnessed were already a thing of the past—a fact which Page 337 would have been totally unregretted had it not been evidence that his strength was also beginning to diminish.

One Ton Camp was found without any difficulty, and having pushed on to Camp 12 it was decided to give the animals a day's rest there, and afterwards to go forward at the rate of 13 geographical miles (15 statute miles) a day. 'Oates thinks the ponies will get through, but that they have lost condition quicker than he expected. Considering his usually pessimistic attitude this must be thought a hopeful view. Personally I am much more hopeful. I think that a good many of the beasts are actually in better form than when they started, and that there is no need to be alarmed about the remainder, always excepting the weak ones which we have always regarded with doubt. Well, we must wait and see how things go.'

Another note from E. Evans was found at One Ton Camp, stating that his party had taken on four boxes of biscuits, and would wait for the main detachment at Lat. 80° 30'. The minimum thermometer left there in the previous year showed -73°, which was rather less than Scott had expected.

After the day's rest the loads were re-organized, the stronger ponies taking on about 580 lbs., while the others had rather over 400 lbs. as their burden; and refreshed by their holiday all of them marched into the next camp without any signs of exhaustion. By this time frost-bites were frequent, both Oates and P.O. Evans being victims, while Meares, when told Page 338 that his nose was 'gone,' remarked that he was tired of it and that it would thaw out by and by!

Hopes and fears concerning the ponies naturally alternated on such a journey, and the latter predominated when Scott wrote on November 18 from Camp 14. 'The ponies are not pulling well. The surface is, if anything, a little worse than yesterday, but I should think about the sort of thing we shall have to expect henceforward.... It's touch and go whether we scrape up to the Glacier; meanwhile we get along somehow.'

During the next two marches, however, the ponies, in spite of rather bad surfaces, did wonderfully well, and both Jehu and Chinaman began to be regarded with real admiration, Jehu being re-christened 'The Barrier Wonder' and Chinaman 'The Thunderbolt.' Again Scott began to take a hopeful view of getting through, unless the surfaces became infinitely worse.

While on the way to Camp 17 Scott's detachment found E. Evans and his party in Lat. 80° 32', and heard that they had been waiting for six days, which they had spent in building a tremendous cairn. All of them looked very fit, but they were also very hungry — an informing fact, as it proved conclusively that a ration which was ample for the needs of men leading ponies, was nothing like enough for those who were doing hard pulling work. Thus the provision that Scott had made for summit work received a full justification, though even with the rations that were Page 339 to be taken he had no doubt that hunger would attack the party.

After some discussion it was decided to take Evans' motor party on in advance for three days, and then that Day and Hooper should return.

Good, steady progress was made on the next two marches, and at Camp 19 they were within 150 geographical miles of the Glacier. 'But it is still rather touch and go. If one or more ponies were to go rapidly down hill we might be in queer street.'

Then at Camp 20 came the end of the gallant Jehu. 'We did the usual march very easily over a fairly good surface, the ponies now quite steady and regular. Since the junction with the Motor Party the procedure has been for the man-hauling people to go forward just ahead of the crocks, the other party following two or three hours later. To-day we closed less than usual, so the crocks must have been going very well. However, the fiat had already gone forth, and this morning (November 24) after the march poor old Jehu was led back on the track and shot. After our doubts as to his reaching Hut Point, it is wonderful to think that he has actually got eight marches beyond our last year limit, and could have gone more. However, towards the end he was pulling very little, and on the whole it is merciful to have ended his life. Chinaman seems to improve and will certainly last a good many days yet. I feel we ought to get through now. Day and Hooper leave us to-night.'

Page 340 Referring to Jehu in his diary Cherry-Garrard re-marked how much Scott felt 'this kind of thing,' and how cut up Atkinson was at the loss of his pony.

After Day and Hooper had turned back the party was re-arranged and started together. The man-haulers, Atkinson, E. Evans and

Lashly, went ahead with their gear on the 10-foot sledge, then came Wright with Chinaman and Keohane with James Pigg, the rest following close behind them. But although the two crocks had not been given their usual start, they stuck to their work so gallantly that at the finish they were less than a quarter of a mile behind.

At Camp 22, in Lat. 81° 35' the Middle Barrier Depôt was made, and as they did not leave until 3 A.M. they were gradually getting back to day-marching. The next stage, however, of their journey was struggled through under the greatest difficulties. At the start the surface was bad, and the man-haulers in front made such heavy weather of it that they were repeatedly overtaken. This threw the ponies out and prolonged the march so much that six hours were spent in reaching the lunch camp. But bad as the first part of the march had been, the latter part was even worse. The advance party started on ski, but had the greatest difficulty in keeping a course; and presently snow began to fall heavily with a rise of temperature, and the ski became hopelessly clogged. At this time the surface was terribly hard for pulling, and the man-haulers also found it impossible to steer. The march of 13 miles was eventually completed, but under Page 341 the most harassing circumstances and with very tired animals.

'Our forage supply necessitates that we should plug on the 13 (geographical) miles daily under all conditions, so that we can only hope for better things. It is several days since we had a glimpse of land, which makes conditions especially gloomy. A tired animal makes a tired man, I find, and none of us are very bright now after the day's march.'

No improvement in the weather was in store for them on the following day (November 28), for snowstorms swept over them, the driving snow not only preventing them from seeing anything, but also hitting them stingingly in their faces. Chinaman was shot on this night, but in struggling on until he was within go miles of the Glacier he had done more than was ever expected of him; and with only four bags of forage left the end of all the ponies was very near at hand.

During the march to Camp 25, Lat. 82° 21', 'the most unexpected and trying summer blizzard yet experienced in this region' ceased, and prospects improved in every respect. While they were marching the land showed up hazily, and at times looked remarkably close to them. 'Land shows up almost ahead now,' Scott wrote on the 29th, 'and our pony goal is less than 70 miles away. The ponies are tired, but I believe all have five days' work left in them, and some a great deal more.... It follows that the dogs can be employed, rested and fed well on the homeward track. We could really get through now with their Page 342 help and without much delay, yet every consideration makes it desirable to save the men from heavy hauling as long as possible. So I devoutly hope the 70 miles will come in the present order of things.'

Snippets and Nobby by this time walked by themselves, but both of them kept a continually cunning eye upon their driver, and if he stopped they at once followed his example. It was, Scott admitted, a relief no longer to have to lead his animal, for fond of Snippets as he was, the vagaries of the animal were annoying when on the march. Thursday, November 30, brought most pleasant weather with it, but the surface was so bad that all of the ponies, with the exception of Nobby, began to show obvious signs of failure. A recurrence of 'sinking crusts' (areas which gave way with a report) was encountered, and the ponies very often sank nearly to their knees.

At Camp 27 Nobby was the only pony who did not show signs of extreme exhaustion, but forage was beginning to get so scarce that even Nobby had nearly reached the end of his life. On this night (December 1) Christopher was shot, and by no possibility could he be much regretted, for he had given nothing but trouble at the outset, and as soon as his spirits began to fail his strength had also disappeared. 'He has been a great disappointment,' Cherry-Garrard wrote, 'even James Pigg has survived him.'

A depôt, called the Southern Barrier Depôt, was left at Camp 27, so that no extra weight was added to the loads of the other ponies. 'Three more marches Page 343 ought to carry us through. With the seven crocks and the dog teams we *must* get through, I think. The men alone ought not to have heavy loads on the surface, which is extremely trying.'

On the morning of the 1st Nobby had been tried in snow-shoes, and for about four miles had traveled splendidly upon them, but then the shoes racked and had to be taken off; nevertheless, in Scott's opinion, there was no doubt that snow-shoes were the thing for ponies, and that if his ponies had been able to use them from the beginning their condition would have been very different from what it was.

From Camp 28, Lat. 83°, Scott wrote, 'Started under very bad weather conditions. The stratus spreading over from the S.E. last night meant mischief, and all day we marched in falling snow with a horrible light.... The ponies were sinking deep in a wretched surface. I suggested to Oates that he should have a roving commission to watch the animals, but he much preferred to lead one, so I handed over Snippets very willingly and went on ski myself.' This he found such easy work, that he had time to take several photographs of the ponies as they plunged through the snow. But in the afternoon they found a better surface, and Scott, who was leading, had to travel at a very steady pace to keep the lead.

When this march had finished they had reached the 83rd parallel, and were 'practically safe to get through.' But with forage becoming scarcer and scarcer poor Bictor — to the great sorrow of Bowers, Page 344 who was very fond of him — had to be shot. Six ponies remained, and as the dogs were doing splendidly, the chances of the party reaching the Glacier were excellent if only they could see their way to it. Wild in his diary of Shackleton's journey remarked on December 15 that it was the first day for a month on which he could not record splendid weather. With Scott's party, however, a fine day had been the exception rather than the rule, and the journey had been one almost perpetual fight against bad weather and bad surfaces.

The tent parties at this date were made up of (1) Scott, Wilson, Oates and Keohane; (2) Bowers, P.O. Evans, Cherry-Garrard and Crean; (3) man-haulers, E. R. Evans, Atkinson, Wright and Lashly. 'We have all taken to horse meat and are so well fed that hunger isn't thought of.'

At 2.30 A.M. on Sunday, December 3, Scott, intending to get away at 5, roused all hands, but their bad luck in the way of weather once more delayed the start. At first there seemed to be just a chance that they might be able to march, but while they were having breakfast a full gale blew up from the south; 'the strongest wind I have known here in summer.' In a very short time the pony wall was blown down, the sledges were buried, and huge drifts had collected. In heavy drift everyone turned out to make up the pony walls, but the flanking wall was blown down three times before the job was completed. About mid-day the weather improved and soon afterwards the clouds broke and the land appeared; and when they got away at Page 345 2 P.M., the sun was shining brightly. But this pleasant state of affairs was only destined to last for one short hour; after that snow again began to fall, and marching conditions became supremely horrible. The wind increased from the S.E., changed to S. W., where for a time it remained, and then suddenly shifted to W.N.W., and afterwards to N.N.W., from which direction it continued to blow with falling and drifting snow. But in spite of these rapid and absolutely bewildering changes of conditions they managed to get 11-1/2 miles south and to Camp 29 at 7 P.M. The man-haulers, however, camped after six miles, for they found it impossible to steer a course. 'We (Scott and Bowers) steered with compass, the drifting snow across our ski, and occasional glimpses of south-easterly sastrugi under them, till the sun showed dimly for the last hour or so. The whole weather conditions seem thoroughly disturbed, and if they continue so when we are on the Glacier, we shall be very awkwardly placed. It is really time the luck turned in our favor—we have had all too little of it. Every mile seems to have been hardly won under such conditions. The ponies did splendidly and the forage is lasting a little better than expected... we should have no difficulty whatever as regards transport if only the weather was kind.' On the following day the weather was still in a bad mood, for no sooner had they got on their gear for the start than a thick blizzard from the S.S.E. arrived. Quickly everyone started to build fresh walls for the ponies, an uninviting task enough in a regular white flowing blizzard, but one which added Page 346 greatly to the comfort of the animals, who looked sleepy and bored, but not at all cold. Just as the walls were finished the man-haulers came into camp, having been assisted in their course by the tracks that the other parties had made.

Fortunately the wind moderated in the forenoon and by 2 P.M. they were off and in six hours had placed 13 more miles to their credit. During this march the land was quite clearly in view, and several uncharted glaciers of large dimensions were seen. The mountains were rounded in outline, very massive, with excrescent peaks, one or two of the peaks on the foothills standing bare and almost perpendicular. Ahead of them was the ice-rounded, boulder-strewn Mount Hope and the gateway to the Glacier. 'We should reach it easily enough on to-morrow's march if we can compass 12 miles.... We have only lost 5 or 6 miles on these two wretched days, but the disturbed condition of the weather makes me anxious with regard to the Glacier, where more than anywhere we shall need fine days. One has a horrid feeling that this is a real bad season. However, sufficient for the day is the evil thereof. We are practically through with the first stage of our journey. Looking from the last Camp (29) towards the S.S.E., where the farthest land can be seen, it seemed more than probable that a very high latitude could be reached on the Barrier, and if Amundsen journeying that way has a stroke of luck, he may well find his summit journey reduced to 100 miles or so. In any case it is a fascinating direction for next year's work, if only fresh transport arrives.'

Page 347 On this day, December 4, the ponies marched splendidly, crossing the deep snow in the undulations without any difficulty, and had food been plentiful enough there was no doubt that they could have gone on for many more miles. As it was 'gallant little Michael' had to be sacrificed when the march was over. 'He walked away,' Cherry-Garrard wrote, 'and rolled on the way down, not having done so when we got in. He died quite instantaneously. He was just like a naughty child all the way and pulled all out; he has been a good friend and has a good record, 83° 22' S. He was a bit done to-day, the blizzard had knocked him.'

By night the weather looked very uninviting, and they woke to find a raging, howling blizzard. Previously the winds that had so constantly bothered them had lacked that very fine powdery snow which is usually an especial feature of a blizzard, but on this occasion they got enough and to spare of it. Anyone who went into the open for a minute or two was covered from head to foot, and as the temperature was high the snow stuck where it fell. The heads, tails and legs of the ponies were covered with ice, and they had to stand deep in snow. The sledges were almost covered, and there were huge drifts about the tent. It was a scene on which no one wanted to look longer than he could help, and after they had rebuilt the pony walls they retreated sadly and soppingly into their bags. Even the small satisfaction of being able to see from one tent to another was denied them, and Scott, while asking what on earth such weather could mean at this Page 348 time of year, stated emphatically that no party could possibly travel against such a wind.

'Is there,' he asked, 'some widespread atmospheric disturbance which will be felt everywhere in this region as a bad season, or are we merely the victims of exceptional local conditions? If the latter, there is food for thought in picturing our small party struggling against adversity in one place whilst others go smilingly forward in sunshine. How great may be the element of luck! No foresight—no procedure—could have prepared us for this state of affairs. Had we been ten times as experienced or certain of our aim we should not have expected such rebuffs.'

Mt. Hope

LOOKING UP THE GATEWAY FROM PONY DEPÔT.
Photo by R. F. Scott.

Mt. Hope

LOOKING SOUTH FROM LOWER GLACIER DEPÔT.

The snowfall on this day (December 5) was quite the greatest that Scott remembered, the drifts about the tents being colossal. And to add to their misery and misfortune the temperature remained so high that the snow melted if it fell on anything except snow, with the result that tents, wind clothes, night boots, &c., were all wet through; while water, dripping from the tent poles and door, lay on the floor, soaked the sleeping-bags, and made the situation inconceivably miserable. In the midst of this slough, however, Keohane had the spirit to make up a rhyme, which is worth quoting mainly, if not solely, because of the conditions under which it was produced:

The snow is all melting and everything's afloat,
If this goes on much longer we shall have to turn the tent
    upside down and use it as a boat.

The next day Scott described as 'miserable, Page 349 utterly miserable. We have camped in the "Slough of Despond."' When within twelve miles of the Glacier it was indeed the most cruel fortune to be held up by such a raging tempest. The temperature at noon had risen to 33°, and everything was more soakingly wet than ever, if that was possible. The ponies, too, looked utterly desolate, and the snow climbed higher and higher about the walls, tents and sledges. At night signs of a break came, but hopes of marching again were dashed on the following morning, when the storm continued and the situation became most serious; after this day only one small feed remained for the ponies, so that they had either to march or to sacrifice all the animals. That, however, was not the most serious part, for with the help of the dogs they could without doubt have got on. But what troubled Scott most intensely was that they had on this morning (December 7) started on their summit rations, or, in other words, the food calculated to take them on from the Glacier depôt had been begun.

In the meantime the storm showed no signs of abatement, and its character was as unpleasant as ever. 'I can find no sign of an end, and all of us agree that it is utterly impossible to move. Resignation to this misfortune is the only attitude, but not an easy one to adopt. It seems undeserved where plans were well laid, and so nearly crowned with a first success.... The margin for bad weather was ample according to all experience, and this stormy December — our finest month — is a thing that the most cautious Page 350 organizer might not have been prepared to encounter.... There cannot be good cheer in the camp in such weather, but it is ready to break out again. In the brief spell of hope last night one heard laughter.'

Hour after hour passed with little or no improvement, and as every hour of inactivity was a real menace to the success of their plans, no one can wonder that they chafed over this most exasperating delay. Under ordinary circumstances it would have been melancholy enough to watch the mottled, wet, green walls of their tents and to hear the everlasting patter of the falling snow and the ceaseless rattle of the fluttering canvas, but when the prospect of failure of their cherished plan was added to the acute discomforts of the situation, it is scarcely possible to imagine how totally miserable they must have been both in body and mind. Nevertheless in the midst of these distressing conditions Scott managed to write, 'But yet, after all, one can go on striving, endeavoring to find a stimulation in the difficulties that arise.'

Friday morning, however, did not bring any cause for hope. The snow was still falling heavily, and they found themselves lying in pools of water that squelched whenever they moved. Under such circumstances it was a relief to get outside, shift the tents and dig out the sledges. All of the tents had been reduced to the smallest space by the gradual pressure of snow, the old sites being deep pits with hollowed, icy, wet centers. The re-setting of them at least made things more comfortable, and as the Page 351 wind dropped about mid-day and a few hours later the sky showed signs of breaking, hope once more revived; but soon afterwards snow was falling again, and the position was rapidly becoming absolutely desperate.

To test the surface the man-haulers tried to pull a load during the afternoon, and although it proved a tough job they managed to do it by pulling in ski. On foot the men sank to their knees, and an attempt to see what Nobby could do under such circumstances was anything but encouraging.

Writing in the evening Scott said, 'Wilson thinks the ponies finished, but Oates thinks they will get another march in spite of the surface, *if it comes to-morrow*. If it should not, we must kill the ponies to-morrow and get on as best we can with the men on ski and the dogs. But one wonders what the dogs can do on such a surface. I much fear they also will prove inadequate. Oh! for fine weather, if only to the Glacier.'

By 11 P.M. the wind had gone to the north, and the sky at last began really to break. The temperature also helped matters by falling to +26°, and in consequence the water nuisance began to abate; and at the prospect of action on the following morning cheerful sounds were once more heard in the camp. 'The poor ponies look wistfully for the food of which so very little remains, yet they are not hungry, as recent savings have resulted from food left in their nose-bags. They look wonderfully fit, all things Page 352 considered. Everything looks more hopeful to-night, but nothing can recall four lost days.' During the night Scott turned out two or three times to find the weather slowly improving, and at 8 o'clock on December 9 they started upon a most terrible march to Camp 31.

The tremendous snowfall had made the surface intolerably soft, and the half-fed animals sank deeper and deeper. None of them could be led for more than a few minutes, but if they were allowed to follow the poor beasts did fairly well. Soon, however, it began to seem as if no real headway could be made, and so the man-haulers were pressed into the service to try and improve matters.

Bowers and Cherry-Garrard went ahead with one 10-foot sledge and made a track—thus most painfully a mile or so was gained. Then when it seemed as if the limit had been reached P.O. Evans saved the situation by putting the last pair of snow-shoes upon Snatcher, who at once began to go on without much pressure, and was followed by the other ponies.

No halt was made for lunch, but after three or four laborious miles they found themselves engulfed in pressures which added to the difficulties of their march. Still, however, they struggled on, and by 8 P.M. they were within a mile of the slope ascending to the gap, which Shackleton called the Gateway. This gateway was a neck or saddle of drifted snow lying in a gap of the mountain rampart which flanked the last curve of the Glacier, and Scott had hoped to be through it at a much earlier date, as indeed he Page 353 would have been had not the prolonged storm delayed him.

By this time the ponies, one and all, were quite exhausted. 'They came on painfully slowly a few hundred yards at a time.... I was hauling ahead, a ridiculously light load, and yet finding the pulling heavy enough. We camped, and the ponies have been shot. Poor beasts! they have done wonderfully well considering the terrible circumstances under which they worked.'

On December 8 Wilson wrote in his journal, 'I have kept Nobby all my biscuits to-night as he has to try to do a march to-morrow, and then happily he will be shot and all of them, as their food is quite done.' And on the following day he added: 'Nobby had all my biscuits last night and this morning, and by the time we camped I was just ravenously hungry.... Thank God the horses are now all done with and we begin the heavy work ourselves.'

This Camp 31 received the name of Shambles Camp, and although the ponies had not, owing to the storm, reached the distance Scott had expected, yet he, and all who had taken part in that distressing march, were relieved to know that the sufferings of their plucky animals had at last come to an end.

CHAPTER VIII

ON THE BEARDMORE GLACIER

In thrilling region of thick ribbed ice
To be imprison'd in the viewless winds
And blown with restless violence round about.
—SHAKESPEARE.

On the death of the ponies at Camp 31 the party was reorganized, and for some days advanced in the following order:

Sledge 1. Scott, Wilson, Oates and P.O. Evans.

Sledge 2. E. Evans, Atkinson, Wright and Lashly.

Sledge 3. Bowers, Cherry-Garrard, Crean and Keohane; with
Meares and Demetri continuing to drive the dogs.

When leaving this Camp Scott was very doubtful whether the loads could be pulled over such an appalling surface, and that success attended their efforts was due mainly to the ski. The start was delayed by the readjustments that had to be made, but when they got away at noon, and with a 'one, two, three together' Scott's party began to pull their sledge, they were most agreeably surprised to find it running fairly easily Page 355 behind them. The first mile was gained in about half an hour, but then they began to rise, and soon afterwards with the slope becoming steeper and the surface getting worse they had to take off their ski. After this the pulling was extraordinarily exhausting, for they sank above their finnesko, and in some places nearly up to their knees.

The runners of the sledges became coated with a thin film of ice from which it was impossible to free them, and the sledges themselves sank in soft spots to the cross-bars. At 5 P.M. they reached the top of the slope, and after tea started on the down grade. On this they had to pull almost as vigorously as on the upward slope, but they could just manage to get along on ski.

Evans and his party, however, were unable to keep up the pace set by the leaders, and when they camped at 9.15 Scott heard some news that thoroughly alarmed him. 'It appears,' he wrote, 'that Atkinson says that Wright is getting played out, and Lashly is not so fit as he was owing to the heavy pulling since the blizzard. I have not felt satisfied about this party. The finish of the march to-day showed clearly that something was wrong.... True, the surface was awful and growing worse every moment. It is a very serious business if the men are going to crack up. As for myself, I never felt fitter and my party can easily hold its own. P.O. Evans, of course, is a tower of strength, but Oates and Wilson are doing splendidly also.'

Round the spot where Camp 32 had been pitched Page 356 the snow was appallingly deep and soft. 'Every step here one sinks to the knees, and the uneven surface is obviously insufficient to support the sledges.' A wind, however, had sprung up, and though under ordinary circumstances it would have been far from welcome, on this occasion it was a blessing because it hardened the snow; and a good surface was all the more necessary because, after half another march, Meares and Demetri were to return with the dogs, and in consequence 200 lbs. would have to be added to each sledge-load.

Before starting from Camp 32 they built a depôt (the Lower Glacier depôt), made it very conspicuous, and left a good deal of gear there. Then at the very beginning of their march they got into big pressure, and must have passed over several crevasses. After four hours, however, they were clear of the pressure, and then they said good-bye to Meares and Demetri, who took back a note from Scott to say that 'Things are not so rosy as they might be, but we keep our spirits up and say the luck must turn. This is only to tell you that I find I can keep up with the rest as well as of old.'

The start after lunch was anxious work, for the question whether they could pull their loads had to be answered. Scott's party went away first, and, to their joy, found that they could make fairly good headway. Every now and again the sledge sank in a soft patch which brought them up, and then they got sideways to the sledge and hauled it out. 'We learned,' Scott wrote on December 11, at Camp 33, Page 357 'to treat such occasions with patience.... The great thing is to keep the sledge moving, and for an hour or more there were dozens of critical moments when it all but stopped, and not a few when it brought up altogether. The latter were very trying and tiring. But suddenly the surface grew more uniform and we more accustomed to the game, for after a long stop to let the other parties come up, I started at 6 and ran on till 7, pulling easily without a halt at the rate of about 2 miles an hour. I was very jubilant; all difficulties seemed to be vanishing; but unfortunately our history was not repeated with the other parties. Bowers came up half an hour after us. They also had done well at the last, and I'm pretty sure they will get on all right. Keohane is the only weak spot, and he only, I think, because temporarily blind. But Evans' party didn't get up till 10. They started quite well, but got into difficulties, did just the wrong thing by straining again and again, and so, tiring themselves, went from bad to worse. Their ski shoes, too, are out of trim.'

During the morning of the 12th they steered for the Commonwealth Range until they reached about the middle of the glacier and then the course was altered for the 'Cloudmaker,' and afterwards still further to the west. In consequence they got a much better view of the southern side of the main glacier than Shackleton's party had obtained, and a number of peaks not noticed previously were observed. On the first stage of this march Scott's party was bogged time after time, Page 358 and do what they could their sledge dragged like a huge lump of lead. Evans' team had been sent off in advance and kept well ahead until lunch-time. Then, when Scott admits being 'pretty well cooked,' the secret of their trouble was disclosed in a thin film with some hard knots of ice on the runners of the sledge; these impediments having been removed they went ahead without a hitch, and in a mile or two resumed their leading position. As they advanced it became more and more evident that, with the whole of the lower valley filled with snow from the storm, they would have been bogged had they been without ski. 'On foot one sinks to the knees, and if pulling on a sledge to half-way between knee and thigh.'

Scott's hope was that they would get better conditions as they rose, but on the next march the surface became worse instead of better, the sledges simply plunging into the soft places and stopping dead. So slow in fact was the progress they made, that on his sledge Scott decided at lunch to try the 10-foot runners under the crossbars, for the sledge was sinking so deeply that the cross-pieces were on the surface and acting as brakes. Three hours were spent in securing the runners, and then Scott's party started and promptly saw what difficulties the other teams were having.

In spite of the most desperate efforts to get along, Bowers and his men were so constantly bogged that Scott soon passed them. But the toil was awful, because the snow with the sun shining and a high temperature Page 359 had become very wet and sticky, and again and again the sledge got one runner on harder snow than the other, canted on its side, and refused to move. At the top of the rise Evans' party was reduced to relay work, and shortly afterwards Bowers was compelled to adopt the same plan. 'We,' Scott says, 'got our whole load through till 7 P.M., camping time, but only with repeated halts and labour which was altogether too strenuous. The other parties certainly cannot get a full load along on the surface, and I much doubt if we could continue to do so, but we must try again to-morrow. I suppose we have advanced a bare four miles to-day and the aspect of things is very little changed. Our height is now about 1,500 feet.'

On the following morning Evans' party got off first from Camp 35, and after stiff hauling for an hour or so found the work much easier than on the previous day. Bowers' contingent followed without getting along so well, and so Scott, whose party were having no difficulty with their load, exchanged sledges with them, and a satisfactory morning's march was followed by still better work in the afternoon, eleven or twelve miles being gained. 'I think the soft snow trouble is at an end, and I could wish nothing better than a continuance of the present surface. Towards the end of the march we were pulling our load with the greatest ease. It is splendid to be getting along and to find some adequate return for the work we are putting into the business.'

At Camp 37, on Friday, December 15, they had Page 360 reached a height of about 2,500 feet, after a march on which the surface steadily improved and the snow covering over the blue ice became thinner and thinner. During the afternoon they found that at last they could start their sledges by giving one good heave, and so, for the first time, they were at liberty to stop when they liked without the fear of horrible jerks before they could again set the sledge going. Patches of ice and hard névé were beginning to show through in places, and had not the day's work been interrupted by a snowstorm at 5 P.M. their march would have been a really good one, but, as it was, eleven more miles had to be put to their credit. The weather looked, however, very threatening as they turned in for the night, and Scott expressed a fervent hope that they were not going to be afflicted by snowstorms as they approached the worst part of the glacier.

As was to be expected after the storm they found the surface difficult when the march was resumed, but by sticking to their work for over ten hours — 'the limit of time to be squeezed into one day' — they covered eleven miles, and altered greatly the aspect of the glacier. Beginning the march as usual on ski, they had to take them off in the afternoon because they struck such a peculiarly difficult surface that the sledges were constantly being brought up. Then on foot they made better progress, though no advance could be made without the most strenuous labour. The brittle crust would hold for a pace or two, and then let them down with a bump, while now and again a leg went down a crack in the hard ice underneath. So Page 361 far, since arriving among the disturbances, which increased rapidly towards the end of the march, they had not encountered any very alarming crevasses, though a large quantity of small ones could be seen.

At the end of the march to Camp 39, Scott was able to write, 'For once we can say "Sufficient for the day is the good thereof." Our luck may be on the turn — I think we deserve it. In spite of the hard work everyone is very fit and very cheerful, feeling well fed and eager for more toil. Eyes are much better except poor Wilson's; he has caught a very bad attack. Remembering his trouble on our last Southern journey, I fear he is in for a very bad time.... I'm inclined to think that the summit trouble will be mostly due to the chill falling on sunburned skins. Even now one feels the cold strike directly one stops. We get fearfully thirsty and chip up ice on the march, as well as drinking a great deal of water on halting. Our fuel only just does it, but that is all we want, and we have a bit in hand for the summit.... We have worn our crampons all day (December 17) and are delighted with them. P.O. Evans, the inventor of both crampons and ski shoes, is greatly pleased, and certainly we owe him much.'

On the 19th, although snow fell on and off during the whole day and crevasses were frequent, a splendid march of 14 miles was accomplished. The sledges ran fairly well if only the haulers could keep their feet, but on the rippled ice which they were crossing it was impossible to get anything like a firm foothold. Still, however, they stuck most splendidly to their Page 362 task, and on the following day even a better march was made to Camp 41.

Starting on a good surface they soon came to a number of criss-cross cracks, into two of which Scott fell and badly bruised his knee and thigh. Then they reached an admirably smooth ice surface over which they traveled at an excellent pace. A long hour was spent over the halt for lunch, during which angles, photographs and sketches were taken, and continuing to make progress in the second part of the day's march they finished up with a gain of 17 miles. 'It has not been a strain except perhaps for me with my wounds received early in the day. The wind has kept us cool on the march, which has in consequence been very much pleasanter.... Days like this put heart in one.'

On Wednesday, December 20, however, the good marches of the previous two days were put entirely into the shade by one of nearly 23 miles, during which they rose 800 feet. Pulling the sledges in crampons was not at all difficult on the hard snow and on hard ice with patches of snow. At night they camped in Lat. 84° 59' 6", and then Scott had to perform a task that he most cordially disliked. 'I have just told off the people to return to-morrow night: Atkinson, Wright, Cherry-Garrard and Keohane. All are disappointed—poor Wright rather bitterly, I fear. I dreaded this necessity of choosing—nothing could be more heartrending. I calculated our program to start from 85° 10' with twelve units of food[1] and Page 363 eight men. We ought to be in this position to-morrow night, less one day's food. After all our harassing trouble one cannot but be satisfied with such a prospect.'

[Footnote 1: A unit of food means a week's supplies for four men.]

The next stage of the journey, though accomplished without accident, was too exciting to be altogether pleasant, for crevasses were frequent and falls not at all uncommon. And at mid-day, while they were in the worst of places, a fog rolled up and kept them in their tents for nearly three hours.

During this enforced delay, Scott wrote a letter which was taken back by the returning party.

'December 21, 1911, Lat. 85° S. We are struggling on, considering all things, against odds. The weather is a constant anxiety, otherwise arrangements are working exactly as planned.

'For your ear also I am exceedingly fit and can go with the best of them.

'It is a pity the luck doesn't come our way, because every detail of equipment is right... but all will be well if we can get through to the Pole.

'I write this sitting in our tent waiting for the fog to clear, an exasperating position as we are in the worst crevassed region. Teddy Evans and Atkinson were down to the length of their harness this morning, and we have all been half-way down. As first man I get first chance, and it's decidedly exciting not knowing which step will give way. Still all this is interesting enough if one could only go on.

'Since writing the above I made a dash for it; got out of the valley out of the fog and away from Page 364 crevasses. So here we are practically on the summit and up to date in the provision line. We ought to get through.'

After the fog had cleared off they soon got out of the worst crevasses, and on to a snow slope that led past Mount Darwin. The pull up the slope was long and stiff, but by holding on until 7.30 P.M. they got off a good march and found a satisfactory place for their depôt. Fortunately the weather was both calm and bright, and all the various sorting arrangements that had to be made before the returning party left them were carried out under most favorable conditions. 'For me,' Scott says, 'it is an immense relief to have the indefatigable little Bowers to see to all detail arrangements of this sort,' and on the following day he added, 'we said an affecting farewell to the returning party, who have taken things very well, dear good fellows as they are.'

Then the reorganized parties (Scott, Wilson, Oates and P.O. Evans; Bowers, E. R. Evans, Crean and Lashly) started off with their heavy loads, and any fears they had about their ability to pull them were soon removed.

'It was a sad job saying good-bye,' Cherry-Garrard wrote in his diary, 'and I know some eyes were a bit dim. It was thick and snowing when we started after making the depôt, and the last we saw of them as we swung the sledge north, was a black dot just disappearing over the next ridge, and a big white pressure wave ahead of them.'

Page 365 Then the returning party set off on their homeward march, and arrived at Cape Evans on January 28, 1912, after being away for three months.

Repairs to the sledgemeter delayed the advancing party for some time during their first march under the new conditions, but they managed to cover twelve miles, and, with the loads becoming lighter every day, Scott hoped to march longer hours and to make the requisite progress. Steering, however, south-west on the next morning they soon found themselves among such bad crevasses and pressure, that they were compelled to haul out to the north, and then to the west. One comfort was that all the time they were rising. 'It is rather trying having to march so far to the west, but if we keep rising we must come to the end of the disturbance some time.' During the second part of this march great changes of fortune awaited them. At first they started west up a slope, and on the top another pressure appeared on the left, but less lofty and more snow-covered than that which had troubled them in the morning. There was temptation to try this, but Scott resisted it and turned west up yet another slope, on the top of which they reached a most extraordinary surface. Narrow crevasses, that were quite invisible, ran in all directions. All of these crevasses were covered with a thin crust of hardened névé which had not a sign of a crack in it. One after another, and sometimes two at a time, they all fell in; and though they were getting fairly accustomed to unexpected falls through being unable to mark the run of Page 366 the surface appearances of cracks, or where such cracks were covered with soft snow, they had never expected to find a hardened crust formed over a crack, and such a surface was as puzzling as it was dangerous and trouble-some.

For about ten minutes or so, while they were near these narrow crevasses, they came on to snow which had a hard crust and loose crystals below it, and each step was like breaking through a glass-house. And then, quite suddenly, the hard surface gave place to regular sastrugi, and their horizon leveled in every direction. At 6 P.M., when they reached Camp 45 (height about 7,750 feet), 17 miles stood to their credit and Scott was feeling 'very cheerful about eve-rything.' 'My determination,' he said, 'to keep mounting irrespective of course is fully justified, and I shall be indeed surprised if we have any further difficulties with crevasses or steep slopes. To me for the first time our goal seems really in sight.'

On the following day (Christmas Eve) they did not find a single crevasse, but high pressure ridges were still to be seen, and Scott confessed that he should be glad to lose sight of such disturbances. Christmas Day, however, brought more trouble from crevasses — 'very hard, smooth névé between high ridges at the edge of crevass-es, and therefore very difficult to get foothold to pull the sledges.' To remedy matters they got out their ski sticks, but this did not prevent several of them from going half-down; while Lashly, disap-pearing completely, had to be pulled out by Page 367 means of the Alpine rope. 'Lashly says the crevasse was 50 feet deep and 8 feet across, in form U, showing that the word "unfathomable" can rarely be applied. Lashly is 44 to-day and as hard as nails. His fall has not even disturbed his equanimity.'

When, however, they had reached the top of the crevasse ridge a better surface was found, and their Christmas lunch — at which they had such luxuries as chocolate and raisins — was all the more enjoy-able because 8 miles or so had already been gained.

In the middle of the afternoon they got a fine view of the land, but more trouble was caused by crevasses, until towards the end of their march they got free of them and on to a slight decline down which they progressed at a swinging pace. Then they camped and prepared for their great Christmas meal. 'I must,' Scott says, 'write a word of our supper last night. We had four courses. The first, pem-mican, full whack, with slices of horse meat flavored with onion and curry powder, and thickened with biscuit; then an arrowroot, cocoa and biscuit hoosh sweetened; then a plum-pudding; then cocoa with raisins, and finally a dessert of caramels and ginger. After the feast it was difficult to move. Wilson and I couldn't finish our share of plum-pudding. We have all slept splendidly and feel thoroughly warm — such is the effect of full feeding.'

The advance, possibly owing to the 'tightener' on Christmas night, was a little slow on the following morning, but nevertheless 15 miles were covered Page 368 in the day and the 86th parallel was reached. Crevasses still appeared, and though they avoided them on this march, they were not so lucky during the next stage to Camp 49.

In fact Wednesday, December 27, was unfortunate owing to several reasons. To begin with, Bowers broke the only hypsometer thermometer, and so they were left with nothing to check their two aneroids. Then during the first part of the march they got among sastrugi which jerked the sledges about, and so tired out the second team that they had great difficulty in keeping up. And, finally, they found more crevasses and disturbances during the afternoon. For an hour the work was as painful as it could be, because they tumbled into the crevasses and got the most painful jerks. 'Steering the party,' Scott wrote at Camp 49, 'is no light task. One cannot allow one's thoughts to wander as others do, and when, as this afternoon, one gets amongst disturbances, I find it very worrying and tiring. I do trust we shall have no more of them. We have not lost sight of the sun since we came on the summit; we should get an extraordinary record of sunshine. It is monotonous work this; the sledgemeter and theodolite govern the situation.'

During the next morning the second sledge made such 'heavy weather' that Scott changed places with E. R. Evans. That, however, did not improve matters much, for Scott soon found that the second team had Page 369 not the same swing as his own team, so he changed Lashly for P.O. Evans, and then they seemed to get on better. At lunch-time they discussed the difficulties that the second party was having, and several reasons for them were put forward. One was that the team was stale, another that all the trouble was due to bad stepping and want of swing, and yet another was that the first's party's sledge pulled much more easily than the second party's.

On the chance that this last suggestion was correct, Scott and his original team took the second party's sledge in the afternoon, and soon found that it was a terrible drag to get it along in soft snow, whereas the second party found no difficulty in pulling the sledge that had been given to them. 'So the sledge is the cause of the trouble, and taking it out, I found that all is due to want of care. The runners ran excellently, but the structure has been distorted by bad strapping, bad loading, &c. The party are not done, and I have told them plainly that they must wrestle with the trouble and get it right for themselves.'

Friday evening found them at Camp 51, and at a height of about 9,000 feet, But they had encountered a very bad surface, on which the strain of pulling was terrific. The hardest work occurred on two rises, because the loose snow had been blown over the rises and had rested on the north-facing slopes, and these heaps were responsible for the worst of their troubles. However, there was one satisfactory result of the Page 370 march, for now that the second party had seen to the loading of their sledge they had ceased to lag.

But the next stage was so exhausting that Scott's fears for the conditions of the second party again arose. Writing from Camp 52, on December 30, he says: 'To-morrow I'm going to march half a day, make a depôt and build the 10-foot sledges. The second party is certainly tiring; it remains to be seen how they will manage with the smaller sledge and lighter load. The surface is certainly much worse than it was 50 miles back. (T. -10°.) We have caught up Shackleton's dates. Everything would be cheerful if I could persuade myself that the second party were quite fit to go forward.'

Camp was pitched after the morning's march on December 31, and the process of building up the 10-foot sledges was at once begun by P.O. Evans and Crean. 'It is a very remarkable piece of work. Certainly P.O. Evans is the most invaluable asset to our party. To build a sledge under these conditions is a fact for special record.'

MAN HAULING CAMP, 87TH PARALLEL.
Photo by Lieut. H. R. Bowers.

Half a day was lost while the sledges were made, but this they hoped to make up for by advancing at much greater speed. A depôt, called 'Three Degree Depôt,' consisting of a week's provision for both units, was made at this camp, and on New Year's morning, with lighter loads, Evans' party led the advance on foot, while Scott's team followed on ski. With a stick of chocolate to celebrate the New Year, and with only 170 miles between them and the Pole, prospects Page 371 seemed to be getting brighter on New Year's night, and on the next evening at Camp 55 Scott decided that E. R. Evans, Lashly and Crean should go back after one more march.

Writing from Camp 56 he says, 'They are disappointed, but take it well. Bowers is to come into our tent, and we proceed as a five-man unit to-morrow. We have 5-1/2 units of food—practically over a month's allowance for five people—it ought to see us through.... Very anxious to see how we shall manage tomorrow; if we can march well with the full load we shall be practically safe, I take it.'

By the returning party Scott sent back a letter, dated January 3, in which he wrote, 'Lat. 87° 32".' A last note from a hopeful position. I think it's going to be all right. We have a fine party going forward and arrangements are all going well.'

On the next morning the returning men followed a little way until Scott was certain that his team could get along, and then farewells were said. In referring to this parting with E. Evans, Crean and Lashly, Scott wrote, 'I was glad to find their sledge is a mere nothing to them, and thus, no doubt, they will make a quick journey back,' and under average conditions they should easily have fulfilled anticipations. But a blizzard held them up for three days before they reached the head of the glacier, and by the time they reached the foot of it E. Evans had developed symptoms of scurvy. At One Ton Camp he was unable to stand without the support of his ski sticks, and Page 372 although, with the help of his companions, he struggled on for 53 more miles in four days, he could go no farther. Rejecting his suggestion that he should be left alone while they pressed on for help, Crean and Lashly pulled him on the sledge with a devotion matching that of their captain years before, when he and Wilson had brought Shackleton, ill and helpless, safely to the *Discovery*.

After four days of this pulling they reached Corner Camp, and then there was such a heavy snowfall that the sledge could not travel. In this crisis Crean set out to tramp alone to Hut Point, 34 miles away, while Lashly stayed to nurse E. Evans, and most certainly was the means of keeping him alive until help came. After a remarkable march of 18 hours Crean reached Hut Point, and as soon as possible Atkinson and Demetri started off with both dog teams to relieve Evans and Lashly. Some delay was caused by persistent bad weather, but on February 22 Evans was got back to the *Discovery* hut, where he was unremittingly tended by Atkinson; and subsequently he was sent by sledge to the *Terra Nova*. So ended the tale of the last supporting party, though, as a sequel, it is good to record that in reward for their gallant conduct both Lashly and Crean received the Albert Medal.

THE SOUTH POLE

> The Silence was deep with a breath like sleep
> As our sledge runners slid on the snow,
> And the fate-full fall of our fur-clad feet
> Struck mute like a silent blow
> On a questioning 'Hush?' as the settling crust
> Shrank shivering over the floe.
> And the sledge in its track sent a whisper back
> Which was lost in a white fog-bow.
>
> And this was the thought that the Silence wrought,
> As it scorched and froze us through,
> For the secrets hidden are all forbidden
> Till God means man to know.
> We might be the men God meant should know
> The heart of the Barrier snow,
> In the heat of the sun, and the glow,
> And the glare from the glistening floe,
> As it scorched and froze us through and through
> With the bite of the drifting snow.

(These verses, called 'The Barrier Silence,' were written by Wilson for the *South Polar Times*. Characteristically, he sent them in typewritten, lest the editor should recognize his hand and judge them on personal rather than literary grounds. Many of their readers confess that they felt in these lines Wilson's own premonition of the event. The version given is the final form, as it appeared in the *South Polar Times*.)

The ages of the five men when they continued the journey to the Pole were: Scott 43, Wilson 39, P.O. Evans 37, Oates 32, Bowers 28.

Page 374 After the departure of the last supporting party Scott was naturally anxious to get off a good day's march, and he was not disappointed. At first the sledge on which, thanks to P.O. Evans, everything was most neatly stowed away, went easily. But during the afternoon they had to do some heavy pulling on a surface covered with loose sandy snow. Nevertheless they covered some 15 miles before they camped, and so smoothly did everything seem to be going that Scott began to wonder what was in store for them. 'One can scarcely believe that obstacles will not present themselves to make our task more difficult. Perhaps the surface will be the element to trouble us.'

And on the following day his supposition began to prove correct, for a light wind from the N.N.W. brought detached cloud and a constant fall of ice crystals, and in consequence the surface was as bad as it could be. The sastrugi seemed to increase as they advanced, and late in the afternoon they encountered a very rough surface with evidences of hard southerly wind. Luckily the sledge showed no signs of capsizing, but the strain of trying to keep up a rate of a little over a mile and a quarter an hour was very great. However, they were cheered by the thought, when they reached Camp 58 (height 10,320 feet), that they were very close to the 88th parallel, and a little more than 120 miles from the Pole.

Another dreadful surface was their fate during the next march on Saturday, January 6. The sastrugi increased in height as they advanced, and presently Page 375 they found themselves in the midst of a sea of fishhook waves, well remembered from their Northern experience. And, to add to their trouble, each sastrugus was covered with a beard of sharp branching crystals. They took off their ski and pulled on foot, but both morning and afternoon the work of getting the sledge along was tremendous. Writing at Camp 59, Latitude 88° 7', Scott said, 'We think of leaving our ski here, mainly because of risk of breakage. Over the sastrugi it is all up and down hill, and the covering of ice crystals prevents the sledge from gliding even on the downgrade. The sastrugi, I fear, have come to stay, and we must be prepared for heavy marching, but in two days I hope to lighten loads with a depôt. We are south of Shackleton's last camp, so, I suppose, have made the most southerly camp.'

During the next day, January 7, they had good cause to think that the vicissitudes of their work were bewildering. On account of the sastrugi the ski were left at Camp 59, but they had only marched a mile from it when the sastrugi disappeared. 'I kept debating the ski question and at this point stopped, and after discussion we went back and fetched the ski; it cost us 1-1/2 hours nearly. Marching again, I found to my horror we could scarcely move the sledge on ski; the first hour was awful owing to the wretched coating of loose sandy snow.' Consequently this march was the shortest they had made on the summit, and there was no doubt that if things remained for long they were, it would be impossible to keep up the Page 376 strain of such strenuous pulling. Luckily, however, loads were to be lightened on the following day by a weight of about 100 lbs., and there was also hope of a better surface if only the crystal deposit would either harden up or disappear. Their food, too, was proving ample. 'What luck to have hit on such an excellent ration. We really are an excellently found party.' Indeed, apart from the strain of pulling, Scott's only anxiety on Sunday, January 7, was that Evans had a nasty cut on his hand.

They woke the next morning to find their first summit blizzard; but Scott was not in the least perturbed by this delay, because he thought that the rest would give Evans' hand a better chance of recovery, and he also felt that a day in their comfortable bags within their double-walled tent would do none of them any harm. But, both on account of lost time and food and the slow accumulation of ice, he did not want more than one day's delay.

'It is quite impossible,' he wrote during this time of waiting, 'to speak too highly of my companions. Each fulfils his office to the party; Wilson, first as doctor, ever on the lookout to alleviate the small pains and troubles incidental to the work; now as cook, quick, careful and dexterous, ever thinking of some fresh expedient to help the camp life; tough as steel on the traces, never wavering from start to finish.

'Evans, a giant worker with a really remarkable head-piece. It is only now I realize how much has been due to him. Our ski shoes and crampons have been Page 377 absolutely indispensable, and if the original ideas were not his, the details of manufacture and design and the good workmanship are his alone. He is responsible for every sledge, every sledge fitting, tents, sleeping-bags, harness, and when one cannot recall a single expression of dissatisfaction with anyone of these items, it shows what an invaluable assistant he has been. Now, besides superintending the putting up of the tent, he thinks out and arranges the packing of the sledge; it is extraordinary how neatly and handily everything is stowed, and how much study has been given to preserving the suppleness and good running qualities of the machine. On the Barrier, before the ponies were killed, he was ever roaming round, correcting faults of stowage.

'Little Bowers remains a marvel — he is thoroughly enjoying himself. I leave all the provision arrangement in his hands, and at all times he knows exactly how we stand, or how each returning party should fare. It has been a complicated business to redistribute stores at various stages of reorganization, but not one single mistake has been made. In addition to the stores, he keeps the most thorough and conscientious meteorological record, and to this he now adds the duty of observer and photographer. Nothing comes amiss to him, and no work is too hard. It is a difficulty to get him into the tent; he seems quite oblivious of the cold, and he lies coiled in his bag writing and working out sights long after the others are asleep.

'Of these three it is a matter for thought and Page 378 congratulation that each is specially suited for his own work, but would not be capable of doing that of the others as well as it is done. Each is invaluable. Oates had his invaluable period with the ponies; now he is a foot slogger and goes hard the whole time, does his share of camp work, and stands the hardships as well as any of us. I would not like to be without him either. So our five people are perhaps as happily selected as it is possible to imagine.'

Not until after lunch on the 9th were they able to break camp, the light being extremely bad when they marched, but the surface good. So that they might keep up the average length of their daily marches Scott wanted to leave a depôt, but as the blizzard tended to drift up their tracks, he was not altogether confident that to leave stores on such a great plain was a wise proceeding. However, after a terribly hard march on the following morning, they decided to leave a depôt at the lunch camp, and there they built a cairn and left one week's food with as many articles of clothing as they could possibly spare.

Then they went forward with eighteen days' food on a surface that was 'beyond words,' for it was covered with sandy snow, and, when the sun shone, even to move the sledge forward at the slowest pace was distressingly difficult. On that night from Camp 62, Scott wrote, 'Only 85 miles (geog.) from the Pole, but it's going to be a stiff pull *both ways* apparently; still we do make progress, which is something.... It is very difficult to imagine what is Page 379 happening to the weather.... The clouds don't seem to come from anywhere, form and disperse without visible reason.... The meteorological conditions seem to point to an area of variable light winds, and that plot will thicken as we advance.'

From the very beginning of the march on January 11 the pulling was heavy, but when the sun came out the surface became as bad as bad could be. All the time the sledge rasped and creaked, and the work of moving it onward was agonizing. At lunch-time they had managed to cover six miles but at fearful cost to themselves, and although when they camped for the night they were only about 74 miles from the Pole, Scott asked himself whether they could possibly keep up such a strain for seven more days. 'It takes it out of us like anything. None of us ever had such hard work before.... Our chance still holds good if we can put the work in, but it's a terribly trying time.'

For a few minutes during the next afternoon they experienced the almost forgotten delight of having the sledge following easily. The experience was very short but it was also very sweet, for Scott had begun to fear that their powers of pulling were rapidly weakening, and those few minutes showed him that they only wanted a good surface to get on as merrily as of old. At night they were within 63 miles of the Pole, and just longing for a better surface to help them on their way.

But whatever the condition of the surface, Bowers continued to do his work with characteristic Page 380 thoroughness and imperturbability; and after this appalling march he insisted, in spite of Scott's protest, on taking sights after they had camped — an all the more remarkable display of energy as he, being the only one of the party who pulled on foot, had spent an even more strenuous day than the others, who had been 'comparatively restful on ski.'

Again, on the next march, they had to pull with all their might to cover some 11 miles. 'It is wearisome work this tugging and straining to advance a light sledge. Still, we get along. I did manage to get my thoughts off the work for a time to-day, which is very restful.

We should be in a poor way without our ski, though Bowers manages to struggle through the soft snow without tiring his short legs.' Sunday night, January 14, found them at Camp 66 and less than 40 miles from the Pole. Steering was the great difficulty on this march, because a light southerly wind with very low drift often prevented Scott from seeing anything, and Bowers, in Scott's shadow, gave directions. By this time the feet of the whole party were beginning, mainly owing to the bad condition of their finnesko, to suffer from the cold. 'Oates seems to be feeling the cold and fatigue more than the rest of us, but we are all very fit. It is a critical time, but we ought to pull through.... Oh! for a few fine days! So close it seems and only the weather to balk us.'

Another terrible surface awaited them on the morrow, and they were all 'pretty well done' when Page 381 they camped for lunch. There they decided to leave their last depôt, but although their reduced load was now very light, Scott feared that the friction would not be greatly reduced. A pleasant surprise, however, was in store for him, as after lunch the sledge ran very lightly, and a capital march was made. 'It is wonderful,' he wrote on that night (January 15), 'to think that two long marches would land us at the Pole. We left our depôt to-day with nine days' provisions, so that it ought to be a certain thing now, and the only appalling possibility the sight of the Norwegian flag forestalling ours. Little Bowers continues his indefatigable efforts to get good sights, and it is wonderful how he works them up in his sleeping-bag in our congested tent. Only 27 miles from the Pole. We *ought* to do it now.'

The next morning's march took them 7-1/2 miles nearer and their noon sight showed them in Lat. 89° 42' S.; and feeling that the following day would see them at the Pole they started off after lunch in the best of spirits. Then, after advancing for an hour or so, Bowers' sharp eyes detected what he thought was a cairn, but although he was uneasy about it he argued that it must be a sastrugus.

'Half an hour later he detected a black speck ahead. Soon we knew that this could not be a natural snow feature. We marched on, found that it was a black flag tied to a sledge bearer; near by the remains of a camp; sledge tracks and ski tracks going and coming and the clear trace of dogs' paws—many dogs.

Page 382 This told us the whole story. The Norwegians have forestalled us and are first at the Pole. It is a terrible disappointment, and I am very sorry for my loyal companions. Many thoughts come and much discussion have we had. To-morrow we must march on to the Pole and then hasten home with all the speed we can compass. All the day-dreams must go; it will be a wearisome return. Certainly also the Norwegians found an easy way up.'

Very little sleep came to any of the party after the shock of this discovery, and when they started at 7.30 on the next morning (January 17) head winds with a temperature of -22° added to their depression of spirit. For some way they followed the Norwegian tracks, and in about three miles they passed two cairns. Then, as the tracks became increasingly drifted up and were obviously leading them too far to the west, they decided to make straight for the Pole according to their calculations. During the march they covered about 14 miles, and at night Scott wrote in his journal, 'The Pole. Yes, but under very different circumstances from those expected.'

That announcement tells its own story, and it would be impertinent to guess at the feelings of those intrepid travelers when they found themselves forestalled. Nevertheless they had achieved the purpose they had set themselves, and the fact that they could not claim the reward of priority makes not one jot of difference in estimating the honours that belong to them.

THE PARTY AT THE SOUTH POLE.
Photo by Lieut. H. R. Bowers.

Page 383 'Well,' Scott continued, 'it is something to have got here, and the wind may be our friend to-morrow.... Now for the run home and a desperate struggle. I wonder if we can do it.'

On the following morning after summing up all their observations, they came to the conclusion that they were one mile beyond the Pole and three miles to the right of it, in which direction, more or less, Bowers could see a tent or cairn. A march of two miles from their camp took them to the tent, in which they found a record of five Norwegians having been there:

'Roald Amundsen
 Olav Olavson Bjaaland
 Hilmer Hanssen
 Sverre H. Hassel
 Oscar Wisting.
    —16 *Dec.* 1911.

'The tent is fine—a small compact affair supported by a single bamboo. A note from Amundsen, which I keep, asks me to forward a letter to King Haakon!'

In the tent a medley of articles had been left: three half bags of reindeer containing a miscellaneous assortment of mitts and sleeping-socks, very various in description, a sextant, a Norwegian artificial horizon and a hypsometer without boiling-point thermometers, a sextant and hypsometer of English make. 'Left a note to say I had visited the tent with companions. Bowers photographing and Wilson sketching. Since lunch we have marched 6.2 miles S.S.E. by compass (i.e. northwards). Sights at lunch gave us 1/2 to 3/4 Page 384 of a mile from the Pole, so we call it the Pole Camp. (Temp. Lunch -21°.) We built a cairn, put up our poor slighted Union Jack, and photographed ourselves — mighty cold work all of it — less than 1/2 a mile south we saw stuck up an old underrunner of a sledge. This we commandeered as a yard for a floorcloth sail. I imagine it was intended to mark the exact spot of the Pole as near as the Norwegians could fix it. (Height 9,500.) A note attached talked of the tent as being 2 miles from the Pole. Wilson keeps the note. There is no doubt that our predecessors have made thoroughly sure of their mark and fully carried out their program. I think the Pole is about 9,500 feet in height; this is remarkable, considering that in Lat. 88° we were about 10,500.

'We carried the Union Jack about 3/4 of a mile north with us and left it on a piece of stick as near as we could fix it. I fancy the Norwegians arrived at the Pole on the 15th Dec. and left on the 17th, ahead of a date quoted by me in London as ideal, viz. Dec. 22.... Well, we have turned our back now on the goal of our ambition and must face our 800 miles of solid dragging — and good-bye to most of the day-dreams!'

Page 385 CHAPTER X

ON THE HOMEWARD JOURNEY

> It matters not how strait the gate,
> How charged with punishments the scroll;
> I am the master of my fate,
> I am the Captain of my soul. — HENLEY.

During the afternoon of Thursday, January 18, they left the Pole 7 miles behind them, and early in the march on the following morning picked up their outward tracks and a Norwegian cairn. These tracks they followed until they came to the black flag that had been the first means of telling them of the Norwegians' success. 'We have picked this flag up, using the staff for our sail, and are now camped about 1-1/2 miles further back on our tracks. So that is the last of the Norwegians for the present.'

In spite of a surface that was absolutely spoilt by crystals they marched 18-1/2 miles on the Friday, and also easily found the cairns that they had built; but until they reached Three Degree Depôt which was still 150 miles away, anxiety, Scott said, could not be laid to rest.

On the next day they reached their Southern Page 386 Depôt and picked up four days' food. With the wind behind them and with full sail they went along at a splendid rate in the afternoon, until they were pulled up by a surface on which drifting snow was lying in heaps; and then, with the snow clinging to the ski, pulling became terribly distressing. 'I shall be very glad when Bowers gets his ski,' Scott wrote at R. 3,[1] 'I'm afraid he must find these long marches very trying with short legs, but he is an undefeated little sportsman. I think Oates is feeling the cold and fatigue more than most of us. It is blowing pretty hard to-night, but with a good march we have earned one good hoosh and are very comfortable in the tent. It is everything now to keep up a good marching pace; I trust we shall be able to do so and catch the ship. Total march, 18-1/2 miles.'

[Footnote 1: A number preceded by R. marks the camps on the return journey.]

A stiff blizzard with thick snow awaited them on the Sunday morning, but the weather cleared after mid-day, and they struggled on for a few very weary hours. At night they had 6 days' food in hand and 45 miles between them and their next depôt, where they had left 7 days' food to take them on the go miles to the Three Degree Depôt. 'Once there we ought to be safe, but we ought to have a day or two in hand on arrival and may have difficulty with following the tracks. However, if we can get a rating sight for our watches to-morrow we should be independent of the tracks at a pinch.'

January 22 brought an added worry in the fact Page 387 that the ski boots were beginning to show signs of wear, but this was nothing compared with the anxiety Scott began to feel about Evans on the following day. 'There is no doubt that Evans is a good deal run down—his fingers are badly blistered and his nose is rather seriously congested with frequent frost-bites. He is very much annoyed with himself, which is not a good sign. I think Wilson, Bowers and I are as fit as possible under the circumstances. Oates gets cold feet.... We are only about 13 miles from our "Degree and half" Depôt and should get there tomorrow. The weather seems to be breaking up. Pray God we have something of a track to follow to the Three Degree Depôt—once we pick that up we ought to be right.'

Another blizzard attacked them at mid-day on the morrow, and so, though only seven miles from their depôt, they were obliged to camp, for it was impossible to see the tracks. With the prospect of bad weather and scant food on the tremendous summit journey in front of them, and with Oates and Evans suffering badly from frost-bites, Scott had to admit that the situation was going from bad to worse. But on the next afternoon, they managed to reach the Half Degree Depôt, and left with 9-1/2 days' provision to carry them the next 89 miles.

During Friday, January 26, they found their old tracks completely wiped out, but knowing that there were two cairns at four-mile intervals they were not anxious until they picked up the first far on their right, and afterwards Bowers caught a glimpse of the second which was far on their Page 388 left. 'There is not a sign of our tracks between these cairns, but the last, marking our night camp of the 6th, No. 59, is in the belt of hard sastrugi, and I was comforted to see signs of the track reappearing as we camped. I hope to goodness we can follow it to-morrow.'

Throughout the early part of the next day's march, however, these hopes were not realized. Scott and Wilson pulling in front on ski, the others being on foot, found it very difficult to follow the track, which constantly disappeared altogether and at the best could only just be seen.

On the outward journey, owing to the heavy mounds, they had been compelled to take a very zigzag course, and in consequence the difficulty of finding signs of it was greatly increased. But by hook or crook they succeeded in sticking to the old track, and during the last part of the march they discovered, to their joy and relief, that it was much easier to follow. Through this march they were helped on their way by a southerly breeze, and as the air was at last dry again their tents and equipment began to lose the icy state caused by the recent blizzards. On the other hand, they were beginning to feel that more food, especially at lunch, was becoming more and more necessary, and their sleeping-bags, although they managed to sleep well enough in them, were slowly but steadily getting wetter.

On Sunday night, at R. 11, they were only 43 miles Page 389 from their depôt with six days food in hand, after doing a good march of 16 miles. 'If this goes on and the weather holds we shall get our depôt without trouble. I shall indeed be glad to get it on the sledge. We are getting more hungry, there is no doubt. The lunch meal is beginning to seem inadequate. We are pretty thin, especially Evans, but none of us are feeling worked out. I doubt if we could drag heavy loads, but we can keep going with our light one. We talk of food a good deal more, and shall be glad to open out on it.

With the wind helping greatly and with no difficulty in finding the tracks, two splendid marches followed; but on the Tuesday their position had its serious as well as its bright side, for Wilson strained a tendon in his leg. 'It has,' Scott wrote, 'given pain all day and is swollen to-night. Of course, he is full of pluck over it, but I don't like the idea of such an accident here. To add to the trouble Evans has dislodged two finger-nails to-night; his hands are really bad, and to my surprise he shows signs of losing heart over it. He hasn't been cheerful since the accident.... We can get along with bad fingers, but it [will be] a mighty serious thing if Wilson's leg doesn't improve.'

Before lunch on Wednesday, January 31, they picked up the Three Degree Depôt, and were able slightly to increase their rations, though not until they reached the pony food depôt could they look for a 'real feed.' After lunch (January 31) the surface, owing to sandy crystals, was very bad, and with Wilson Page 390 walking by the sledge to rest his leg as much as possible, pulling was even more toilsome work than usual. During the afternoon they picked up Bowers' ski, which he had left on December 31. 'The last thing we have to find on the summit, thank Heaven! Now we have only to go north and so shall welcome strong winds.'

Pulling on throughout the next day they reached a lunch cairn, which had been made when they were only a week out from the Upper Glacier Depôt. With eight days' food in hand Scott hoped that they would easily reach it, for their increased food allowance was having a good effect upon all of them, and Wilson's leg was better. On the other hand, Evans was still a cause for considerable anxiety.

All went very well during their march to R. 16 on February 2 until Scott, trying to keep the track and his feet at the same time on a very slippery surface, came 'an awful purler' on his shoulder. 'It is horribly sore to-night and another sick person added to our tent — three out of five injured, and the most troublesome surfaces to come. We shall be lucky if we get through without serious injury.... The extra food is certainly helping us, but we are getting pretty hungry.... It is time we were off the summit — Pray God another four days will see us pretty well clear of it. Our bags are getting very wet and we ought to have more sleep.'

On leaving their sixteenth camp they were within 80 miles or so of the Upper Glacier Depôt under Mount Darwin, and after exasperating delays in searching for Page 391 tracks and cairns, they resolved to waste no more time, but to push due north just as fast as they could. Evans' fingers were still very bad, and there was little hope that he would be able for some time to help properly with the work, and on the following day an accident that entailed the most serious consequences happened.

'Just before lunch,' Scott wrote at R. 18, 'unexpectedly fell into crevasses, Evans and I together — a second fall for Evans,[1] and I camped. After lunch saw disturbance ahead.... We went on ski over hard shiny descending surface. Did very well, especially towards end of march, covering in all 18.1.... The party is not improving in condition, especially Evans, who is becoming rather dull and incapable. Thank the Lord we have good food at each meal, but we get hungrier in spite of it. Bowers is splendid, full of energy and bustle all the time.'

[Footnote 1: Wilson afterwards expressed an opinion that Evans injured his brain by one of these falls.]

On Monday morning a capital advance of over 10 miles was made, but in the afternoon difficulties again arose to harass them. Huge pressures and great street crevasses partly open barred their way, and so they had to steer more and more to the west on a very erratic course. Camping-time found them still in a very disturbed region, and although they were within 25 to 30 miles of their depôt there seemed to be no way through the disturbances that continued to block their path. On turning out to continue their march they went straight for Mount Darwin, but almost at once Page 392 found themselves among huge open chasms. To avoid these they turned northwards between two of them, with the result that they got into chaotic disturbance. Consequently they were compelled to retrace their steps for a mile or so, and then striking to the west they got among a confused sea of sastrugi, in the midst of which they camped for lunch. A little better fortune attended them in the afternoon, and at their twentieth camp Scott estimated that they were anything from 10 to 15 miles off the Upper Glacier Depôt. 'Food is low and weather uncertain,' he wrote, 'so that many hours of the day were anxious; but this evening (February 6), though we are not so far advanced as I expected, the outlook is much more promising. Evans is the chief anxiety now; his cuts and wounds suppurate, his nose looks very bad, and altogether he shows considerable signs of being played out. Things may mend for him on the Glacier, and his wounds get some respite under warmer conditions. I am indeed glad to think we shall so soon have done with plateau conditions. It took us 27 days to reach the Pole and 21 days back — in all 48 days — nearly 7 weeks in low temperature with almost incessant wind.'

February 7, which was to see the end of their summit journey, opened with a very tiresome march down slopes and over terraces covered with hard sastrugi. However, they made fairly good progress during the day, and between six and seven o'clock their depôt was sighted and soon afterwards they were camped close to it. 'Well,' Scott wrote at R. 21, Page 393 'we have come through our 7 weeks' ice camp journey and most of us are fit, but I think another week might have had a very bad effect on P.O. Evans, who is going steadily downhill.'

On the next morning they started late owing to various re-arrangements having to be made, and then steered for Mt. Darwin to get specimens. As Wilson was still unable to use his ski, Bowers went on and got several specimens of much the same type—a close-grained granite rock which weathers red; and as soon as Bowers had rejoined the party they skidded downhill fairly fast, Scott and Bowers (the leaders) being on ski, Wilson and Oates on foot along-side the sledge, while Evans was detached.

By lunch-time they were well down towards Mt. Buckley, and decided to steer for the moraine under the mountain. Having crossed some very irregular steep slopes with big crevasses, they slid down towards the rocks, and then they saw that the moraine was so interesting that, after an advance of some miles had brought escape from the wind, the decision was made to camp and spend the rest of the day in geologising.

'It has been extremely interesting. We found ourselves under per-pendicular cliffs of Beacon sandstone, weathering rapidly and car-rying veritable coal seams. From the last Wilson, with his sharp eyes, has picked several plant impressions, the last a piece of coal with beautifully traced leaves in layers, also some excellently pre-served impressions of thick stems, Page 394 showing cellular struc-ture. In one place we saw the cast of small waves in the sand. To-night Bill has got a specimen of limestone with archeo-cyathus—the trouble is one cannot imagine where the stone comes from; it is evidently rare, as few specimens occur in the moraine. There is a good deal of pure white quartz. Altogether we have had a most interesting afternoon, and the relief of being out of the wind and in a warmer temperature is inexpressible. I hope and trust we shall all buck up again now that the conditions are more favorable.... A lot could be written on the delight of setting foot on rock after 14 weeks of snow and ice, and nearly 7 out of sight of aught else. It is like going ashore after a sea voyage.'

On the following morning they kept along the edge of the mo-raine to the end of Mt. Buckley, and again stopping to geologise, Wilson had a great find of vegetable impression in a piece of lime-stone. The time spent in collecting these geological specimens from the Beardmore Glacier, and the labour endured in dragging the additional 35 lbs. to their last camp, were doubtless a heavy price to pay; but great as the cost was they were more than willing to pay it. The fossils contained in these specimens, often so inconspicuous that it is a wonder they were discovered by the collectors, proved to be the most valuable obtained by the expedition, and promise to solve completely the questions of the age and past history of this portion of the Antarctic continent. At night, after a difficult day among bad ice pressures, Scott almost apologizes for Page 395 being too tired to write any geological notes, and as the sledgemeter had been unshipped he could not tell the distance they had traversed. 'Very warm on march and we are all pretty tired.... Our food satisfies now, but we must march to keep on the full ration, and we want rest, yet we shall pull through all right, D. V. We are by no means worn out.'

On the night of Friday, February 10, they got some of the sleep that was so urgently needed, and in consequence there was a great change for the better in the appearance of everyone. Their progress, however, was delayed during the next afternoon by driving snow, which made steering impossible and compelled them to camp. 'We have two full days' food left,' Scott wrote on the same evening, 'and though our position is uncertain, we are certainly within two outward marches from the middle glacier depôt. However, if the weather doesn't clear by to-morrow, we must either march blindly on or reduce food.'

The conditions on Sunday morning were utterly wretched for the surface was bad and the light horrible, but they marched on until, with the light getting worse and worse, they suddenly found themselves in pressure. Then, unfortunately, they decided to steer east, and after struggling on for several hours found themselves in a regular trap. Having for a short time in the earlier part of the day got on to a good surface, they thought that all was going well and did not reduce their lunch rations. But half an hour after lunch they suddenly got into a terrible ice mess.

Page 396 For three hours they plunged forward on ski, first thinking that they were too much to the right, and then too much to the left; meanwhile the disturbance got worse and worse, and there were moments when Scott nearly despaired of finding a way out of

the awful turmoil in which they found themselves. At length, arguing that there must be a way out on the left, they plunged in that
direction, only to find that the surface was more icy and crevassed.

'We could not manage our ski and pulled on foot, falling into crevasses every minute — most luckily no bad accident. At length we
saw a smoother slope towards the land, pushed for it, but knew it
was a woefully long way from us. The turmoil changed in character,
irregular crevassed surface giving way to huge chasms, closely
packed and most difficult to cross. It was very heavy work, but we
had grown desperate. We won through at 10 P.M., and I write after
12 hours on the march. I *think* we are on or about the right track
now, but we are still a good number of miles from the depôt, so we
reduced rations to-night. We had three pemmican meals left and
decided to make them into four. To-morrow's lunch must serve for
two if we do not make big progress. It was a test of our endurance
on the march and our fitness with small supper. We have come
through well.'

On leaving R. 25, early on Monday morning, everything went
well in the forenoon and a good march was made over a fair surface. Two hours before lunch they were cheered by the sight of their
night Page 397 camp of December 18 (the day after they had made
their depôt), for this showed them that they were still on the right
track. In the afternoon, refreshed by tea, they started off confidently
expecting to reach their depôt, but by a most unfortunate chance
they kept too far to the left and arrived in a maze of crevasses and
fissures. Afterwards their course became very erratic, and finally, at
9 P.M., they landed in the worst place of all.

'After discussion we decided to camp, and here we are, after a
very short supper and one meal only remaining in the food bag; the
depôt doubtful in locality. We *must* get there to-morrow. Meanwhile we are cheerful with an effort.'

On that night, at Camp R. 26, Scott says that they all slept well in
spite of grave anxieties, his own being increased by his visits outside the tent, when he saw the sky closing over and snow beginning
to fall. At their ordinary hour for getting up the weather was so
thick that they had to remain in their sleeping-bags; but presently
the weather cleared enough for Scott dimly to see the land of the

Cloudmaker. Then they got up and after breakfasting off some tea and one biscuit, so that they might leave their scanty remaining meal for even greater emergencies, they started to march through an awful turmoil of broken ice. In about an hour, however, they hit upon an old moraine track where the surface was much smoother, though the fog that was still hanging over everything added to their difficulties.

Page 398 Presently Evans raised their hopes with a shout of depôt ahead, but it proved to be nothing but a shadow on the ice, and then Wilson suddenly saw the actual depôt flag. 'It was an immense relief, and we were soon in possession of our 3-1/2 days' food. The relief to all is inexpressible; needless to say, we camped and had a meal.'

Marching on in the afternoon Scott kept more to the left, and closed the mountain until they came to the stone moraines, where Wilson detached himself and made a collection, while the others advanced with the sledge. Writing that night (Tuesday, February 13) at 'Camp R. 27, beside Cloudmaker' Scott says, 'We camped late, abreast the lower end of the mountain, and had nearly our usual satisfying supper. Yesterday was the worst experience of the trip and gave a horrid feeling of insecurity. Now we are right, but we must march. In future food must be worked so that we do not run so short if the weather fails us. We mustn't get into a hole like this again.... Bowers has had a very bad attack of snow-blindness, and Wilson another almost as bad. Evans has no power to assist with camping work.'

A good march followed to Camp R. 28, and with nearly three days' food they were about 30 miles away from the Lower Glacier Depôt. On the other hand, Scott was becoming most gravely concerned about the condition of the party, and especially about Evans, who seemed to be going from bad to worse.

Page 399 And on the next evening, after a heavy march he wrote, 'We don't know our distance from the depôt, but imagine about 20 miles. We are pulling for food and not very strong evidently.... We have reduced food, also sleep; feeling rather done. Trust 1-1/2 days or 2 at most will see us at depôt.'

Friday's march brought them within 10 or 12 miles of their depôt, and with food enough to last them until the next night; but anxiety about Evans was growing more and more intense. 'Evans has nearly broken down in brain, we think. He is absolutely changed from his normal self-reliant self. This morning and this afternoon he stopped the march on some trivial excuse.... Memory should hold the events of a very troublesome march with more troubles ahead. Perhaps all will be well if we can get to our depôt to-morrow fairly early, but it is anxious work with the sick man.'

On the following morning (Saturday, February 17) Evans looked a little better after a good sleep, and declared, as he always did, that he was quite well; but half an hour after he had started in his place on the traces, he worked his ski shoes adrift and had to leave the sledge. At the time the surface was awful, the soft snow, which had recently fallen, clogging the ski and runners at every step, the sledge groaning, the sky overcast, and the land hazy. They stopped for about an hour, and then Evans came up again, but very slowly. Half an hour later he dropped out again on the same plea, and asked Bowers to lend Page 400 him a piece of string. Scott cautioned him to come on as quickly as he could, and he gave what seemed to be a cheerful answer. Then the others were compelled to push on, until abreast the Monument Rock they halted and, seeing Evans a long way behind, decided to camp for lunch.

At first there was no alarm, but when they looked out after lunch and saw him still afar off they were thoroughly frightened, and all four of them started back on ski. Scott was the first to meet the poor man, who was on his knees with hands uncovered and frost-bitten and a wild look in his eyes. When asked what was the matter, he replied slowly that he didn't know, but thought that he must have fainted.

They managed to get him on his feet, but after two or three steps he sank down again and showed every sign of complete collapse. Then Scott, Wilson and Bowers hastened back for the sledge, while Oates remained with him.

'When we returned he was practically unconscious, and when we got him into the tent quite comatose. He died quietly at 12.30 A.M.'

THE LAST MARCH

Men like a man who has shown himself a pleasant companion
through a week's walking tour. They worship the man who,
over thousands of miles, for hundreds of days, through renewed
difficulties and efforts, has brought them without friction,
arrogance or dishonour to the victory proposed, or to the higher
glory of unshaken defeat. — R. KIPLING.

After this terrible experience the rest of the party marched on later in the night, and arrived at their depôt; there they allowed themselves five hours' sleep and then marched to Shambles Camp, which they reached at 3 P.M. on Sunday, February 18. Plenty of horse meat awaited them, with the prospect of plenty to come if they could only keep up good marches. 'New life seems to come with greater food almost immediately, but I am anxious about the Barrier surfaces.'

A late start was made from Shambles Camp, because much work had to be done in shifting sledges[1] and fitting up the new one with a mast, &c., and in packing Page 402 horse meat and personal effects. Soon after noon, however, they got away, and found the surface every bit as bad as they expected. Moreover Scott's fears that there would not be much change during the next few days were most thoroughly justified. On the Monday afternoon they had to pullover a really terrible surface that resembled desert sand. And the same conditions awaited them on the following day, when, after four hours' plodding in the morning, they reached Desolation Camp. At this camp they had hoped to find more pony meat, but disappointment awaited them. 'Total mileage for day 7,' Scott wrote at R. 34, 'the ski tracks pretty plain and easily followed this afternoon.... Terribly slow progress, but we hope for better things as we clear the land.... Pray God we get better traveling as we are not so fit as we were, and the season is advancing apace.'

[Footnote 1: Sledges were left at the chief depôts to replace damaged ones.]

Again, on Wednesday, February 21, the surface was terrible, and once more Scott expressed a devout hope that as they drew away from the land the conditions might get better; and that this improvement should come and come soon was all the more necessary because they were approaching a critical part of their journey, in which there were long distances between the cairns. 'If we can tide that over we get on the regular cairn route, and with luck should stick to it; but everything depends on the weather. We never won a march of 8-1/2 miles with greater difficulty, but we can't go on like this.'

Page 403 Very fresh wind from the S.E., with strong surface drift, so completely wiped out the faint track they were trying to follow during the next stage of their struggle homewards, that lunch-time came without a sight of the cairn they had hoped to pass. Later in the day Bowers, feeling sure that they were too far to the west, steered out, with the result that another pony camp was passed by unseen. 'There is little doubt we are in for a rotten critical time going home, and the lateness of the season may make it really serious.... Looking at the map to-night there is no doubt we are too far to the east. With clear weather we ought to be able to correct the mistake, but will the weather clear? It's a gloomy position, more especially as one sees the same difficulty recurring even when we have corrected this error. The wind is dying down to-night and the sky clearing in the south, which is hopeful. Meanwhile it is satisfactory to note that such untoward events fail to damp the spirit of the party.'

The hopes of better weather were realized during the following day, when they started off in sunshine and with very little wind. Difficulties as to their course remained, but luckily Bowers took a round of angles, and with the help of the chart they came to the conclusion that they must be inside rather than outside the tracks. The data, however, were so meager that none of them were happy about taking the great responsibility of marching out. Then, just as they had decided to lunch, Bowers' wonderfully Page 404 sharp eyes detected an old double lunch cairn, and the theodolite telescope confirmed it. Camp R. 37 found them within 2-1/2 miles of their depôt. 'We cannot see it, but, given fine weather, we cannot miss it. We are, therefore, extraordinarily relieved.... Things are again looking up, as we are on the regular line of cairns, with no gaps right home, I hope.' In the forenoon of Saturday, February 24, the depôt was reached, and there they found the store in order except for a shortage of oil. 'Shall have to be *very* saving with fuel.'

[Indeed from this time onward the party were increasingly in want of more oil than they found at the depôts. Owing partly to the severe conditions, but still more to the delays caused by their sick comrades, they reached the full limit of time allowed for between the depôts. The cold was unexpected, and at the same time the actual amount of oil found at the depôts was less than Scott anticipated.

The return journey on the summit was made at good speed, for the party accomplished in 21 days what had taken them 27 days on the outward journey. But the last part of it, from Three Degree to Upper Glacier Depôt, took nearly eight marches as against ten, and here can be seen the first slight slackening as P.O. Evans and Oates began to feel the cold. From the Upper Glacier to the Lower Glacier Depôt there was little gain on the outward journey, partly owing to the conditions but more to Evans' gradual collapse. And from that time onward the marches Page 405 of the weary but heroic travelers became shorter and shorter.

As regards the cause of the shortage of oil, the tins at the depôts had been exposed to extreme conditions of heat and cold. The oil in the warmth of the sun — for the tins were regularly set in an accessible place on the top of the cairns — tended to become vapour and to escape through the stoppers without damage to the tins. This process was much hastened owing to the leather washers about the stoppers having perished in the great cold.

The tins awaiting the Southern party at the depôts had, of course, been opened, so that the supporting parties on their way back could take their due amount. But however carefully the tins were re-stoppered, they were still liable to the unexpected evaporation and leakage, and hence, without the smallest doubt, arose the shortage which was such a desperate blow to Scott and his party.]

Apart from the storage of fuel everything was found in order at the depôt, and with ten full days' provisions from the night of the 24th they had less than 70 miles between them and the Mid-Barrier depôt. At lunch-time Scott wrote in a more hopeful tone, 'It is an immense relief to have picked up this depôt, and, for the time, anxieties are thrust aside,' but at night, after pulling on a dreadful surface and only gaining four miles, he added, 'It really will be a bad business if we are to have this plodding all through. I don't know what to think, but the rapid closing Page 406 of the season is ominous.... It is a race between the season and hard conditions and our fitness and good food.'

Their prospects, however, became a little brighter during the following day, when the whole march yielded 11.4 miles, 'The first double figures of steady dragging for a long time.' But what they wanted and what would not come was a wind to help them on their way. Nevertheless, although the assistance they so sorely needed was still lacking, they gained another 11-1/2 miles on their next march, and were within 43 miles of their next depôt. Writing from 'R. 40. Temp. -21°' on Monday night, February 26, Scott said, 'Wonderfully fine weather but cold, very cold. Nothing dries and we get our feet cold too often. We want more food yet, and especially more fat. Fuel is woefully short. We can scarcely hope to get a better surface at this season, but I wish we could have some help from the wind, though it might shake us up badly if the temp. didn't rise.'

Tuesday brought them within 31 miles of their depôt, but hunger was attacking them fiercely, and they could talk of little else except food and of when and where they might possibly meet the dogs. 'It is a critical position. We may find ourselves in safety at next depôt, but there is a horrid element of doubt.'

On the next day Scott decided to increase the rations, and at R. 42, which they reached after a march of 11-1/2 miles in a blightingly cold wind, they had a 'splendid pony hoosh.' The temperatures, however, Page 407 which varied at this time between -30° and -42°, were chilling them through and through, and to get their foot-gear on in the mornings was both a painful and a long task. 'Frightfully cold starting,' Scott wrote at lunch-time on Thursday, February 29, 'luckily Bowers and Oates in their last new finnesko; keeping my old ones for the present.... Next camp is our depôt and it is exactly 13 miles. It ought not to take more than 1-1/2 days; we pray for another fine one. The oil will just about spin out in that event, and we arrive a clear day's food in hand.'

On reaching the Middle Barrier Depôt, however, blow followed blow in such quick succession that hope of pulling through began to sink in spite of all their cheerfulness and courage. First they found such a shortage of oil that with the most rigid economy it could scarcely carry them on to their next depôt, 71 miles away. Then Oates disclosed the fact that his feet, evidently frost-bitten by the recent low temperatures, were very bad indeed. And lastly the wind, which at first they had greeted with some joy, brought dark overcast weather. During the Friday night the temperature fell to below -40°, and on the next morning an hour and a half was spent before they could get on their foot-gear. 'Then on an appalling surface they lost both cairns and tracks, and at lunch Scott had to admit that they were 'in a very queer street since there is no doubt we cannot do the extra marches and feel the cold horribly.'

Afterwards they managed to pick up the track Page 408 again, and with a march of nearly 10 miles for the day prospects brightened a little; but on the next morning they had to labour upon a surface that was coated with a thin layer of woolly crystals, which were too firmly fixed to be removed by the wind and caused impossible friction to the runners of the sledge. 'God help us,' Scott wrote at mid-day, 'we can't keep up this pulling, that is certain. Amongst ourselves we are unendingly cheerful, but what each man feels in his heart I can only guess. Putting on foot-gear in the morning is getting slower and slower, therefore every day more dangerous.'

No relief whatever to the critical situation came on Monday, March 4, and there was in fact little left to hope for except a strong drying wind, which at that time of the year was not likely to come. At mid-day they were about 42 miles from the next depôt and had a week's food; but in spite of the utmost economy their oil could only last three or four days, and to pull as they were doing and be short of food at the same time was an absolute impossibility. For the time being the temperature had risen to -20°, but Scott was sure that this small improvement was only temporary and feared that Oates, at any rate, was in no state to weather more severe cold than they were enduring. And hanging over all the other misfortunes was the constant fear that if they did get to the next depôt they might find the same shortage of oil. 'I don't know what I should do if Wilson and Bowers weren't so determinedly cheerful over things.'

Page 409 And it must in all truth have been as difficult as it was heroic to be cheerful, for weary and worn as they were their food needed such careful husbanding, that their supper on this night (March 4) consisted of nothing but a cup of cocoa and pemmican solid with the chill off. 'We pretend to prefer the pemmican this way,' Scott says, and if any proof was needed of their indomitable resolution it is contained in that short sentence. The result, however, was telling rapidly upon all of them, and more especially upon Oates, whose feet were in a terrible condition when they started to march on the morning of the 5th. Lunch-time saw them within 27 miles of their next supply of food and fuel, but by this time poor Oates was almost done.

'It is pathetic enough because we can do nothing for him; more hot food might do a little, but only a little, I fear. We none of us expected these terribly low temperatures, and of the rest of us Wilson is feeling them most; mainly, I fear, from his self-sacrificing devotion in doctoring Oates' feet. We cannot help each other, each has enough to do to take care of himself. We get cold on the march when the trudging is heavy, and the wind pierces our worn garments. The others, all of them, are unendingly cheerful when in the tent. We mean to see the game through with a proper spirit, but it's tough work to be pulling harder than we ever pulled in our lives for long hours, and to feel that the progress is so slow. One can only say "God help us!" and plod on our weary way, cold and Page 410 very miserable, though outwardly cheerful. We talk of all sorts of subjects in the tent, not much of food now, since we decided to take the risk of running a full ration. We simply couldn't go hungry at this time.'

On the morning of the 6th Oates was no longer able to pull, and the miles gained, when they camped for lunch after desperate work, were only three and a half, and the total distance for the day was short of seven miles. For Oates, indeed, the crisis was near at hand. 'He makes no complaint, but his spirits only come up in spurts now, and he grows more silent in the tent.... If we were all fit I should have hopes of getting through, but the poor Soldier has become a terrible hindrance, though he does his utmost and suffers much I fear.' And at mid-day on the 7th, Scott added, 'A little worse I fear. One of Oates' feet *very* bad this morning; he is wonderfully brave. We still talk of what we will do together at home.'

At this time they were 16 miles from their depôt, and if they found the looked-for amount of fuel and food there, and if the surface helped them, Scott hoped that they might get on to the Mt. Hooper Depôt, 72 miles farther, but not to One Ton Camp. 'We hope against hope that the dogs have been to Mt. Hooper; then we might pull through.... We are only kept going by good food. No wind this morning till a chill northerly air came ahead. Sun bright and cairns showing up well. I should like to keep the track to the end.'

Another fearful struggle took them by lunch-time Page 411 on the 8th to within 8-1/2 miles of their next goal, but the time spent over foot-gear in the mornings was getting longer and longer. 'Have to wait in night footgear for nearly an hour before I start changing, and then am generally first to be ready. Wilson's feet giving trouble now, but this mainly because he gives so much help to others.... The great question is, what shall we find at the depôt? If the dogs have visited it we may get along a good distance, but if there is another short allowance of fuel, God help us indeed. We are in a very bad way, I fear, in any case.'

On the following day they managed to struggle on to Mount Hooper Depôt. 'Cold comfort. Shortage on our allowance all round. I don't know that anyone is to blame. The dogs which would have been our salvation have evidently failed.'

[For the last six days Cherry-Garrard and Demetri had been waiting with the dogs at One Ton Camp. Scott had dated his probable return to Hut Point anywhere between mid-March and early April, and calculating from the speed of the other return parties Atkinson expected him to reach One Ton Camp between March 3 and 10. There Cherry-Garrard met four days of blizzard, with the result that when the weather cleared he had little more than enough dog food to take the teams home. Under these circumstances only two possible courses were open to him, either to push south for one more march and back with imminent risk of missing Scott on the way, or to stay two days at the Camp where Scott was bound to come, Page 412 if he came at all. Wisely he took the latter course and stayed at One Ton Camp until the utmost limit of time.]

With the depôt reached and no relief to the situation gained, Scott was forced to admit that things were going 'steadily downhill,' but for the time being Oates' condition was by far the most absorbing trouble. 'Oates' foot worse,' he wrote on the 10th. 'He has rare pluck and must know that he can never get through. He asked Wilson if he had a chance this morning, and of course Bill had to say he didn't know. In point of fact he has none. Apart from him, if he went under now, I doubt whether we could get through. With great care we might have a dog's chance, but no more.... Poor chap! it is too pathetic to watch him; one cannot but try to cheer him up.'

On this same day a blizzard met them after they had marched for half an hour, and Scott seeing that not one of them could face such weather, pitched camp and stayed there until the following morning. Then they struggled on again with the sky so overcast that they could see nothing and consequently lost the tracks. At the most they gained little more than six miles during the day, and this they knew was as much as they could hope to do if they got no help from wind or surfaces. 'We have 7 days' food and should be about 55 miles from One Ton Camp to-night, 6 X 7 = 42, leaving us 13 miles short of our distance, even if things get no worse.'

Oates too was, Scott felt, getting very near the end. 'What we or he will do, God only knows. We Page 413 discussed the matter after breakfast; he is a brave fine fellow and understands the situation, but he practically asked for advice. Nothing could be said but to urge him to march as long as he could. One satisfactory result to the discussion: I practically ordered Wilson to hand over the means of ending our troubles to us, so that any of us may know how to do so. Wilson had no choice between doing so and our ransacking the medicine case.'

Thus Scott wrote on the 11th, and the next days brought more and more misfortunes with them. A strong northerly wind stopped them altogether on the 13th, and although on the following morning they started with a favorable breeze, it soon shifted and blew through their wind-clothes and their mitts. 'Poor Wilson horribly cold, could not get off ski for some time. Bowers and I practically made camp, and when we got into the tent at last we were all deadly cold.... We *must* go on, but now the making of every camp must be more difficult and dangerous. It must be near the end, but a pretty merciful end.... I shudder to think what it will be like to-morrow.'

Up to this time, incredible as it seems, Scott had only once spared himself the agony of writing in his journal, so nothing could be more pathetic and significant than the fact that at last he was unable any longer to keep a daily record of this magnificent journey.

'Friday, March 16 or Saturday 17. Lost track of dates, but think the last correct,' his next entry begins, but then under the most unendurable Page 414 conditions he went on to pay a last and imperishable tribute to his dead companion.

'Tragedy all along the line. At lunch, the day before yesterday, poor Titus Oates said he couldn't go on; he proposed we should leave him in his sleeping-bag. That we could not do, and we induced him to come on, on the afternoon march. In spite of its awful nature for him he struggled on and we made a few miles. At night he was worse and we knew the end had come.

'Should this be found I want these facts recorded. Oates' last thoughts were of his Mother, but immediately before he took pride in thinking that his regiment would be pleased with the bold way in which he met his death. We can testify to his bravery. He has borne intense suffering for weeks without complaint, and to the very last was able and willing to discuss outside subjects. He did not — would not — give up hope till the very end. He was a brave soul. This was the end. He slept through the night before last, hoping not to wake; but he woke in the morning — yesterday. It was blowing a blizzard. He said, "I am just going outside and may be some time." He went out into the blizzard and we have not seen him since.

'I take this opportunity of saying that we have stuck to our sick companions to the last. In case of Edgar Evans, when absolutely out of food and he lay insensible, the safety of the remainder seemed to demand his abandonment, but Providence mercifully removed him at this critical moment. He died Page 415 a natural death, and we did not leave him till two hours after his death.

'We knew that poor Oates was walking to his death, but though we tried to dissuade him, we knew it was the act of a brave man and an English gentleman. We all hope to meet the end with a similar spirit, and assuredly the end is not far.

'I can only write at lunch and then only occasionally. The cold is intense, -40° at mid-day. My companions are unendingly cheerful, but we are all on the verge of serious frost-bites, and though we constantly talk of fetching through I don't think anyone of us believes it in his heart.

'We are cold on the march now, and at all times except meals. Yesterday we had to lay up for a blizzard and to-day we move dreadfully slowly. We are at No. 14 pony camp, only two pony marches from One Ton Depôt. We leave here our theodolite, a camera, and Oates' sleeping-bags. Diaries, etc., and geological specimens carried at Wilson's special request, will be found with us or on our sledge.'

At mid-day on the next day, March 18, they had struggled to within 21 miles of One Ton Depôt, but wind and drift came on and they had to stop their march. 'No human being could face it, and we are worn out *nearly*.

'My right foot has gone, nearly all the toes — two days ago I was the proud possessor of best feet. These are the steps of my downfall. Like an ass I mixed a spoonful of curry powder with my melted pemmican — it Page 416 gave me violent indigestion. I lay awake and in pain all night; woke and felt done on the march; foot went and I didn't know it. A very small measure of neglect and have a foot which is not pleasant to contemplate.

'Bowers takes first place in condition, but there is not much to choose after all. The others are still confident of getting through — or pretend to be — I don't know! We have the last *half* fill of oil in our primus and a very small quantity of spirit — this alone between us and thirst.'

On that night camp was made with the greatest difficulty, but after a supper of cold pemmican and biscuit and half a pannikin of cocoa, they were, contrary to their expectations, warm enough to get some sleep.

Then came the closing stages of this glorious struggle against persistent misfortune.

'*March* 19.—Lunch. To-day we started in the usual dragging manner. Sledge dreadfully heavy. We are 15-1/2 miles from the depôt and ought to get there in three days. What progress! We have two days' food but barely a day's fuel. All our feet are getting bad—Wilson's best, my right foot worst, left all right. There is no chance to nurse one's feet till we can get hot food into us. Amputation is the least I can hope for now, but will the trouble spread? That is the serious question. The weather doesn't give us a chance; the wind from N. to N. W. and -40 temp. to-day.

we shall stick it out
to the end but we
are getting weaker of
course and the end
cannot be far.
It seems a pity but
I do not think I can
write more —

R Scott

Last Entry —

For Gods Sake look

after our people

Page 417 During the afternoon they drew 4-1/2 miles nearer to
the One Ton Depôt, and there they made their last camp. Through-

out Tuesday a severe blizzard held them prisoners, and on the 21st Scott wrote: 'To-day forlorn hope, Wilson and Bowers going to depôt for fuel.'

But the blizzard continued without intermission. '22 and 23. Blizzard bad as ever — Wilson and Bowers unable to start — to-morrow last chance — no fuel and only one or two of food left — must be near the end. Have decided it shall be natural — we shall march for the depôt with or without our effects and die in our tracks.'

'*March* 29. — Since the 21st we have had a continuous gale from W.S.W. and S.W. We had fuel to make two cups of tea apiece, and bare food for two days on the 20th. Every day we have been ready to start for our depôt 11 *miles* away, but outside the door of the tent it remains a scene of whirling drift. I do not think we can hope for any better things now. We shall stick it out to the end, but we are getting weaker, of course, and the end cannot be far.

'It seems a pity, but I do not think I can write more.

'R. SCOTT.

'Last entry For God's sake look after our people.'

Page 418 After Cherry-Garrard and Demetri had returned to Hut Point on March 16 without having seen any signs of the Polar party, Atkinson and Keohane made one more desperate effort to find them. When, however, this had been unsuccessful there was nothing more to be done until the winter was over.

During this long and anxious time the leadership of the party devolved upon Atkinson, who under the most trying circumstances showed qualities that are beyond all praise. At the earliest possible moment (October 30) a large party started south. 'On the night of the 11th and morning of the 12th,' Atkinson says, 'after we had marched 11 miles due south of One Ton, we found the tent. It was an object partially snowed up and looking like a cairn. Before it were the ski sticks and in front of them a bamboo which probably was the mast of the sledge...

'Inside the tent were the bodies of Captain Scott, Doctor Wilson, and Lieutenant Bowers. They had pitched their tent well, and it had withstood all the blizzards of an exceptionally hard winter.'

Wilson and Bowers were found in the attitude of sleep, their sleeping-bags closed over their heads as they would naturally close them.

'THE LAST REST'.

The grave of Capt. Scott, Dr. Wilson, and Lieut. Bowers.
Photo by Lieut. T. Gran.

Scott died later. He had thrown back the flaps of his sleeping-bag and opened his coat. The little wallet Page 419 containing the three notebooks was under his shoulders and his arm flung across Wilson.

Among their belongings were the 35 lbs. of most important geological specimens which had been collected on the moraines of the Beardmore Glacier. At Wilson's request they had clung on to these to the very end, though disaster stared them in the face.

'When everything had been gathered up, we covered them with the outer tent and read the Burial Service. From this time until well into the next day we started to build a mighty cairn above them.'

Upon the cairn a rough cross, made from two skis, was placed, and on either side were up-ended two sledges, fixed firmly in the snow. Between the eastern sledge and the cairn a bamboo was placed, containing a metal cylinder, and in this the following record was left:

'November 12, 1912, Lat. 79 degrees, 50 mins. South. This cross and cairn are erected over the bodies of Captain Scott, C.V.O., R.N., Doctor E. A. Wilson, M.B. B.C., Cantab., and Lieutenant H. R. Bowers, Royal Indian Marine—a slight token to perpetuate their successful and gallant attempt to reach the Pole. This they did on January 17, 1912, after the Norwegian Expedition had already done so. Inclement weather with lack of fuel was the cause of their death. Also to commemorate their two gallant comrades, Captain L. E. G. Oates of the Inniskilling Dragoons, who walked to his death in a blizzard to Page 420 save his comrades about eighteen miles south of this position; also of Seaman Edgar Evans, who died at the foot of the Beardmore Glacier.

'"The Lord gave and the Lord taketh away; blessed be the name of the Lord."'

Page 421 With the diaries in the tent were found the following letters:—

To Mrs. E. A. Wilson

My DEAR MRS. WILSON,

If this letter reaches you Bill and I will have gone out together. We are very near it now and I should like you to know how splendid he was at the end—everlastingly cheerful and ready to sacrifice himself for others, never a word of blame to me for leading him into this mess. He is not suffering, luckily, at least only minor discomforts.

His eyes have a comfortable blue look of hope and his mind is peaceful with the satisfaction of his faith in regarding himself as part of the great scheme of the Almighty. I can do no more to comfort you than to tell you that he died as he lived, a brave, true man—the best of comrades and staunchest of friends.

My whole heart goes out to you in pity.

Yours,
R. SCOTT.

To Mrs. Bowers

My DEAR MRS. BOWERS,

I am afraid this will reach you after one of the heaviest blows of your life.

I write when we are very near the end of our journey, and I am finishing it in company with two gallant, noble gentlemen. One of these is your son. He Page 422 had come be one of my closest and soundest friends, and I appreciate his wonderful upright nature, his ability and energy. As the troubles have thickened his dauntless spirit ever shone brighter and he has remained cheerful, hopeful, and indomitable to the end.

The ways of Providence are inscrutable, but there must be some reason why such a young, vigorous and promising life is taken.

My whole heart goes out in pity for you.

Yours,
R. SCOTT.

To the end he has talked of you and his sisters. One sees what a happy home he must have had and perhaps it is well to look back on nothing but happiness.

He remains unselfish, self-reliant and splendidly hopeful to the end, believing in God's mercy to you.

To Sir J. M. Barrie

My DEAR BARRIE,

We are pegging out in a very comfortless spot. Hoping this letter may be found and sent to you, I write a word of farewell.... More practically I want you to help my widow and my boy—your godson. We are showing that Englishmen can still die with a bold spirit, fighting it out to the end. It will be known that we have accomplished our object in reaching the Pole, and that we have done everything Page 423 possible, even to sacrificing ourselves in order to save sick companions. I think this makes an example for Englishmen of the future, and that the country ought to help those who are left behind to mourn us. I leave my poor girl and your godson, Wilson leaves a widow, and Edgar Evans also a widow in humble circumstances. Do what you can to get their claims recognized. Goodbye. I am not at all afraid of the end, but sad to miss many a humble pleasure which I had planned for the future on our long marches. I may not have proved a great explorer, but we have done the greatest march ever made and come very near to great success. Goodbye, my dear friend.

Yours ever,
R. SCOTT.

We are in a desperate state, feet frozen, etc. No fuel and a long way from food, but it would do your heart good to be in our tent, to hear our songs and the cheery conversation as to what we will do when we get to Hut Point.

Later.—We are very near the end, but have not and will not lose our good cheer. We have four days of storm in our tent and no where's food or fuel. We did intend to finish ourselves when things proved like this, but we have decided to die naturally in the track.

As a dying man, my dear friend, be good to my wife and child. Give the boy a chance in life if the State won't do it. He ought to have good stuff in him.... I never met a man in my life whom I admired and Page 424 loved more than you, but I never could show you how much your friendship meant to me, for you had much to give and I nothing.

To the Right Hon. Sir Edgar Speyer, Bart.

Dated March 16, 1912. Lat. 79.5°.

My DEAR SIR EDGAR,

I hope this may reach you. I fear we must go and that it leaves the Expedition in a bad muddle. But we have been to the Pole and we shall die like gentlemen. I regret only for the women we leave behind.

I thank you a thousand times for your help and support and your generous kindness. If this diary is found it will show how we stuck by dying companions and fought the thing out well to the end. I think this will show that the spirit of pluck and the power to endure has not passed out of our race....

Wilson, the best fellow that ever stepped, has sacrificed himself again and again to the sick men of the party....

I write to many friends hoping the letters will reach them some time after we are found next year.

We very nearly came through, and it's a pity to have missed it, but lately I have felt that we have overshot our mark. No one is to blame and I hope no attempt will be made to suggest that we have lacked support.

Goodbye to you and your dear kind wife.

Yours ever sincerely,
R. SCOTT.

Page 425*To Vice-Admiral Sir Francis Charles Bridgeman, K.C.V.O., K.C.B.*

My DEAR SIR FRANCIS,

I fear we have slipped up; a close shave; I am writing a few letters which I hope will be delivered some day. I want to thank you for the friendship you gave me of late years, and to tell you how extraordinarily pleasant I found it to serve under you. I want to tell you that I was *not* too old for this job. It was the younger men that went under first.... After all we are setting a good example to our countrymen, if not by getting into a tight place, by facing it like men when we were there. We could have come through had we neglected the sick.

Good-bye, and good-bye to dear Lady Bridgeman.

Yours ever,
  R. SCOTT.

Excuse writing—it is -40°; and has been for nigh a month.

To Vice-Admiral Sir George le Clerc Egerton, K.C.B.

My DEAR SIR GEORGE,

I fear we have shot our bolt—but we have been to Pole and done the longest journey on record.

I hope these letters may find their destination some day.

Subsidiary reasons for our failure to return are due to the sickness of different members of the party, but Page 426 the real thing that has stopped us is the awful weather and unexpected cold towards the end of the journey.

This traverse of the Barrier has been quite three times as severe as any experience we had on the summit.

There is no accounting for it, but the result has thrown out my calculations, and here we are little more than 100 miles from the base and petering out.

Good-bye. Please see my widow is looked after as far as Admiralty is concerned.

  R. SCOTT.

My kindest regards to Lady Egerton. I can never forget all your kindness.

To Mr. J. J. Kinsey-Christchurch.

March 24th, 1912.

MY DEAR KINSEY,

I'm afraid we are pretty well done—four days of blizzard just as we were getting to the last dopôt. My thoughts have been with you often. You have been a brick. You will pull the Expedition through, I'm sure.

My thoughts are for my wife and boy. Will you do what you can for them if the country won't.

I want the boy to have a good chance in the world, but you know the circumstances well enough.

If I knew the wife and boy were in safe keeping I should have little to regret in leaving the world, for I feel that the country need not be ashamed of us—our Page 427 journey has been the biggest on record, and nothing but the most exceptional hard luck at the end would have caused us to fail to return. We have been to the S. pole as we set out. God bless you and dear Mrs. Kinsey. It is good to remember you and your kindness.

Your friend,
R. SCOTT.

Letters to his Mother, his Wife, his Brother-in-law (Sir William Ellison Macartney), Admiral Sir Lewis Beaumont, and Mr. and Mrs. Reginald Smith were also found, from which come the following extracts:

The Great God has called me and I feel it will add a fearful blow to the heavy ones that have fallen on you in life. But take comfort in that I die at peace with the world and myself—not afraid.

Indeed it has been most singularly unfortunate, for the risks I have taken never seemed excessive.

...I want to tell you that we have missed getting through by a narrow margin which was justifiably within the risk of such a journey.... After all, we have given our lives for our country—we have actually made the longest journey on record, and we have been the first Englishmen at the South Pole.

You must understand that it is too cold to write much.

...It's a pity the luck doesn't come our way, because every detail of equipment is right.

Page 428 I shall not have suffered any pain, but leave the world fresh from harness and full of good health and vigour. This is decided already—when provisions come to an end we simply stop unless we are within easy distance of another depôt. Therefore you must not imagine a great tragedy. We are very anxious of course, and have been for weeks, but our splendid physical condition and our appetites compensate for all discomfort.

Since writing the above we got to within 11 miles of our depôt, with one hot meal and two days' cold food. We should have got through but have been held for *four* days by a frightful storm. I think the best chance has gone. We have decided not to kill ourselves, but to fight to the last for that depôt, but in the fighting there is a painless end. So don't worry. The inevitable must be faced. You urged me to be leader of this party, and I know you felt it would be dangerous.

Make the boy interested in natural history if you can; it is better than games; they encourage it at some schools. I know you will keep him in the open air.

Above all, he must guard and you must guard him against indolence. Make him a strenuous man. I had to force myself into being strenuous as you know—had always an inclination to be idle.

There is a piece of the Union Jack I put up at the South Pole in my private kit bag, together with Amundsen's black flag and other trifles. Send a small Page 429 piece of the Union Jack to the King and a small piece to Queen Alexandra.

What lots and lots I could tell you of this journey. How much better has it been than lounging in too great comfort at home. What tales you would have for the boy. But what a price to pay.

Tell Sir Clements I thought much of him and never regretted his putting me in command of the *Discovery*.

Page 430 MESSAGE TO THE PUBLIC

The causes of the disaster are not due to faulty organization, but to misfortune in all risks which had to be undertaken.

1. The loss of pony transport in March 1911 obliged me to start later than I had intended, and obliged the limits of stuff transported to be narrowed.

2. The weather throughout the outward journey, and especially the long gale in 83° S., stopped us.
3. The soft snow in lower reaches of glacier again reduced pace.

We fought these untoward events with a will and conquered, but it cut into our provision reserve.

Every detail of our food supplies, clothing and depôts made on the interior ice-sheet and over that long stretch of 700 miles to the Pole and back, worked out to perfection. The advance party would have returned to the glacier in fine form and with surplus of food, but for the astonishing failure of the man whom we had least expected to fail. Edgar Evans was thought the strongest man of the party.

The Beardmore Glacier is not difficult in fine weather, but on our return we did not get a single completely fine day; this with a sick companion enormously increased our anxieties.

As I have said elsewhere we got into frightfully rough ice and Edgar Evans received a concussion of Page 431 the brain — he died a natural death, but left us a shaken party with the season unduly advanced.

But all the facts above enumerated were as nothing to the surprise which awaited us on the Barrier. I maintain that our arrangements for returning were quite adequate, and that no one in the world would have expected the temperatures and surfaces which we encountered at this time of the year. On the summit in lat. 85°, 86° we had -20°, -30°. On the Barrier in lat. 82°, 10,000 feet lower, we had -30° in the day, -47° at night pretty regularly, with continuous head wind during our day marches. It is clear that these circumstances come on very suddenly, and our wreck is certainly due to this sudden advent of severe weather, which does not seem to have any satisfactory cause. I do not think human beings ever came through such a month as we have come through, and we should have got through in spite of the weather but for the sickening of a second companion, Captain Oates, and a shortage of fuel in our depôts for which I cannot account, and finally, but for the storm which has fallen on us within 11 miles of the depôt at which we hoped to secure our final supplies. Surely misfortune could scarcely have exceeded this last blow. We arrived within 11 miles of our old One Ton Camp with fuel for one last meal and food for two days. For four days we have been unable to leave the tent—the gale howling about us. We are weak, writing is difficult, but for my own sake I do not regret this journey, Page 432 which has shewn that Englishmen can endure hardships, help one another, and meet death with as great a fortitude as ever in the past. We took risks, we knew we took them; things have come out against us, and therefore we have no cause for complaint, but bow to the will of Providence, determined still to do our best to the last. But if we have been willing to give our lives to this enterprise, which is for the honour of our country, I appeal to our countrymen to see that those who depend on us are properly cared for.

Had we lived, I should have had a tale to tell of the hardihood, endurance, and courage of my companions which would have stirred the heart of every Englishman. These rough notes and our dead bodies must tell the tale, but surely, surely, a great rich country like ours will see that those who are dependent on us are properly provided for.

R. SCOTT.

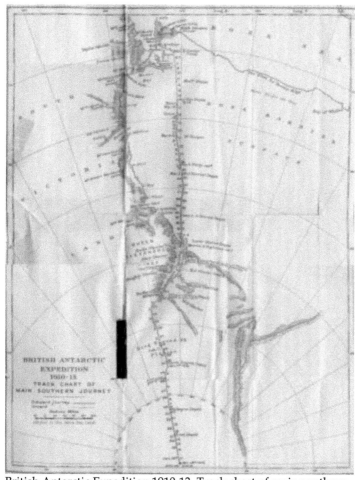

British Antarctic Expedition 1910-13. Track chart of main southern journey.